The Poet Chronicles

Cecilia,

To a fellow writer
and kindred spirit!

Best to you!

The Poet Chronicles

Tim McHugh

Cover photos: Charles Cantrell © 2004.
Cover design: Karen Parker © 2004.

ISBN: 0-9723706-2-5
Library of Congress Control Number: Pending

Tim McHugh
The Poet Chronicles
First KSB printing (May, 2004).

Printed in the United States of America

Kearney Street Books
Po Box 2021
Bellingham, WA 98227
360-738-1355
www.grmckinney.com

To Kristina, whose love and patience knows no bounds.

Special thanks to: Kristina McHugh, Casey and Morgan McHugh, Gary McKinney, Charles Cantrell, Karen Parker, Dana Lyons, Perry Mills, Tim Johnson, R.W. Goodwin, Mitch Friedman, Sam Andrew and Jim Lortz, not to mention the countless music people I've known over the last twenty-five years who helped inspire this story.

"I don't know anything about music.
In my line of work you don't have to."
—*Elvis Presley*

"All is but illusion and disaster."
—*Voltaire*

Prologue

Sunny says this time we're close. Really close. She should know. She's been there. To the top, that is. Or near the top. I know for a fact that she's been *on* the mountain and that's more than I can say for most people. The way I've always figured it, if someone like Sunny could just get us out of Bellingham at least then we could start climbing. I mean, how do you get lost when the only direction is up? Of course if you're Ollie the answer is easy, but I didn't ask Ollie to play drums for The Cosmic Poets because I thought he was the next Edmund Hillary—I asked him because in spite of his madness, he's quite good. For that matter, we're all quite good. In fact, Sunny says we're the next big thing.

You've probably already read the following press release issued by Sunny telling the world about our big West Coast tour but in case you haven't, here it is:

Bellingham's own musical sensation, The Cosmic Poets, launch a major twelve city West Coast tour to promote their incredible new demo to major labels. This tour will be the last opportunity to see this phenomenal group in an intimate setting as they are currently negotiating with several record companies and it appears that a bidding war to sign them has begun. See them tonight at Boundary Bay Brewery so they can thank all their fans for the support that has made this historic occasion possible. According to their manager, Former RCA Record's President Frank Strong, a contract should be signed by early August and that negotiations are going extremely well. Move aside Pearl Jam and make room for the next big Northwest band...

Did I tell you that one of those gigs is with Bonnie Raitt and Neil Young in Arcata, California—to save the Redwoods? Sunny says that we'll be signed to a major label and on the road with U2 in a few short months. So long Bellingham. We're outta here. Don't get me wrong. Bellingham's not a bad place to live. If you love drum circles, suicidal poets and lots of rain, you'll love Bellingham. Just don't move here and tell us all about it. We've been trying to get out of here forever.

The plan is to tour south to the Bay Area and perhaps even as far south as Los Angeles, though I do have a slight confession to make: we actually have only *five* gigs lined up on this tour, two of which are in Seattle and one in Bellingham. None of the jerks booking the California clubs even bothered to call me back. I must admit, though, these gigs do look good on paper. To hell with 'em I say. I remember some famous musician once saying that it's not whether or not you book a lot of club gigs in California, it's whether or not you have Frank Strong on your side. Or something like that. Besides, you can't expect everything to go just the way you plan it and if Sunny and Frank do their job we'll have A&R reps drooling all over us as we rock the masses in Arcata while saving the Redwoods! At that point, the rest of the tour won't even matter. The way I see it the job of a leader is to act like he knows what he's doing and to keep group morale high at all costs. If that means stretching the truth a little from time to time then so be it. One thing I've learned over the years is that if you look and act busy, people actually think you are.

Tonight we rock Bellingham. Tomorrow it's off to Seattle where we'll be opening for the late Janis Joplin's legendary band Big Brother and the Holding Company. From there we'll swoop on down to the Oregon Country Fair and after that to Arcata for our date with destiny...

But first things first. We have one last practice this afternoon. Tolstoy himself proclaimed that unless the uncompromising standard of complete perfection was laid out before humanity, there would be no motivation for any enlightened endeavor. Since the making of music is an enlightened endeavor and since it is a known fact that a minority of people believe that rock musicians are indeed part of the human family, it makes sense to practice. After all, practice does make perfect...

One

Where the hell is Ollie?" asks Star as she plugs her guitar into her effects unit before glancing at her watch. "I knew we should've fired his lazy ass and gotten another drummer for the tour! He's thirty seven minutes late." Before anyone can comment, she cranks up her amplifier and lets loose a screaming Hendrix-like riff. My ears shriek in pain.

Suddenly Ollie does appear and behind his wire spectacles and electric wild hair, he looks frightened—like he knows he's blowing it yet again. "Sorry," he says, "but I was out putting up posters for tonight's gig and I ran into Steve Sampson down at Stuart's and while we were having coffee he started telling me about how his brother got this weird disease after the Gulf War...Did you know that the Pentagon destroyed a bunch of documents on the government's use of—"

"Not now, Ollie," I say.

"...and then we started talking about coffee plantations in third world countries which made me start thinking about how caffeine affects my tempo which made me remember we had practice...Funny how all things are connected, huh?"

"Ollie," hisses Star, white-faced and fuming, "you are *so* absolutely unprofessional. I don't think I can work with you anymore."

"Oh, here you go with your elitist trip again, Star. You going home in your Lear jet again tonight?"

"Quit while you're ahead," says Angel.

As Star's amp erupts in another angry burst of distorted lead guitar, I'm reminded yet again that making music is a great way for people to keep from killing each other. The Cosmic Poets' practice is underway.

Ollie's child-like blue eyes are now smiling as he pounds on his kit. In the corner, Zen's slender fingers pluck along on his bass strings, a six-pack of beer rocking precariously on top of his speaker cabinet. Zen gazes upon Star, his eyes feral and bird-like, though there is also a sadness behind them. Zen's youthful face and bushy unkempt hair make him appear to be much younger then he probably is. Large quantities of intoxicants likely contribute to Zen's calm demeanor; yet whatever brought him to this place, he is utterly worthy of his name.

Star, Bellingham's best-dressed tomboy, wears her jeans tight and her silky black shirt loose. A shaggy mop of blonde hair hangs over her guitar while she slouches indifferently, drowning out everyone else in a wall of distortion, only breaking from her Axel Rose imitation long enough to expel some chew spit from her swollen bottom lip into the plastic bucket behind her amplifier.

Angel grooves in front of her organ and through the sultry air I smell the sweetness of her patchouli. She is stunning in a very renaissance way. Her straight, raven-black hair spills elegantly over her shoulders, contrasting a set of sharp brown eyes that betray a frightening intelligence. Her clothing is awash in colors. A silver bracelet jangles loosely around her left ankle and she is, as usual, barefoot. As the jam progresses her eyes flitter with both orgiastic delight and flashes of panic. The happy, burbling reggae sounds of organ cause my mind to drift and now there is a ringing in my ears growing louder as I see thousands of hippies dancing in front of a giant, outdoor stage. There is a woman in the distance playing a keyboard. *My God, the ringing is growing louder. It's her! It's her! Somebody do something!* Then all is silence except for the sound of wind in my ears.

"What's wrong with Angus?"

It takes a moment for my eyes to refocus. "Nothing, Angel."

"Well, you just keep staring at me. You're not even playing."

"Oh, I wasn't? I thought I was."

"Did I do anything wrong?"

"Not exactly...it's just..."

"What?"

"Come on, Angel."

"I have no idea what you're getting at, Angus."

"No idea?" I point at her organ. "We go through this every time."

"Angus," she says, quietly, "maybe it's *your* fault for signing our agreement."

"Maybe it is, Angel," I plead, "but your singing's what I love. Can't you please just sing?"

"I told you if I don't get to play organ on at least two songs, I'm quitting! It's in our contract."

"Don't you think you're being a little rash?" says Star to her. "Try to be more professional about things." She looks at me. "Can we practice, now?"

"Sure, Star."

We begin practicing *Blue Sunday*, during which time Ollie keeps changing his drum part on the chorus.

I signal a stop, then plead with him. "Ollie, you are a great drummer and this is in no way a criticism of your good ear, but could you please try going, 'chi chi fwap chi chi chi fwap' as we're coming into the chorus instead of those frenetic little fills? I think it works better."

Ollie rolls his eyes. "Tell you what, Angus, you play guitar and I'll play drums. How about that?"

"But you're rushing the tempo on the transition."

"Me? I'm just following you! Your guitar keeps speeding up there."

"No, it's not, Ollie," snaps Star. "It's your drumming."

"What the hell do you know about rhythm, Star?"

"More than you think. Try going, 'chi bu bu bu chi bu bu bu chi' and then switch—"

"Look, Star, do I try to tell you how to play that...that thing?" Ollie asks, motioning to the saxophone she's now holding. Ollie's eyes drift up to the ceiling and soon he's off to the races about the time he drummed for Black Rabbits in Heat before discovering they were but a carefully disguised front for a local Amway distributor after he was tricked into playing at a Tupperware party. He then describes the fight he got into with Rick Smith after the singer hurled his floor tom across the living room...

"Like I'm about to do if you don't shut your mouth and get back to practice," says Angel. "I want to work on my organ part, not listen to you babble on about some argument you had with a guy ten years ago. Deal with it and move on!"

"Yeah, Ollie," pleads Star. "Nobody's attacking you. I was only asking you to try something different. But I see that's asking a lot." They all continue arguing while Zen and I guzzle beer. In the end, Ollie is apologizing to everyone for being so unreasonable. Finally we're back to practicing.

Blue Sunday actually starts flowing pretty well and the harmonies are good. Our spirits are lifted even though we're all aware that Angel's organ solo is fast approaching. *Eight bars and closing,* I think as her cheeks are now twitching nervously. The solo arrives, immediately disintegrating into a spasmodic, disjointed warbling that causes her to jump back from her organ as if she had just scorched her fingers on a hot stove. She wails, clutching her black hair in tight fists as the song crash lands.

"You were doing great," says Star as we all stand in silence, heads bowed.

"It's his fault," says Angel, turning to me. "He makes me so *fucking* self conscious."

"I don't mean to, Angel."

"I need your support, Angus."

"Sure, Angel."

We try again and this time she keeps a semi-coherent lead for about fifteen seconds before disintegrating into chaos.

"Don't you think she's doing great, Zen?" asks Star, happily.

"Fabulously well," says Zen, not looking at me.

"The organ doesn't work," I say, quietly.

"Fuck it," snarls Angel. "I quit! I'm not kidding you, Angus. This time it's for real!"

"You can't quit! Sunny and Frank said no line-up changes until after the tour! This band is your biggest chance of ever breaking out of Bellingham. Wait 'til Frank gets us signed, then quit."

"Angus, Angus, Angus," Angel sings. "Nobody else has a problem with my organ." She yanks the speaker plug from the back of her keyboard, her cheeks flushed and trembling. "You and the fucking patriarchy won't keep me down forever!"

"My, my," exclaims a voice from the door. "A little creative tension?" It's Sunny, wearing the same heavy leather coat and super-tight jeans she was wearing the night we met her in

Bellingham a few months back. Her frizzy, bleach blonde hair and thick eyeliner make her seem ageless. She totters over and plants a smoke-flavored kiss on my cheek. I can tell by the way she chews her lips and fidgets that she's baked. As she touches cheeks with Angel and Star, her lover, Peaches—a plump, dwarf-like fellow with overblown green hair and wrinkly blue eyes—materializes in the doorway. "You all know Peaches," she says, taking his hand like she's showing off some kind of a casino door prize.

"Peaches!" I say, watching him lustfully eye Star and Angel.

"Peaaaches neeeds a huuug," he bleats. He holds out his pudgy arms and waddles over to Star and then Angel, indifferent to the terror in their eyes, moaning and trembling as he squeezes each of them tightly against his protruding belly. Finally it's over and he's snorting and rubbing his nose while Star and Angel recoil.

"How's it going, Peaches?" I ask.

"Good maaan! You exciiited about the tour?"

"You bet we are."

"What's up with you, Zen?" asks Sunny with great concern.

None of us had noticed Zen standing in the corner, tears dribbling from his eyes. "Nothing," he whispers.

"Come on," coaxes Angel. "Tell us, please."

"Elvis died."

"Elvis died?" I am stunned. We all are.

There is a long silence before Zen finally says, "I think I killed him."

"For God's sakes, Zen! How?"

"I changed food brands to this high fiber and protein mix and he bloated."

We all stand in silence out of respect for our departed pink-haired, Mohawked, punk-rock pygmy goat.

"Oh, that's *so* sad," cries Angel, tears welling in her eyes.

"Yeah, that's sad," says Star, curtly. "So Sunny, what's the big news?" We all stare at her. "What? What am I supposed to say? We have a gig tonight and we have to be professional about things." Then, after a moment, she softens. "I *am* really sorry, Zen. I'll miss your little goat as much as anybody—I know he meant a lot to you."

"Thanks, Star," says Zen quietly, yet I can't really tell what he feels. I'm lost for words anyway. It's hard to know what to say to someone when his goat dies.

"Well I got some big news, kids," says Sunny, "and we can't let a small tragedy thwart y'all's mission."

"You talked with Frank?" I ask.

"Yes, I did."

"And?"

She takes a long breath and slowly exhales. "You're on the doorstep."

Everybody stares at her in tense anticipation. Sunny's sense of drama and timing is deliberate and calculated.

"Bob Stills called Frank this week."

"Bob Stills?"

"Bob Stills. He just happens to be the president of A&R at RCA Records in Los Angeles."

"He heard the demo?"

"He must have," she says. "Plus some buzz about the tour."

We all wait in silence, Star's eyes dreamy and far away.

"And?"

Sunny lights a smoke, smiling at Peaches. "He said that he hasn't heard a band as unique as y'all in a long, long time. There is, as he put it, much commercial potential."

"*Commercial* potential?"

"Don't take it wrong," she says.

"Yeaaah," echoes Peaches. "It don't mean it's a baaad thing."

"I'm gonna be *huge*!" squeals Star. We all stare at her. "I mean...we're *all* gonna make it...together."

"So Bob's coming out to see *us*?"

"Yes he is," says Sunny. "He and June Farrow are gonna try to make it to Arcata to hear you warm up for Bonnie Raitt. You should hear Frank. He's very excited." Sunny stares at everybody for a long moment. "It's really happening, kids."

Star pulls out another chew, unable to hide the excitement in her eyes.

"Depending on how the tour goes, of course," she continues. "You've done your part in setting it up, Angus, and I must say I'm impressed. Eleven dates down the West Coast finishing off with your Battle of Seattle at the Showbox. The least I can do is get you off on a good start."

"Yeah, Angus," says Star, beaming. "Great job getting us into the *hottest* clubs on the West Coast. How'd you pull it off so fast?"

"Just a lot of persistence," I say, feeling sick.

"Did you know Phish used to play at Rock City in Berkeley before they were famous?" asks Ollie.

"Yeah," says Star. "The Whiskey à Go Go in Los Angeles will be amazing, too. Most bands pay to play there, but Angus got us on as a headliner." She turns and shoots a brown stream of tobacco juice into her bucket.

"I think The Doors were the house band there at one time," says Ollie. "Gosh, Star, don't you ever worry about lip cancer?"

"There's no such thing as lip cancer," answers Star. "It's mouth cancer that gets into your lip."

"What's the difference, anyway?" I blurt. "There are a million different ways to go down! We all pick our poison!"

"What the hell are you talking about, Angus?" asks Star. "You're not making sense."

"Are you all right, Angus?" asks Sunny. "You look strange."

"I'm okay," I say, forcing a smile. "Look Sunny, we probably won't even need those club gigs if Frank gets his people out to hear us at the Redwood show."

"You can't always count on the big shows, Angus," says Sunny. "Those club dates you booked are worth their weight in gold."

"Sorry, I guess I'm just sick of talking about 'em. Let's just go out and see what happens...starting tomorrow at the Ballard Firehouse."

"Excellent score there," Sunny smiles. "Big Brother and the Holding Company are huge in the classic rock circuit. They really pack'em in. The buzz is there's interest in them again from the record companies."

She turns to Zen. "I saw your tour bus on the way in. It looks road-worthy. I'd say the Cosmic Poets are ready to rock!"

Zen smiles modestly. But, really, he did a fabulous job fixing up his father's molded and mildewed '71 Kampworld Deluxe Motor-Home. If you like vehicles with personality, it's a thing of beauty—beige panels streaked with green and pink algae from years parked under a bunch of cedar trees.

"And you've got a PA system in case you need one?"

Zen shrugs. "Yeah. We're ready."

I am glad no one has asked me thus far about our finances for the tour. Our band fund, which I cashed in today, totals a whopping one hundred seventy-eight dollars and sixty-two cents. Yet this should get us well into California, at least to Arcata. I'm also bringing an emergency credit card with a one thousand five hundred dollar limit. Hopefully I won't have to use it. This is all the money I have left in the world, as it also cost me three thousand dollars on my other credit card to sign with Sunny—something else I haven't bothered to share with my mates. Besides, once the bidding war kicks in, we'll all be rolling in advance money—even though most of it will go to Sunny and Frank for their hard work. We have the opportunity that most bands never dream of getting: having our music presented to major labels by the legendary Frank Strong. We can't blow it now. We've worked too hard to get this far and there's no way I'm gonna let this chance slip away. Any questions I once may have had about Sunny are gone. She's for real. The question now is: are we?

Two

Are you okay, Angus?"

The deep, melancholy eyes of a lovely maiden are slowly coming into focus while the familiar sounds and smells of Boundary Bay Brewery return. I have no idea how long I've been sitting at the back table whispering to a lukewarm cup of coffee. I know she'll hear the tremble in my voice as my mind races for some pre-prepared line—some rehearsed bit of false confidence. "I'm okay, Lily. Thanks for coming to our gig tonight."

Her eyes, amused, also betray a tired, wearisome distance. "Actually, Angus," she says, "I've got plans with Nathan, tonight. I just came to say goodbye."

"You're not gonna stay and hear us?" I fight the tears stinging my eyes.

"Angus," she chastises softly, ignoring my question. "Why are you drinking coffee? You know the way caffeine affects you."

"You're right. You're always right, Lily."

"What's wrong, Angus?" She sits down across from me. "You look sad."

"Nothing, Lily. You should stay and listen tonight. Sunny's really got things cooking for us. It cost me a little money but it's worth it. Sunny says you got to give a little to get a lot."

"How much did it cost you, Angus?"

"Sunny was a big-shot music promoter down in Florida and she's got Frank Strong on board."

"How much, Angus?"

There is a strange buzzing in my head and my breath is labored. "Did you know that Frank was a legend at RCA and he thinks we'll be as big as U2. He's got the contacts to make it happen."

She stares at me without speaking.

"Oh, come on, Lily. What's money, anyway? We gotta pay our dues. We're in the big leagues, now."

"Angus?"

"Three thousand dollars, okay? It's no big deal. I put it on a card and Sunny says I'll get it all back once we're signed. Please just don't tell anyone else."

"Angus!" She shakes her head.

"It's for us, Lily, " I say. "I...I did it for us."

"Why didn't you talk to *me*, first? Nathan is a personal friend of REM. He has contacts all over the music business."

Nathan. The very name sends a shudder of rage through me. Nathan the writer...Nathan the spoiled trust-fund brat...Nathan the condescending all-knowing vegan who always has the last word on everything. It's always Nathan this and Nathan that. When Lily first moved to Bellingham with him they came to a Cosmic Poets' gig. Lily said by the time we were through with our third set she had fallen deeply in love with me and knew Nathan and she would never work. I was a revolutionary romantic who had captured her heart in a special way. I had a vision. A vision for *what* she never said, but it didn't matter at the time. She dumped Nathan while I became her new idol, a poet who became quickly addicted to all the attention she was giving me. She was convinced that I was destined for fame and glory.

But soon she grew weary of me. First it was my eating habits—too much meat for her politics. Then, it was my car—a smashed up Coronet that always pulled to the right. Eventually she came to realize that I was just another lost idealist who'd never figure out how to make a buck. But, as was true with most girls I'd dated, the more she pulled away the more beautiful she became. Some might have called it love. In the depths of my heart I knew it was something else. Now the tables were turning and she was going back. To *Nathan*.

"I'm happy for you, Angus. I really am. You're not a fool. You're a dreamer."

"What's the difference, Lily? I want you. Doesn't that make me a dreamer *and* a fool?"

"I told you not to have any expectations," she whispers. "I don't know where I'm going to land when this is over."

"I know," I say, weakly, "but I still love you."

"I love you too," she says with a sad smile. "I know we'll always be friends."

"But I don't want to be just friends. I want another chance. Please. I'll quit meat *and* coffee this time. I promise."

"Don't change your life for my benefit, Angus," she says. "You shouldn't get so emotional, either."

"I need to know where we stand. Is it Nathan? Are you going back to him?"

"You've got to quit being so jealous. I'll always love him. I told you that when we got together."

"Then tell me it's over and I'll move on."

"I'll hurt you, Angus. Stay away until you're strong."

"Hurt me," I gasp.

But she's no longer looking at me. She's looking past me, a curious smile growing on her lips. "Hi, Ollie," she says, finally.

"Well, hello there, Lily. Angus? How's it going?"

"Great, Ollie," I sigh, not looking at him.

"Sorry to butt in, but what time is soundcheck?"

"8:00, Ollie." I turn to Lily. "You really should stay for this one. This might be one of the last Bellingham gigs we do in quite a while."

"Did Angus tell you about the big tour?" asks Ollie. "Of course he did. By the way, you know you shouldn't be drinking coffee, Angus. You know, I was reading in the *Utne Reader* about a coffee cooperative in Brazil that fell prey to—"

"Not this again, Ollie," I say.

"Why not?" asks Lily. "It sounds like he's got something interesting to say."

"When doesn't Ollie have something interesting to say? I don't have time to listen to some tirade about coffee plantations right now."

"Don't get so defensive, Angus," says Ollie. "We're all in this together. I should quit coffee myself, actually. Did you know that the long-term effects of caffeine wreak havoc on—"

"Enough!" I yell. "I was hoping you wouldn't find me. Why do you always *find* me, Ollie?"

"You should be nicer to your drummer," says Lily. "I'll listen to your story, Ollie."

"What was I saying?" Ollie asks in deep thought. "I forgot."

"It was about coffee plantations."

"Oh yeah, coffee plantations. Did you know that Adolph Hitler was a personal friend of Henry Ford and that the Nazi Empire rose to power only because of the help of American Industrialists like Ford?"

"What does *that* have to do with coffee plantations?"

"Nothing, but that's information people need to know, don't you think?" Ollie stares at her and I feel a pang of jealousy rip through my soul.

"That's incredible," she gasps. "I didn't know that."

"It's true," says Ollie. "If you read the best-selling book, *IBM and the Holocaust* you'll find that Ford wasn't alone in his disdain for Jews and when you stop to think about it..."

I quietly excuse myself to go to the bar for a pint. I find Zen there getting happily smashed.

"The rest of 'em here?" asks Zen.

"Not yet but Ollie is," I say, quietly.

"Well that's a first."

"Bastard's hanging out with Lily."

"She doesn't deserve you, Angus. Let her go." Just then the bartender shows up and Zen orders three pints of stout. He looks at me. "You want anything, Angus?"

~

It's 8:45 and we hope to begin rocking Bounday Bay at 9:30. We have practiced tightening up our set by jumping from song to song without awkward tuning breaks. I'm having Jed Barnes tune my spare guitar so, theoretically, when a song ends and the audience is still cheering, he'll hand it to me and I'll be able to slam into the next song without having to tune. We tried it once in practice and as long as he's not drinking I should be in good shape.

Jed Barnes is a short, pot-bellied man with a big laugh. Because he plays guitar himself, I think he's a good man for the job, though there have been mixed results depending on his level of alcohol consumption. I told him earlier how important this gig was going to be, and how he wasn't to drink at all until after the show, so when he comes staggering up to me, beer in hand, I've got a bad feeling.

"I thought I told you no drinking," I say. His grin fades.

"I'm okay," he slurs. His mouth is all greasy and he seems to be chewing on something.

I look around. The club is already three-quarters filled, and we're not playing for another forty-five minutes.

"Are you sure you're okay?" I ask.

He responds by pulling a half-cooked, bloody piece of meat from his pocket, holding it out to me. Stuck to the meat is an old napkin.

"Some venison?"

"No thanks," I say. "You're gonna wash your hands before you touch my guitars, aren't you?"

"Of course," he says.

Ollie is now back in the club, his hair wet from his before-gig shower ritual. Zen, Angel and Star are up on stage talking about someone. Probably me, I think as they burst out laughing.

Ian Eisner materializes before me, leather jacket, cheap cologne, slicked back, graying hair and his usual air of self-importance. He studies me for a moment. "Sound's like you got some things cooking."

"We do," I say.

"I can still get you on Letterman."

Yeah, bullshit, I think as I look into his blood-shot eyes. This is the same guy who was road manager for Pink Floyd on their *Animals* tour in '77, got Van Halen signed a few years later, played drums on Jackson Browne's debut album, managed Bonnie Raitt, broke U2 into the United States, and co-owns a ranch with Willie Nelson. It just so happens that he now lives at the Lighthouse Mission. Go figure.

"Well, Ian," I say, trying to be polite, "all of our business affairs are now going through Sunny Rickshire. Talk to her about Letterman."

"Does she know what she's doing?" he asks. "I've been in the biz twenty-five years and I've seen a lot of phonies."

I look at him in amazement. "Yeah, she damn well knows what she's doing, Ian. She has *Frank Strong* shopping us to the big boys. I'd say that's pretty damn good, wouldn't you?"

"Frank Strong...hmmm...doesn't ring a bell," Ian says.

"Talk to Sunny if you have any other questions," I say.

"All I'm saying, Angus, is be careful. People aren't always what they seem in this business."

"Hey, Angus, I just heard you got signed by Sony Records," says Jim Douglas, one of our long time groupies. Jim's a disgruntled Viet Nam Vet who keeps to himself a lot.

"No, not yet," I say, amazed at how fast the rumors are flying around. Sunny's tactic is really working and by the time we're ready to seize the stage, eight different people have come up to me looking star-struck. They all think we've actually signed a record contract. I tell them we're not quite there yet, though their excitement is infectious. The air almost crackles with excitement.

We take the stage, self-confident, swaggering and full of ourselves, ready to kick butt. The hometown crowd is huge and they are screaming and cheering before we even start to play. It's one of those rare nights when I look to Star, Angel, Zen, and Ollie and love them all. My heart swells with pride. They can do no wrong and when we blast into our first song, it sounds good. We plow through it and as the last cymbal crash fades into the sound of applause I look for my guitar and notice it still on its stand. Jed's about twenty feet away, beer in hand, yakking with someone out in the crowd. He's already forgotten he's got a job to do. I call to him over the house PA and he comes running up, beer sloshing all over himself, mumbling an apology as he takes my guitar while handing me the other.

I pull the strap over my head and as I slide my hand down the neck I feel a warm, sticky goo on my hand. I examine it and see remnants of blood and flesh. The bastard didn't wash his hands, and now I've got venison blood all over my Taylor! Before I can say anything, he's tuning my other guitar and I realize it's a lost cause.

We play the next song and the crowd is freaking out. Unfortunately I'm still locked in a mortal struggle with venison grease. At the next changeover I yell for him to wash his hands, but he only smiles. He's too far gone to reason with. As I pull my guitar over my head I strike the bone above my eyelid and instantly I feel warm blood flowing down my face. I'm pretending not to notice it, but as I tune my guitar and turn to face the audience, Star looks at me with great concern. "Angus, you're bleeding all over yourself."

"Oh, am I?" I put my hand to my head and when I pull it away it's streaked with blood. Most of our fans don't seem to notice though I see Sunny and Peaches staring at me in disbelief. I put my guitar down and whisper to Angel to do one of her songs.

"I can't," she says, panicked, and I can't tell if it's because of the blood. Zen and Ollie hardly seem to notice, and I mumble something about a break before going back-stage to find a towel. Jed finds me one and after holding it to my head for a few minutes, the bleeding stops. The rest of the band plays a long version of *Peter Gunn*. After it finishes, I take the stage again, greeted by a rousing ovation. I strum the guitar that Jed has just tuned for me and find it tuned in a way I can't quite comprehend.

I look out into the crowd and find Jed's stocky figure talking and laughing with Peaches. I want to tell him to stop messing with my guitars, but I can't. I fix the tuning and catch a glimpse of Sunny glaring at me. I take my rage out on the next few songs and the band picks up on it. Twenty minutes later the crowd is worked into a sweating frenzy, and I see that I've won Sunny over again—she's smiling and chewing her lips.

We're well into our last set and things are raging. We're feeling this synergy and know that no force other than God Himself is going to keep us from a record deal. We're too damn good. Then disaster strikes.

I should have told Jed to lay off on the tuning and to leave my guitars alone. I should have had someone drive him home. I should have paid him to stand outside. As we're peaking out on our last epic jam I hear something horribly wrong. I look at Angel and Star. Neither of them is playing. Finally it registers. It is the sound of another guitar...a lead being played in a different key, a different dimension. I look around and everybody in the band is looking at each other, bewildered. Then I see Jed, tucked behind Zen's bass cabinet, playing my other guitar with closed, squinting eyes. To his credit he's really into it. In a kind of ecstatic trance he wanders out onto the stage trying to play the guitar while Zen and Ollie are locked in a desperate struggle to hold the groove together.

"What are you doing, Jed?" I holler as he comes closer to me. Star just stands behind him, astonished.

Instead of answering he just smiles and rips off another horribly discordant lead. Finally Angel unplugs him and the audience roars as his lead guitar solo evaporates. He stands there staring at me like he's all offended and tries to force the guitar into a stand before turning to me. "Fuck you, Angus, and see if I ever tune your guitars again."

"You're a loser, Jed!" I scream.

He turns to me like he's gonna come after me, but he's so crocked that the simple turning motion causes him to lose his balance and he falls backward, knocking my guitar and stand to the floor in a mighty crash. Finally some of our burly male fans escort him from the stage; one of them picks up my guitar and places it carefully back in its stand. All is confusion and disarray, but somewhere in the surrealistic clamor, Zen and Ollie are still pounding out a groove, and when I finally look out into the crowd, I see three hundred and fifty-people swaying like one amorphous, gelatinous mass. When I start pounding on my guitar again, the whole place explodes with cheering and clapping. I know after Jed sleeps off his drunk he'll have forgotten about the whole ordeal.

We are called back for two encores and this gorgeous brunette woman keeps smiling and flirting with me. I wish Lily could see how much the crowd likes us. Perhaps then she might come around. As the last notes fade into the thunderous applause of the audience, I'm sad. I miss her terribly, knowing she's with Nathan.

It seems weird to be sad when people are cheering for you. Maybe that's just the way it always is. Or maybe it's just because I know I've become a liar. Sometimes you gotta lie to get what you want. Four shows in eleven days isn't terrible. Especially the Redwood concert. I can't risk having Sunny and Frank pull the plug after we've worked so hard to get where we are. It's my only chance for Lily.

Several of our groupies are hanging around while we're breaking down and someone asks if we're gonna have a party afterwards. Ollie, Zen and Angel say they're up for it, but I'm not. I need sleep and some alone time. We're about to embark upon a great journey. I've placed all the eggs I've ever owned into the basket and now the basket wavers precariously on the edge of the Great Abyss. But hey, what are a few stupid eggs?

Three

We are slated to be on the road at noon which will put us into Seattle at about three this afternoon. One of the agreements I made with Zen is that while on tour I do most of the driving so he can drink and sleep. Of course getting on the road at noon doesn't happen. It's not entirely Ollie's fault, either. As we're nearing the I-5 cutoff Angel suddenly decides she needs to see her boyfriend Preston alone for a couple of hours.

"Maybe you should just stay home," I say, immediately wishing that I hadn't.

"It would be just like you to leave me behind," she says, coldly. "You'll probably try to ditch me somewhere."

"Angel," I say, "I'm sorry I said that and I'd never ditch you on purpose."

Then Ollie starts obsessing about a junk filled room; cleaning it out might mean the difference in saving his marriage. Like most musicians, Ollie has stuff left over from childhood that he's never unpacked.

"Geeze, Ollie," I say, gently. "Don't you think it's a little late to be unpacking all that crap? Besides, she'll probably just throw it away anyway while we're on tour." I recall Ollie's confused expression when after dropping him off at home after practice a few weeks back, we found his cherished and extensive album collection distributed all over the front yard and some even in the top of his cherry tree. They were like black Frisbees, thrown everywhere. Many were shattered and cracked.

Now Ollie is sitting in the back of our tour bus looking panicked while Star consoles him to no avail. "No, I gotta do it. I'm sorry, but I really gotta clean that room. I've got important papers in there."

Given he and Angel's precarious emotional states, we all agree to get a later start and drop them both off at their respective destinations.

Zen, Star and I decide to go bowling since it's a good chance for getting some aggression out. Aggression, when channeled appropriately, can be a healthy thing. It's funny: I'm not uptight or even mad at Angel or Ollie. I've come to accept these kinds of things and only lament that things might be tight getting to Seattle. But even that will be all right. It's all good as they say.

Zen bowls a two twenty, Star a one eighteen, and I an eighty-nine. Afterwards we order a pitcher of generic beer and sit around a table.

"How are you guys feeling?" I ask.

"I miss Elvis," says Zen.

"He would have wanted it this way, Zen," says Star. "Elvis was a pro."

"We all gotta leave our personal shit at the door," I say. "I mean, if we want to be pros, too."

We sit in silence, watching the little carbonated bubbles break loose from the side of the pitcher, floating lazily upward and suddenly Star says in a very wobbly voice, "Excuse me, I gotta go make a phone call." She hurriedly arises and I can tell she's about to lose it.

Now it's just Zen and me staring at bubbles and I'm feeling weaker by the second as an irrational, leaden cloak of depression smothers me. "Zen, please excuse me. I must go make a phone call as well." He smiles sadly as I arise and search my pockets for some change. I know that by the time I get back, the pitcher will be history.

The phone rings once, twice, three times and then the phone machine clicks on and I hear her soft voice: "I'm sorry I missed you...please leave a message and I'll call you right back. I promise..." As I hear the beep, I slam the phone down. She doesn't really mean she's sorry she missed me. Or is she? Maybe she is. I dial the number again. This time I'm startled when she answers on the first ring.

"Hello?"

"Hi."

"Oh...hi. I wasn't expecting to hear from you. Did you just try to call?"

You thought it would be Nathan, didn't you? "Uh, no. We're about to hit the road and I just thought I'd say goodbye. Sunny's talking like we're gonna have a deal on the table any day now."

"I'm happy for you."

"Look, I just wanted to say goodbye," I say, angrily. "I don't have time to talk, anyway."

"I'll miss you, Angus. I guess I won't see you for a couple of weeks."

"Maybe I'll call you from the road sometime to check in, but you know how crazy things can get. It's too bad you couldn't have stayed last night. Jed Barnes smeared venison blood all over the neck of my guitar and I gashed my eye. That was before he invited himself up to play on a song. He's the worst guitar player I've ever heard and now that Elvis is dead I don't know what's going to happen."

"You are so *funny*," she laughs. "You know, I hope we'll always be friends. I love you so much."

"What do you mean, you *love* me?"

"I mean, I love you. You don't want to hear the truth?"

"No, I guess I don't," I say, feeling a surge of delight. She *does* love me. She just needs time alone.

"Well, it's true. I know we'll always be close friends."

Ah, the dagger. I know what she really means—she means nothing. "I gotta go," I sigh.

"You guys are gonna be really big," she says, quickly. "I just know Sunny's gonna score. You totally deserve it, too."

"Thanks."

I mean it, Angus. I hope you find a woman worthy of you."

"I only want to be with you," I say, quietly.

"It's hard right now, but it'll get better. You'll see. Be safe out there. I really do love you, Angus. You mean the world to me."

I gently place the receiver back in its cradle and when I check the clock, it's 2:34 P.M. Time to go.

When I return, Zen's well into our second pitcher. I really have nothing to say, and he doesn't expect me to. We drink in silence until Star shows up. Her face is streaked with red. We all understand. She too has a breaking heart.

Star wants marriage and stability in her life, which makes her quest to become famous a great irony. She believes that the power in getting what she wants lies in refining and perfecting the strength of her will. She still has a ways to go. She isn't married and the band isn't famous, yet. Like most of us, she fears a life of insignificance and believes that only by becoming the cultural icon of the millennium will she find joy and inner peace.

We drive back across town to find Angel and her boyfriend, Preston, engaged in a tragic goodbye. Angel cries, as gentle winds blow her raven hair about her face.

"All over a stupid male," says Star as we wait for Angel and Preston to finish.

"Give her a break," says Zen from the back. Ollie sits next to him reading a copy of a *Rolling Stone* dated October, 1971, and is lost in thought. He didn't even get close to cleaning out his secret room. He instead became absorbed in some old magazines and grabbed a bunch for the trip. Nonetheless, he seems to be feeling better.

"Aw, come on, Angel," I say, leaning on the horn.

She turns her attention from her green-eyed dream boy only long enough to wave us off.

Star begins chanting, "*An*-gel, *An*-gel, *An*-gel," and soon, the motor-home is rocking.

Preston shoots us the bird, yelling something in our direction before storming away. Angel climbs aboard, furious.

"You guys are so rude!" she yells.

"Get it together, baby," I scream, feeling sudden sense of liberation. "We gotta gig with Bonnie Raitt to save the Redwoods."

"Have you no compassion?" yells Ollie.

I gun the engine up Old Fairhaven Parkway's I-5 on-ramp. I emulate a Morrison scream, drowning out Angel's cries. We are finally on our way.

Four

"Alger or bust!" I holler as we top out at fifty miles-per-hour and the air is electric with trees blowing in the summer wind and clouds racing through the sky. On tour at last...

On tour. The phrase evokes images of a posh, coach-liner bus surrounded by several semi-trucks full of equipment cruising through the desert on the way to the next arena gig. Or a beat up hippie van stuffed with shirtless freaks on their way to the next Rainbow Gathering. On tour. The freedom of the road. The beginning of possibility, the mythical place where dreams come true, where bands bond, where inspiration grows, where great songs are written, where love is expressed in unspeakable ways, where the fullness of life is....

"Can you close the fucking window?" screeches Star. "I'm fucking freezing!"

I look in the rear view mirror and see Angel and Star in the back engaged in some deep conversation. We make it as far south as Alger when Zen informs us that he has to give birth to a Republican, and since the toilet is one part of the motor-home that is not functional, we are required to stop at The Alger Tavern, a scant fifteen miles southeast of Bellingham. It's actually a good thing that the bathroom isn't functional since I've heard horror stories about getting splashed with excrement while sitting on the throne. When you're on tour to get famous like we are, you can't afford to be getting splashed with excrement, even if it's your own.

Since it is determined that a celebration beer is in order, we all go in. We put a ten-minute limit on the stop and Zen uses up the whole ten minutes but seems to be feeling better upon his return. Everybody drinks beer but me. I instead drink a cup of coffee that tastes like it's been on the burner a week.

"Being on tour is exciting, huh?" I ask the crew. Angel is in much better spirits; we all are. We finish our beverages and Zen buys a six-pack for the road.

"There's something that's been troubling me," I say as we assemble outside.

"What?" asks Zen.

"We haven't named our road machine," I say. "It needs a name."

"Elvis," says Zen without hesitation.

"Elvis," I whisper. "That's a great idea."

Ollie looks slowly around at each of us as if he's suddenly afraid to speak. "Are you sure you want to name the motor-home after a deceased icon that died such a horrible death?" he asks.

"Elvis," says Angel, smiling while her eyes mist over. "Zen, what a great idea."

"It sure is," says Star, reaching for a chew.

Ollie has no further argument. He certainly knows there are to be much more worthwhile things to fight about later on in the tour. It is 3:32 P.M. as we pile into Elvis, and secure ourselves for the two-hour drive south. Finally, we're really and truly on our way.

~

We pull into Seattle at about 5:00 P.M. and make it a few blocks off of the freeway heading for Ballard on West 80th when Elvis overheats again. Load-in is at 6:30 and though our plan is to stop at Ivar's for some fish & chips before our big Seattle debut, it's now doubtful there will be time. We pull over at 80th and Phinney while my grudge against Seattle grows as quickly as the cloud of steam pouring out from under the hood. We all pile out of the rig and for a few moments stare at it in dejected silence.

"I thought you said you fixed it, Zen," says Angel.

"That's what I heard," says Star.

"It works fine as long as you don't go over fifty-five."

Cars rush by as I look around noticing we've at least reached the business section of Phinney Ridge, a few miles from the club.

"I noticed you were going sixty-three back in Everett, Angus," says Ollie. "I should have said something. I remember Nixon's famous speech on June 9, 1973 when he announced the mandatory fifty-five mile-per-hour national speed limit. There was a study done back then that showed we would actually save a million barrels of oil per year if—"

"Stop it, Ollie," says Zen.

"And now you'd think with global warming and all that people would be more conscious, but it's just the opposite—"

"Don't go there, Ollie," says Zen.

"I'm serious, Zen. Did you know that OPEC wields more power to regulate the entire global economy than any other entity in the entire world and that when Reagan was in office he was privately arming the same Iranian militants who were responsible for the suicide bombing of—"

"Ollie!" Zen yells. "Shut up!"

"I can't believe this is happening again," says Star. "Angus, how could you be so stupid?"

"Thai food," says Angel. "I need Thai food."

"One hundred and sixty-three U.S. Marines dead, all because Reagan—"

"I said I *need* Thai food."

"And, Zen, sometimes you seem to fall predictably in line with mainstream public opinion and given all the information I've presented to you—"

"Angus, I need Thai food, goddamnit!" screams Angel. "How do you expect me to sing when I'm feeling so fucking invalidated?"

"I'm pretty hungry myself, Angel," says Zen, upbeat. "And I could sure use a drink. I saw a Thai place a couple of blocks back." He and Angel begin walking back up the street.

"I need a bathroom," Ollie says. "I should have said something awhile ago. Maybe I should go with them."

"Come on, Ollie," I say. "Just wait 'til this thing cools down. We'll go find a bathroom together."

"I'm perfectly capable of finding a bathroom on my own, Angus."

"You'll be lost in five minutes."

"Oh let him go," sighs Star. "Zen'll make sure he doesn't get lost." We both watch Ollie shuffling up the block until he's out of sight.

"So much for the big Seattle debut," I sigh.

"You have to quit worrying so much," says Star. Then as an afterthought: "What about Elvis? Why does he keep over-heating?"

"Zen says it's nothing that a little duct tape can't fix. We just have to wait for him to cool."

We wait. We wait some more. A half-hour passes and I pop the radiator cap and add water. In moments Elvis is running smoothly again. But, of course, our comrades have not returned. "Let's cruise back down the block and pick 'em up at the restaurant."

We find the Thai place a few blocks back up the street and after searching the restaurant, I reconnoiter with Star at the van. "Classic," I say. "I knew this was gonna happen."

"Let's circle the block again," she says, her eyes dark with anger.

We do, and to no avail. We can't find them anywhere.

"Ah, to hell with 'em," says Star. "Let's go to the Firehouse and play as a duo."

We drive west on 80th toward Ballard and I envision Zen and Angel having a drink in some dark, smoky cocktail lounge with Ollie lost and wandering around someone's back yard on Phinny Ridge. Star is surprisingly tranquil. She reaches into her bag.

"Must you do that in the rig?" I ask as she pops a wad of wintergreen chew under her lower lip and spits into a paper cup.

"I won't spill any this time, I promise. You want me to relax, don't you?"

"Why don't you smoke a cigarette instead?"

"Smoking's hard on the lungs."

"Yeah, but do you know what that stuff does to your lips and teeth?"

"I'm too stressed to quit right now," she says. "Fire Ollie, and then maybe I'll think about quitting." She looks at me and her clear eyes betray a subtle wildness.

"In case you forgot, we're officially on tour, Star. Besides, where would we find a drummer as good as him? He's got us over a barrel."

"Yeah, but I can't put anymore energy into baby-sitting him. Not to mention the fact that the bell of his ride cymbal's been killing me lately."

We drive on in silence for a few blocks. "How did Janis die?" she asks after awhile.

"Heroin overdose. Ollie knows the details."

"Have you ever tried heroin?"

"No," I say, truthfully. "My life's already screwed up enough as it is."

"How do you mean?" Her sudden interest flatters me.

"Lily's dumping me. It's my fault, really."

"Why do you say that?"

"I wasn't there for her when she said she really needed me."

"I think you're being way too hard on yourself."

Oh, please don't start getting tender hearted, Star. I can't handle it.

"I really do," she continues. "You're one of the nicest, most gentle guys I've known and if you ask me the bitch doesn't deserve a second chance with you." She spits loudly into her cup for emphasis. "Trust me, Angus, if I ever see that old money New England priss again I'll knock her fucking teeth out."

"Well, gee...thanks, Star. That's really nice of you. But she's not as bad as I probably make it seem." I pull into the Ivar's parking lot, deeply moved by her sensitivity. It's so strange. We've lost three band members and we're having our best conversation ever. I'm not even worried anymore.

We go inside and order. Star's sudden earthiness and child-like innocence seem to make her face glow, and were it not for her swollen bottom lip I'd find her quite attractive. "Do you swallow that stuff?" I ask.

"You bet," she says.

Our food arrives and between bites of fish and swigs of root beer, we go over the set list we'll play as a duo. I'm excited at the prospect of pulling it off without the band. "We don't need a drummer, anyway," she says. "I can see why bands get heavily into drugs. Maybe that's what happened to Janis. Maybe she was just fine and normal before she got her band together."

"No musician who's any good is normal," I say, wondering what Star would actually consider normal to be. "Personally, I'm sick of Angel and her whining. She's drives me nuts."

Star's blue eyes are suddenly big with concern. "Do *I*?"

"I can't believe they charge you for extra tartar sauce here," I reply, looking away.

"Answer the question, Angus. *Do* I?"

"Well, sometimes, but I'm sure I get on your nerves, too."

"Oh, you'd better believe you do, Angus. You're way too passive. If I were you, I'd fire the whole band except for Zen and me."

"Are you serious? You'd fire Angel?"

"You think I gave up two years of my life to be in this band only to have some prima donna fuck up my chances for success? We've got the former President of RCA shopping us to labels, a publisher and music promoter who knows what it takes to get to the top. With my artistic brilliance...and your great song writing too," she adds as a quick afterthought, "the sky's the limit. Dump her, but just make sure that Ollie is in the bowl with her before you flush."

I look at her with a sudden fear as she hurriedly wipes a spot of tartar sauce with a napkin that's rolled up in the tightest of balls. She throws it down, cupping her face in both hands. "I just wanted this stupid band to work...I've invested so much of myself in it, Angus. Doesn't anybody give a shit?" She slams her hand on the tray sending her root beer cup airborne. "Where *are* those assholes?"

"We'd better go now, Star," I say, getting up and putting my arm gently around her shoulders. "We don't need a band, remember?" People are now staring at us.

"Sorry," she sniffles. "I'm kind of losing it, I guess."

"It's okay, Star," I say with compassion.

Five

We pull into The Ballard Firehouse parking lot at a quarter-to-seven. An actual former fire station, its redbrick exterior and old architecture give it a flavor that, in my opinion, is perfect for classic rock. The place is dark and almost looks abandoned, though the marquee does read: Tonight: Big Brother and the Holding Company! Even though we are supposed to be the exclusive opening act for these venerable 60's icons, our name is conspicuously absent.

I walk over to the entrance. It's locked.

"Doesn't open till seven," says a harshed-out male voice. I turn and see a red, '67 Ford van with tinted windows and a wiry little guy with sunken eyes and a pubescent mustache staring at me from the passenger seat. "Who are you?" he asks.

"Angus Keegan," I say. "My band is opening up for Big Brother."

"Oh, really? So are we."

"No shit?" I ask. "I didn't know there was another opener."

I hear laughter coming from within the dark recesses of the van and I smell pot smoke. "Three," wire-arms says and there is more laughter.

"What?"

"There are *three* other opening acts besides yourselves."

"You've got to be kidding me."

"Hell, Roy wanted to book four, but I talked him out of it," wire-arms says. "You want a beer?"

"No thanks," I say, still in shock. The dude has a hideous tattoo of a boa with a large rodent hanging out of its mouth. "So you guys had to sell thirty tickets to get this gig?" I ask.

"Not even, dude," he says. "I'm a friend of Roy's and he knows we draw. I think it's just Goon Squad and you guys that sold tickets. You're kind of mad, aren't you dude?"

"What time is Roy showing up?" I ask, ignoring his question.

"About seven. Oh my," he says in sudden astonishment, looking past me.

I turn and see Star walking slowly and seductively up the sidewalk toward us. She has changed her clothes and is now wearing a red, lacy silk shirt with a black mini-skirt. Her hair is all frizzy and the tops of her breasts protrude tauntingly. I hear a commotion in the van and suddenly the side door opens and three other seedy-looking males appear, looking like they've just awakened from a two-day nap under the Lake Washington Ship Canal Bridge.

"Hi, fellas," she says, before turning to launch a dark stream of tobacco juice from her lips toward some bushes.

"Right *on*!" one of the trio says. "Got any more of that?"

"You bet," she says pulling the can from her purse. "Are you guys with Big Brother?"

More stoned laughter erupts, and one of the stinky males says, "Why, you wanna see Janis's corpse?"

"No, we're not from Big Brother," says rodent breath. "My homey here's just being a smartass." He extends his hand to me. I hardly notice as I am consumed with fury.

"What's the name of your band?"

"Ratfuck," says the dude which gets Star choking and spitting madly.

"Are you serious?" she asks after recovering a bit. "What kind of music do you play?"

"Psychedelic-grunge with industrial overtones," he says, proudly.

"Cool," she says, but when she's informed that there are now *four* opening acts, including us, and we're only one of two bands who sold six hundred dollars worth of tickets out which we'll be paid seventy-five dollars for services rendered, she doesn't think it is very cool at all. In fact, she is livid.

"Welcome to Seattle," someone says. As I'm imagining what I'll say to that son-of-a-bitch Roy, he comes pulling up on a Harley in rattling, popping rage. As his engine dies the chunky, burly-armed-biker-booking-agent gets off of his bike. I imagine his variety of responses to me telling him he's an asshole—among them, I imagine having my neck casually snapped like a Sunday chicken. Nothing personal of course.

Introductions are brief and clarification comes quickly. Yes, there are four opening bands. Yes, competition is very heavy to play in Seattle. Yes, advance ticket sales are a common practice. Seattle is the land of the desperate musician and the parasitic booking-agent. And, finally, yes, the sets will be short, one half-hour maximum with the order of the bands to be determined by a coin toss. Except for a band called Groovetribe who goes on right before Big Brother.

And no, not even Star is going to argue with this mangy tripe who smells like stale bacon grease. He just got up to go to work and is in no mood to argue with whiny, prima donnas like us. Besides, I don't have a band, anyway—just one chew-spitting rocker-queen who is waiting for the world to bow down in worship before those slick, black boots of hers.

We begin load-in and once inside this huge dude with purple hair and silver nose ring introduces himself as Bruce, the bass player and lead singer for Goon Squad. He asks if I want to do the coin flip.

"Nah," I say. "We'll go on first." At least this means we might get a sound check.

"How's it going, sweetie?"

I turn, feeling the blood fall from my head. "Sunny, I didn't know you were coming."

Sunny stands before me licking her lips while trying to keep her balance. She's still wearing the same leather coat and doesn't look like she's been to sleep in days. "I thought I'd surprise y'all."

"It *is* a surprise."

Peaches stands next to her, smiling while his eyes dart back and forth, searching the dark corners of the club for signs of Star and Angel.

"Where's the rest of the band?" Sunny asks.

"They're around here somewhere," I say, casually.

Then, as if on cue, out in the hall comes the sound of drunken shouting and here's Angel standing before me in her elegant, flowing clothes. Her bare feet are filthy. "It's just like you to abandon me, Angus!" she pants. "Why'd you ditch us?"

Zen comes in behind her, a bit wobbly himself. "Yeah, Angus, why?"

"We looked all over for you guys," I say. Sunny and Peaches stare at all of us, puzzled. Angel picks up on it and calms down.

"We had problems," I say to Sunny. "They're all fixed now."

Angel looks at Sunny as if noticing her for the first time. "Give me a hug, sister," she says. They both head for the bar.

"What happened, Zen?" I ask.

"We were attempting to transcend the physical and material realm by altering the nature of cosmic reality and in the process we lost Ollie. He never made it to the restaurant. We were hoping he was with you."

"He never made it to the restaurant? We went there looking for you guys. We didn't see you there either."

"We were there," Zen sputters, and as he says this, I realize that I really don't want to try to piece together what happened. Besides nobody's going to remember what happened tomorrow, anyway. Sunny is off having drinks with Star, Angel and Peaches, and now Zen joins them. They're all talking with Roy, our burly-armed booking agent. "Blue Oyster Cult played here last week," I hear him say, and a moment later some laughter erupts.

The other bands' members are now drifting in. A fat guy with rainbow-colored, frizzy hair is hauling some drums to the center of the floor. After chatting with the amiable, but slightly high-strung fellow, I learn that he is the drummer for Goon Squad. But still no sign of Big Brother. It doesn't matter. With four openers, they won't be going on until at least midnight, and we'll be long gone by then, heading south for our meeting with destiny in Arcata. I manage to distract Angel and Star from the big city glam-fest long enough to get them to haul their equipment, including Angel's organ, to the stage. Now Sunny is standing before me, smiling. Behind her stand Zen, Angel and Star.

"Guess what?" she asks.

"What?"

"Roy told me this place is gonna be crawling with labels tonight." She waits for my response.

"Did Frank set this up?" I ask, getting excited.

"He must have," she says.

"Who are they?"

"Probably Warner Brothers, Virgin, Island, Sony, MCA. You know, those guys."

"Oh yeah, *those* guys," I say. For once, Star and Angel are speechless and Zen looks like he just wants to sober up.

"This is your big shot. Play good tonight." Then she looks around quickly and asks, "Where's Ollie?"

"He's outside," I say. It is a fact and it also buys time. Zen, Star and Angel look to me for leadership.

"Let me know when he comes in; I need to talk with him." Sunny rubs her nose as she heads back toward the bar.

"We'll do it as a four-piece," I say, once Sunny's out of earshot.

Angel has this tense, strained look in her eyes, and she won't look at me.

'We'll rock," Star hisses. "Ollie's been sucking on the drums lately, anyway."

Angel's eyes keep avoiding me. I know why. But there is too much on the line this time. This isn't child's play anymore.

I breathe deeply, preparing myself to speak. She knows it's coming and we both know it's going to get ugly. "Angel?"

"What, Angus?" she says, not looking at me.

"We're not playing *Blue Sunday*, so you won't need to set up your organ."

"Oh, my organ's already set up," she says really quick-like while looking at the others with pleading eyes. "It's been sounding good, hasn't it Star?"

Star looks at her, and as her eyes slowly drift toward Zen, she says to me in a barely audible voice, "Let her play; it's been sounding fine."

"Zen?" asks Angel, feeling more confidence.

"It's been sounding all right to me," says Zen, staring at his shoes.

"Come on you guys; it's been shaky as hell." I feel my voice trembling. "Our ass is on the line tonight. I say we play to our strengths."

"Yeah, the same old boring songs," Angel says with disgust. She climbs onto the stage to stand protectively next to her organ. "They're tight," I retort. "And they're not old to label people who have never heard them before."

"Fine, Angus," she says in her sing-song voice, and I lip-sync with her as she says: "I'm gonna quit this fucking band. I gave my heart and soul to you for this bullshit?" Then she grabs onto her speaker cord, and yanks hard on it. It comes flying out of the organ, and she tries to whip me with it just as Star is jumping up on the stage. The metal jack smacks Star squarely in the forehead with a sickening thud.

"Owww, goddamnit!" Star grabs her head while crumpling to her knees.

"Oh my God, Star. I'm so sorry!" Angel cries, rushing over to examine the reddening welt forming on Star's forehead. "Are you all right?"

"I coulda' lost an eye!" she hisses. She then turns to me. "Just let her play her fucking organ you moron. I swear, you're as clueless as a bag of hammers!"

Suddenly we hear him outside in the hall, approaching fast. Ollie enters the room with a tall dude with a ponytail, laughing eyes and a slick leather coat.

"So was Newport the largest gig you guys ever played?" Ollie asks.

"No, Monterey Pop was by far the biggest," the man says.

"Ollie!" I yell. "What the hell happened this time?"

Ollie looks at us rather blankly as if nothing's wrong and nothing should be wrong. "Hey you guys, this is Sam Andrew, the lead guitarist for Big Brother and the Holding Company. He's a legend."

"Nice to meet you Sam," I say, taking his hand.

"Nice to meet *you*," says Sam, smiling as we all crowd around him in awe, forgetting that moments before we were in the midst of a life and death battle. It all seems so trivial now, anyway. Even Star has made a remarkable recovery, standing next to Sam with a big, goofy smile though she does keep gingerly touching the strawberry-sized lump on her forehead. Certainly this battle wound will only add to her mystique. We chat superficially, trying not to act too blown away, and out of this conversation we learn what happened to Ollie—and why.

Six

After Elvis had overheated and Zen and Angel left for the restaurant, Ollie had, in fact, followed them up the block. But for reasons unknown, he lost sight of them. Perhaps he was distracted by someone walking a dog across the street that looked like a girl with whom he had attended junior-high school twenty-five years ago. Or, perhaps, someone honked and he peered out into the street amazed at how the traffic had gotten so bad since the time he lived in the Wallingford District in his early twenties.

Whatever the reason, by the time he neared the restaurant he could no longer see them. However, he did notice a sign pointing to a new Larry's Market, a scant half-block away. He figured he could grab a macaroni salad and a corn dog for about a third the price of Phad Thai (considering the tip and all), not to mention the fact that Thai food didn't always agree with him. These considerations weighed heavily on his mind, as did the fact that it would probably take him half the time to get served at Larry's. After conferring with himself for a few minutes, he decided to go for it.

He found the main entrance, no problem, but it seemed to take him forever to find the deli and by the time he did, he remembered that he had to take a leak, and then it took awhile to find someone who could tell him where the bathroom was (he asked several people who all turned out to be non-employees) and then there was the actual finding of the bathroom, which, in itself, took some time, even with directions.

By the time he was back in line at the deli for his macaroni salad special, he had been in the store about a half-hour. By this time, he knew we might be getting worried. As he was pondering this possibility his eyes kept drifting back to a lone figure eating a piece of pizza and some coleslaw. The guy looked strangely familiar. Where had Ollie seen him before? Then his brain spasmed and cramped, taking him back to 1967: he was sitting in front of a black and white television watching *The Ed Sullivan Show*. Ed was welcoming the television audience and behind him were some beatniks with some very, very long hair. In the midst of them was a tough-looking girl with a frizzy mop. "Ladies and gentlemen," said Mr. Sullivan. "Please welcome Janis Joplin with Big Brother and the Holding Company."

The eerie, opening guitar melody of *Summertime* came floating across the television's little speakers and Ollie was transfixed on not the charismatic Janis, but on the tall, lanky freak playing those beautiful lines...and there he was some three decades later sitting in a Larry's Market deli, a strand of mozzarella hanging from his lip—Sam Andrew, the legendary guitarist from Big Brother and the Holding Company!

Ollie paid for his macaroni salad and made a beeline toward an empty table across from Sam. There he ate and stared, which after a few moments made the guitarist a bit nervous. "Excuse me," he had said, "but do you need something?"

"Oh, sorry for staring. You look like someone I know." Ollie's embarrassment was not enough to overcome his sense of urgency. There was too much at stake.

"Are you okay, man?" the man had asked.

"Oh, I'm sorry. Say, excuse me for asking, but are you Sam Andrew?"

The guy had stood up, choking and coughing loudly. After composing himself, he had asked, "How the hell did you know? Nobody ever recognizes me."

"I saw you on the Ed Sullivan show in August of '67, right after the Monterey Pop Festival. Say, you've got some cheese hanging from your lip," and saying this, Ollie had made a wiping motion on his own lip. Then, before Sam could speak, Ollie told him how much he loved his guitar playing.

"Well, thanks," Sam had responded.

Then Ollie began his inquisition for details regarding Janis's personal life and Sam, flattered and amazed at Ollie's in-depth knowledge of the Haight-Ashbury scene in the sixties, gladly provided them. After perhaps an hour or so, Sam informed Ollie that he had to meet the rest of his band over at the Ballard Firehouse for a gig that night, and Ollie asked if he could catch a ride with Sam since the band he was playing with called The Cosmic Poets was opening up for them.

"You're playing a gig with us tonight?" Sam had asked, shaking his head. "This is too weird."

They drove Sam's rental car back up the block to where the van was parked, but Ollie wasn't surprised that we had left; after all, he had been gone an hour-and-a-half. So they both drove to the Firehouse, and here they are. And here *we* are staring at the legendary Sam Andrew. All is well. Angel, especially, is star-struck, and has conveniently forgotten that she had just quit the band.

~

In a matter of forty-five minutes, the Firehouse is filled to capacity with an interesting mix of aging hippies, bikers, and multi-colored leather-clad punks with nose rings. The intensity level is high, and I'm actually glad that we are going on first. My acoustic guitars look impressive on their stands under the lights. I notice Sunny up at the bar talking to another freaky-looking dude and I wonder if he's from a record company. The thought of being watched by the mythical A&R people is exciting. Sunny had told me beforehand that we'd never actually know who the A&R people are. Like undercover cops, they try to hide their real identities. This gig could be huge. Some say that Seattle is just crawling with label people these days, kind of like the new Liverpool.

"You guys are on in five minutes," says a short guy with a deep voice whose black bandanna makes him look like a bandit.

Zen is near the stage drinking coffee. The place is really buzzing now; the room is filled to near capacity. A smoky, blue haze hangs over the room, drenching the crowd in its carcinogenic vapor. It is sweltering. "You guys ready?" I ask Angel, Star and Zen.

Zen nods, and the other two don't even hear me.

"Angel," I say. "Don't panic if anything goes wrong." I am imagining her annoying habit of jumping up and down while slapping herself in the head when the monitors aren't loud enough.

"I know, Angus," she says.

"Star, remember to lay off on the leads during the vocals."

"Yeah, sure, whatever you say, Angus." Star says dreamily, staring into the crowd that is now pressing up against the stage.

"Okay, you guys are up!" the bandit yells, jumping up on the stage.

"Where the hell is Ollie?"

"Has anyone seen him?"

"I heard him say he was going for a piss."

"You ready?" Bandit yells.

No, thanks to Ollie. Everything's in slow motion. This is Seattle—spawning grounds for Nirvana, Soundgarden, Pearl Jam, Heart, and Hendrix. This is our biggest gig ever.

Ollie returns to Star yelling, "I'm gonna put a fucking leash on you!"

"Did you give it a good shake?" mocks Zen.

Before Ollie can respond, we hear the big voice over the sound system saying, "From Bellingham, this group plays a delightful blend of organic, cutting edge folk-rock with bluesy textures..." We all turn in time to see him squinting at a piece of paper in his hand. I cringe.

"He's reading from our promo flyer," Star whispers. "How humiliating."

"...Please welcome The Cosmic Poets."

The bandit jumps from the stage and although there are probably three hundred and fifty people in the room, there is only a spattering of applause. We take the stage and I feel like we're walking out in front of a firing squad. The hands that reach down to grab my guitar look familiar, but feel much different now. Have they ever played a guitar before? Everything is slow and dream-like and I wonder why Ollie is wailing on his kick drum until I realize that it is my heart.

I see each band member swirl by in a surrealistic kaleidoscope, frozen in strange and desperate anticipation. The faces of the audience are scowling, indifferent and excited, yet all somehow restrained in a toxic, sultry ambivalence. I reach down for my guitar cord and see a shaking hand pick it up. I poke the end of my guitar, trying to find the jack when it slips through my fingers and falls to the floor, causing a loud buzz through the sound system. *Which of you assholes is Sony*, I wonder. I scan the audience packed up against the stage before picking up the guitar cord to try again.

Now it is my pick that falls through my fingers, landing somewhere on the gray, well-worn rug. I bend over, looking for it, but because it's the same color as the rug, I'm having trouble.

"Are you okay? What's wrong?" Star hisses.

I do not answer but continue on hands and knees looking for that damned pick. Aha, there it is. I'm amazed at how far it has bounced. Now the challenge is picking it up and since I've got no fingernails, I'm having difficulty. Are those boos I'm starting to hear?

You're blowing it, Angus. I catch a glimpse of a glaring Sunny and Peaches standing out in the seething mass of lunacy before me. When I look again, they're gone.

The sound of Zen's bass startles me, and I call upon Angel to assist in my pick retrieval.

"That was nice of you to help me," I say as she hands me the pick. "You have such beautiful, clean fingernails, Angel. How do you keep them so clean?"

Angel looks at me, concerned. Now I hear Ollie's nervous drum fills and the sound of distorted electric guitar. Star is poised next to me, ready to conquer. I hear my guitar over the sound system. Good. "Hi, Seattle," I say, timidly checking the microphone.

"Hi, Seattle?" laughs Angel.

"Start the song," commands Ollie.

All eyes are upon me. Here goes.

I start thrashing and banging out the opening guitar intro, and when the bass and drums come in I am completely engulfed in a wall of sound. Just when I think it can't get any louder, enter Star's saxophone which sounds to me like a giant fingernail raking a piece of slate. In fact, all I hear is that fingernail, and when the vocals arrive they are absent from the monitors.

That's when Angel begins her panic dance, jumping around in circles and boxing her ears and mouth simultaneously. What she is really doing is trying to communicate to the sound man that she can't hear herself—but she does it so fast she looks like she's playing her head like a marimba. So much for subtlety. We finish plowing through the song and to my surprise, the audience is cheering loudly. They like it. How about that?

We start our next song which kind of sounds like Lou Reed jamming with Jimi Hendrix. It is a loose, industrial space-jam with spoken word over the top of it. It starts quietly, then it builds. Star has now switched back to electric guitar and is noodling wildly while Angel thumps along on a tambourine next to her. Behind me Ollie and Zen form the gravitational force that holds us to the ground. This is a poetic ode to Armageddon and the great global computer crash that will trigger mass upheavals and famine.

After the poem part is complete, Star is going off with her double whammy2 Octave Bender and wah-wah pedal. We peak out to the point where we cannot take it any farther. It's critical mass, the moment of high drama when the volume will drop to a whisper, triggering a roar of approval from the crowd. It doesn't happen that way—though some of us do try.

Star, in her Hendrix seance with the great beyond, continues playing at the same volume, oblivious that the bottom has dropped out. The audience roars their approval as she goes off on her own, and we are forced to raise the volume. I mean, who needs a supporting cast anyway? I try to catch her attention and this time I think I do. We attempt the dynamic shift again, and the result is the same. It appears that Star has discovered a new universe.

I look back at Ollie and Zen and see Ollie shrug his shoulders while somehow holding down the groove. Here lies the greatest irony; Ollie's the one who holds us together on stage.

In the meantime Star has entered a new dimension, unforeseen by even Rod Serling. We cannot end the song until Star has decided we can. A group of sweaty, lizard-like guys have gathered before her, seething and writhing while slipping all over each other, staring up at her like faces from Hades, eyes burning with wild lust. She stands over them in her scanty black skirt, one leg up on a monitor. As she finally allows us to end the song, they go wild and I wonder if it's because she's not wearing underwear.

"Thank-you very much," I scream into the microphone.

"Thanks, you guys!" yells Angel, followed by Zen who yells, "Ello Sea'le!" in his mock Cockney. It's now clear that Star has helped us win over the crowd in a big way, and though my ears are ringing painfully, I'm grateful. Up yours, all of you Seattle music critics out there. What the hell do you know about real art? For that matter, what the hell do I know about real art? Now I notice Angel standing behind her organ. She has this strange, tense expression on her face as she protectively hovers over it, the way a wolverine might protect its kill.

Please keep it together, Angel, and, as if in response, the house speakers suddenly roar with the jangly theme song from the Redford/Newman classic *The Sting*. The audience laughs and cheers as Angel spasmodically slaps at the various buttons on her keyboard, trying to turn off the sampler button she had accidentally hit. I see Zen and Ollie laughing too while Star just kind of stares off into her own little dream world.

"I need your support!" Angel hisses to me, oblivious that she is hissing directly into the microphone and that her comments are broadcast to the entire room.

"We support you babe!" someone yells from the back of the room while people cheer loudly, but we're losing them fast.

"All right," I say into my microphone. "This one's called *Blue Sunday...*"

"Wait," says Angel, "I'm not ready." She is fiddling with her speaker cord, the same one she ripped out of her organ earlier that hit Star. It isn't working now. She looks up, panicked. "I can't hear my keyboard," she says to the soundman over her microphone.

Immediately out of the restless-growing crowd materializes the soundman. He is a short, nervous-looking guy with an afro, and he jumps up on stage with her.

"I can't believe this piece of shit," she says—again into her microphone.

"Angel," I whisper. "Don't talk into the microphone."

"But I can't hear my fucking *organ*," she says directly into the microphone while slapping the back of her keyboard and fiddling with a cord. Suddenly the speakers crackle like there is a full-blown thunderhead in the room followed by a high-pitched electronic squeal. The audience gasps and now there are boos starting to rain down upon us.

"Geeze, Louise," I say to Ollie.

Angel shoots another cold stare my way again as the clear, warbly sound of the organ fills the monitors again. We are ready to rock.

"I need your support *now* Angus," Angel says, this time off-mic and smiling.

"Whatever you say, Angel," I reply. We crash into the song and all I hear now is Zen's bass and Angel's organ. The soundman *is* deaf, I think. Many of them are. When it comes time to sing there are no vocals in the monitors and I can't hear my own guitar. Them's the breaks.

Angel grooves back and forth in front of her keyboard, trying to smile. We sing, guessing our notes, and it must sound terrible. But Angel pours her heart out. She really does. And what she's now playing sounds musical. Then a very strange thing happens as the song ends: the audience is cheering. They like it.

We slam right into the next song, and our fears have been conquered. This is another rocker, and I'm amazed at how good Zen's bass is sounding in the monitors. Zen should, by all rights, be the best musician in the band, but due to a drug-induced malfunction of the long-term memory bank, he even forgets my name from time to time, though we've played together for years. Yet he's still our unsung hero and spirit guide.

As the song progresses I look at Angel who is bouncing along with a bubbly joy and afterglow which is the result of her musical orgasm on the keyboard, and I'm happy for her. I'll never understand her, either. She has the raw potential to be an absolute superstar if she only knew how to play to her strengths and not offend people everywhere she goes.

The song is nearing its climax and, on the right of me, Star gyrates wildly. When it appears she can go no farther, as evidenced by the sweaty, lizard-pit that has been worked into a foaming frenzy before her, she sends a brown stream of chew spit that arcs gracefully, landing in the center. In a gesture of idolatrous appreciation, the beneficiaries of this special sacrifice rub the tobacco juice all over themselves. Then the whole room erupts in a roar as the goddess looks down on them, smiling strangely—a mythical figure seemingly trapped in her own tortured, Plexiglas reality, sweating like a 7-11 sausage under a heat lamp.

What do you think now, Seattle, I wonder as an intoxicating power courses through me. I stand, poised and confident in front of the crowd that is going wild again.

We blast into the next song and I'm starting to believe this was worth the price of admission. The monitors now crackle and there are the vocals, clear as the Northwest sky after a November rain. Better late than never, though it really doesn't matter because nobody listens to lyrics anyway.

Just when it seems too good to be true, Star plays a lead line right through the heart of the chorus and we cannot hold our notes. Nobody seems to care and when we finish the song the whole room is going crazy and it does feel like Liverpool in '63 and we are gonna be huge, just like Sunny had said we would. I'm humbled and grateful that Sunny and Frank are on board to take us to the top.

We are now well into the heart of our last jam when somewhere out in the middle of the crowd there is a flurry of activity followed by loud cheering. Logically, I think that it's because of the great music. It slowly dawns on me that the excitement has nothing to do with us. It is, however, something very familiar.

As the crowd parts, I catch a glimpse of Peaches' plump little dwarf-like figure whirling across the dance floor toward Sunny in a surreal, retro-disco glory. His green hair glows silver under the lights, his face is pouring sweat. The circle widens and the two are now center-stage facing each other like a pair of rock crabs, stalking each other sideways to the music, each smiling in a drunken and dangerous way, waiting to see who might make the first move. I can't tell who does, but suddenly they collide in the center of the floor in an embrace of deep, mashing kisses and grinding hips.

I drop my pick again, but this time I find it without too much trouble and when I look up they're back to crab stalking. This ritual continues as our groove evolves into a reggae kind of thing, but this only seems to make them more intense. They collide, arms and legs thrashing, flailing as they have become one awkward, drunken organism galumphing across the floor, trying to maintain the rhythm of the song. Although it's a real crowd pleaser, I find the whole thing disturbing, like I'm trapped in a scene from a David Lynch movie. Star plays on unscathed, as does Zen and

Ollie. Angel just stares on in horror. We finish our set to a standing ovation. Actually the crowd has been standing the whole time, but at least some of them seem to be clapping.

After a few moments backstage we return for an encore. That is *four* of us return for an encore. Somewhere behind the stage I hear Ollie fishing for a compliment though I cannot see him.

"You know, I think I was rushing the tempo on that last song...Oh, you didn't notice? Oh, you really think it was good? Well, that's nice of you to say so....Yeah, I've been playing twenty years...Yeah, I did see The Who back in the Coliseum ...November 18, 1976...Keith Moon's last tour...A shame really...Tickets were only six bucks...Can you believe Ticketmaster these days? Anyway, he was right in the middle of a drum solo when owww..."

I hear Star yelling and the muffled thump of fist on flesh with Ollie's panicked voice saying, "Gotta go..." and they're both back on stage, smiling. We play our last song and leave the audience clapping loudly, feeling pretty cocksure of ourselves. I head for the door, needing some fresh air, and am mobbed by new fans asking about the band. This adoration is nice.

~

Once outside the hot sweat on my shirt turns cold, but the fresh air feels good. People are milling about on the sidewalk while a few elegant-looking hippies unload equipment from a carefully hand-painted ex-Greyhound Coachliner. One hippie in particular is standing by, dressed in loose balloon pants and a black tank top. The others seem to be working for him. He has well-combed, dark, glossy hair and swollen blue eyes. He kind of wanders over my way; once he's close enough, I extend my hand to him. "Hi, my name's Angus."

He looks at me and his eyes seem to question my motivation. "My name's Matt," he finally says. "Who are you with?"

"The Cosmic Poets," I say with pride. "We just warmed up for Big Brother."

"Oh, really," he says rather coldly, sizing me up. "We're playing tonight, too." He takes out an American Spirit and without offering me one, lights it up.

"Got an extra one of those?"

He hands me one and lights it for me. In a second I'm coughing and dizzy as hell. "What's in this thing?"

"Sage," he replies. "A sacred plant with the Native Americans. What's with the name, Cosmic Poets?"

"We're trying to find the true nature of cosmic reality by transcending the material realm," I cough. "You guys from around here?"

"We are originally," he confesses. "I pulled my guys off the road for a break. We just played with Phish down in Santa Fe. After this we're back on tour down the West Coast. I hated asking my guys to open for Big Brother, but Roy's a friend. It's hard to find good opening acts these days. No offense."

"What's the name of your band?" I ask, stung by his insinuation. As far as I can tell, this is but a pseudo-progressive bunch of spoiled hippie brats whose parents probably foot the bill for everything.

"Groovetribe," he says. "You haven't heard of us?"

"We're from Bellingham," I say.

"We've played Bellingham before," he says. He pauses deliberately. "There's not a place in Bellingham big enough for us anymore. Too bad, too. Bellingham's a cool town."

"Funny, I've never heard of you guys," I say, really trying not to hate him. "What do you play?"

"Nothing," he says with a laugh. "I'm the manager. I'm glad you're gonna get to hear us 'cause this is one of the last clubs we're ever gonna do."

"Why?"

"Because, Arnold—"

"Angus."

"Sorry. Because, Angus, we're about to be signed to a major label. Do you guys tour?"

"Oh yeah," I say. "We're actually on tour down the West Coast right now. The past President of RCA Records is our manager, and Sunny says we'll be jamming with U2 in a couple of months."

We stare at each other in silence before a little tanned Rasta-style dude with a Cheshire cat-like smile comes over and whispers something in Matt's ear. They laugh and I hear Matt refer to him as Sequoia. Sequoia ignores me while Matt sighs and says, "Nice talking with ya, but I gotta get to work." He and Sequoia walk into the club, and before going in the door, he looks back as an afterthought, and says, "Good luck, Arthur. It's a rough road to the top."

"It's Angus." I hear the bitterness in my voice. "My name is Angus." I feel a sudden depression coming on and since I'm cold and dizzy from the cigarette, I crush the butt and turn to follow them inside.

Now the heat, smoke and red lights of the club feel good and people are still coming up to me, complimenting me on our killer set. I regret my negative feelings toward Groovetribe. Any creative endeavor involving a group of people, no matter who they are, is worthy of respect. In my heart I wish them well.

Next up is Ratfuck. They thrash and wail their hearts out and there are a few dudes in helmets who seem to be their groupies. After them is Goon Squad and as the rainbow-haired drummer takes his place behind his set, I notice a Native American female cello player with glossy black hair take the stage in front of him. I can tell right away that they are playing for each other and not the crowd and it works—they move me.

Celia, the Indian cellist, is an eloquent lyricist and her poem called *Teacher* is a powerful story about losing her father to drugs and alcohol before he was finished teaching her a song of peace that was given to him by his elders. She tells of how she has spent her whole life trying to figure out an ending for it, but hasn't been able to, and doesn't know if she ever will. People do applaud after the song, but I can't tell whether or not they get it. Celia possesses a simple beauty and inner strength and there's something intensely familiar about her. I respect her courage and honesty. It's not easy being real. After their set I am forced to admit to myself that there are much more worthy bands than us out there trying to make it, though I wonder of their chances with a name like Goon Squad, as funny as it is.

~

As Groovetribe begins setting up their elaborate array of percussion equipment, I go in search of beer and more praise for our awesome set, which, in my heart I know really wasn't all that awesome. On the way to the bar, I meet Sam Andrew and of course, standing next to him, is Ollie.

"You guys were *fantastic*," says Sam to me.

"You can't imagine what that means to hear that, coming from an artist like yourself," I say to him, blushing. Ollie is smiling at me and I can tell he has fished for much praise, likely to the point of irritation. Still, it does feel sweet.

"Course I'd be hard-pressed to name an artist that I *don't* like. I mean even Hitler did some very nice landscapes and had a real feel for the quaintness of life in his time. Should've stuck to his palette and brushes, don't you think?"

"Yeah, he probably should have," I say, blankly.

"But I haven't heard a band like yours in a long time. Don't stop doing what you're doing." He then whispers to me, "You really ought to let your organ player sing more lead."

"Yeah, I probably should," I say, feeling my cheeks blush.

The lights flicker once and it's time for Groovetribe. I hadn't noticed until now the elegant display of candles that have been set up on stage, and the blue light that shines out from underneath the drum set. Then all the lights in the room go out and the crowd roars, probably thinking it's Big Brother.

Four young, athletic-looking, shirtless hippies come out onto the stage looking very stylish—ersatz druids who have spent much of their lives combing their flowing hair. They take their places and begin pounding away on their various percussion instruments while the tiny muscle man with the big voice and Cheshire smile named Sequoia comes out naked, save for a pair of sweatshorts.

He is writhing to the beat of this pop-culture ritual given to us with great celebration, and now there is a spotlight washing over his sweating body. He screams, "Namaste!" into the microphone, sanskrit for "I bow to the divine in you." The crowd goes wild.

There are dozens of young, well-dressed hippies who seem to have come out of nowhere and it's apparent that Groovetribe is quite popular in these parts. When Sequoia opens his mouth to sing I'm surprised at his baritone. His voice is so low that it seems to rattle the whole room, and the combination of his movements, singing and the tribal-rhythm they have going with a bass guitar funking it up...well, it's kind of cool, actually. Soon the audience is swooning in ecstasy. Were they like this for us? I cannot remember. It occurs to me that I'm jealous of the attention they're receiving. Maybe I'd feel differently if they didn't seem so arrogant.

They finish their set with a song about saving the children that everyone seems to love and I know I'll be glad to strike the memory of their existence from my mind. They are just too cool for meepy old Bellingham. One thing is for sure: the stench of body odor is now much stronger in the Firehouse and if that is any indication of their success, they've scored big-time.

By the time Big Brother and the Holding Company take the stage it's about midnight, and though we are absolutely thrilled to have been one of four opening bands for this legendary act, we need to drive some distance south tonight in order to stay on schedule. We've decided to check out only a few of their songs.

I'm glad they open with *Summertime* and find myself more fascinated watching Ollie staring up at the stage than watching Sam Andrew play. I know he's too far gone to communicate with, but I poke him in the side nonetheless while he just kind of stands there, fingers twitching on his legs to the beat. In his mind he probably sees Ed Sullivan somewhere behind that dark-blue, smoky haze. After the song is over, Sam thanks the cheering crowd, and tells the story of how he met Ollie in the deli section of a Larry's Market, and how Ollie had recognized him. The room erupts with laughter while Ollie just stands there looking embarrassed. I am proud of Ollie and find myself glowing even more when Sam tells the crowd what an honor it is to have an opening band like The Cosmic Poets warm up for them. Not Groovetribe. Not Goon Squad. Not Ratfuck. He is talking about The Cosmic Poets.

"Sam sure is a nice guy," I say to Ollie who just smiles back without taking his eyes from the stage.

"They're all nice," he finally says, and it's true. They're also really into their music and their female lead singer is good. Although she covers Janis beautifully, she's not afraid to be herself. Wow. A great gig at last.

Just when I'm wondering about the record labels who are supposed to be here, I find Sunny standing at my side.

"You're gonna be huge," she mumbles, pulling my ear into her lips while I try not to choke on the stench of cheap perfume, smoke and liquor. "Are you excited about what I'm doing for you?"

"Oh, yeah," I say, trying not to stare at the sweat swollen rivers of streaking mascara flowing down her face.

"Then don't fuck it up, Angus. You got a message for the world and we're counting on you."

"Yaaah," Peaches stutters. "You should be exciiited. I liiike your lyrics. I can't tell what you're saaaying, but I can tell they're deeep."

"Wow, thanks, Peaches," I say. "Great dancing." I turn to Sunny. "Any word from the label people? Were they here?"

"You'd better believe they were here," she says, suddenly sounding sober. "Now you just go have yourself a great tour and leave the rest to us—Frank and I are in control."

Seven

Outside, we sit in the van, ready to drive south to a rest area just beyond Olympia. Angel, however, is not here. We wait. We wait some more. The welt on Star's forehead has swollen quite a bit, and the makeup she has smeared on the bump can't hide it anymore. "Christ, my head is killing me," she murmurs to no one in particular.

"You did a great job in spite of it, Star," I say.

"Yeah, Star," Ollie echoes. "Great job. Sorry I got lost."

"At least you got to meet Sam Andrew," I say. "That almost makes it worth it, though you just about lost your job." Zen is snoring away in the back.

"You gotta back off on the bell of your stupid ride cymbal," snarls Star, turning back to Ollie. "You're making me deaf."

Normally Ollie would argue, but he wisely keeps his mouth shut.

"The sound was lousy on stage, anyway," I say.

"Where *is* she?" Star yells, waking Zen up. "That's it!" She jumps from the van and storms back into the club. Moments later she comes stomping back. She plants herself in the passenger seat and slams the door as hard as she can.

"Is she coming?" I ask.

"I don't know. She's talking to the Groovy Vibes."

"You mean Groovetribe? Is that who she's talking to?"

Star's angry silence is an affirmative.

"What did you think of Groovetribe?" asks Zen, groggily.

"I thought they were a bit arrogant, actually," I say. "Their manager says they're on tour down the West Coast. He thinks they're gonna be signed by August.

"Yeah," says Ollie. "They were good musicians though the percussion ensemble kept dragging on the second half of the fourth song, right after the bridge...I'll go get Angel, now."

He leaves and I fall back into the seat, reliving Sunny and Peaches's crab dance. I try to push the image from my mind to focus on something more pleasant, but can't.

"Boy, Sunny and Peaches put on quite a show," says Zen while Star laughs.

"Yeah, they're pretty talented," I say. Star laughs even harder, but suddenly stops. Here comes Ollie and Angel. As they climb aboard, I pull into traffic, heading south. Angel reaches over and pinches Ollie hard.

"Ouch," he cries. "What's *that* all about?"

"It's for being such a geek," she yells. "Don't pester me when I'm talking to someone. That was Sequoia, the lead singer for Groovetribe." Her tone reveals that they had more than a casual conversation.

"I don't care who it was," snaps Star. "You kept us waiting for a half-hour plus you almost took my eye out during your hissy fit."

"Don't talk to me like that, Star!" hollers Angel. "I didn't mean to hit *you*."

"You're getting kind of abusive, now aren't you Angel?" says Zen, sarcastically. "Angel, have you...have you been drinking?"

"Nooo," she howls, drunkenly.

Star is not at all amused. She sighs quietly, "I sure made a lot of fans tonight."

"Yeah," says Angel, picking up on the game. "Sequoia was asking me what the hell I was doing singing back-up in The Cosmic Poets. With a voice like mine, I should be on the cover of Rolling Stone. Sequoia said he wants *me* to sing with *him* sometime. He says there's a psychic connection between us and we're destined to be together. He's so beautiful."

"Yeah, I sure did make a lot of fans tonight," Star says, loudly. "Did you see that group of guys below me? They were on their knees, just begging for it."

"I think Peaches and Sunny stole the show with their crab dance," says Zen, trying to lighten things up.

"You think they looked like a couple of crabs too, Zen?" I ask. "That's exactly what I saw."

"That head of yours is sure getting big, Star!" cries Angel.

"At least I didn't let my goddamned organ ruin our set," hisses Star.

"In case you didn't notice, Star, the *soundman* screwed up my organ."

"Soundman my ass."

"Angel, wasn't the bad cord yours?" I ask as we pull onto southbound I-5.

"It sure was," Star says. "I'm sure the cord was just fine before you ripped it out of your organ! And how could all you idiots get lost before we even got to Ballard?"

"Sorry, you guys," says Ollie. "It's my fault. I should've stuck with—"

"No, it's not your fault, Ollie," says Angel looking at me. "*You're* the ones who ditched *us*. Besides, there weren't any labels there."

"Labels were there tonight, Angel."

"Did any labels come up to you?"

"Well...no," I say. "But Sunny says they'll never tell you who they really are."

"There were no labels there tonight. I guarantee it," says Angel. "I wouldn't have approached us, even if I was a label."

"Sixty-five! You're going sixty-five!"

The stench of antifreeze is coming on strong as steam pours out from under the hood. I pull over onto the shoulder. Everyone is silent. "Well," I say, cheerfully, "looks like we're gonna have to wait for things to cool down a little."

"Sorry to bring this up, now," mumbles Ollie, "but I really need to find a bathroom."

Eight

Sleep. Ah, yes. Sleep comes at last. Dreams come like dry, restless fall leaves, blowing in unpredictable directions. I am on a dark, winter street, walking quietly past a bunch of suburban mansions.

1404 Deer Park Lane. It's funny how developers always name their developments after whatever it is they had to destroy. Aha, this is the house. I walk up the steps. Predictably, there is a nice Lexus parked in the driveway. Damn, it's chilly. My right hand fingers curl comfortably around a cold '45 and I ring the bell. Soon, I hear footsteps.

"Who is it?" she asks, and I tell her it's me. "Nathan," I hear her say. "It's for you."

A tall, muscular, well-cultured guy with blonde curly hair and a carefully trimmed goatee comes sauntering to the door. His eyes are rat-like and close together. "Can I help you?" he asks cautiously.

"Yeah, are you Nathan Sempleton?"

"Yes, I am." His eyes flicker with a trace of fear.

"Don't you know me?" I ask, calmly. "You should."

"From where?" he asks. "I've never seen you before."

"No, but you reviewed my demo-tape in *The Herald*." I pull the gun from my pocket, pointing it at him before he can close the door. "I wanna talk about a few things you said."

"Lily?" he yells, not taking his eyes from me as he backs away from the door. "We have company." He motions me inside and soon we're standing in his living room. "Would you like some tea or something?" He is more polite than I would have expected.

"Some tea would be fine," I say, keeping the barrel of the gun trained on his head.

"Lily, this is Angus Keegan. I reviewed his tape and he stopped by to talk about it."

"Hi, nice to meet you," she says, forcing a smile before disappearing into the kitchen. Why does she act like she's never seen me before? I hear her voice from the other room say, "Nathan, would you like a beer?"

"Sure," he says, motioning me to sit down. "So, what's the problem, Angus?"

"Gosh, Nathan," I say. "I don't know. Maybe you can tell me." I look around the living room and am impressed by the tastefulness of the décor: plants in graceful vases and lots of framed paintings on the walls. "You must do pretty good as a music writer to afford a place like this."

"It's not a bad life," he says. "I'm trying to remember your music. Sorry, it's been awhile."

"I was the one whose songs were, as you put it, self-absorbed musical rantings strangled by an obviously stunted emotional development though you did commend me for my sincerity. I'll admit, the 'pass the Vivarin' comment was really funny." I glare at him. "It's assholes like you who destroyed Nick Drake."

"Nick's dead, man; get over it."

"You're pretty cocky for someone *else* about to be dead." My hand shakes, but he doesn't seem rattled.

"Thanks, Lily," he says as she comes in from the other room with a tray and hands him a beer. She then gives me my tea, smiling, rolling her eyes.

"Thanks, Lily," I say. "You know I still love you, don't you?"

"Can I get you anything else?" she asks.

"No thanks," I sigh, then turn my attention back to Nathan. "Why did you have to say such mean things about my music?"

He gulps his beer. "The truth hurts, doesn't it?"

"What truth you snide little weasel? Your truth? You said some very mean things and now I am going to kill you." My hand is shaking even harder.

"It doesn't matter, Angus. There are plenty more like me, and you can't kill us all. For every idiot who might like your style, there are ten of us who will gladly humiliate you and love every second of it. It's what makes Bellingham cool, and it's what we get paid to do."

"You could have been nice. It didn't have to be mean."

"You think people want to read nice reviews? Do you really think the world would be better off if everyone were nice?" He laughs. "Give me a break. Kill me if it makes you feel better. You still suck."

"Okay, Nathan." I cock the gun and he flinches a little. "If you're an expert, what are the essences of good music?"

"Craftsmanship," he says, smugly. "Skill, versatility and craftsmanship. Those are essentials."

"That's all? Skill, versatility and craftsmanship?"

"That's all," he burps. "Oh, and theory. You do need theory. I forgot theory."

"Oh yeah, theory. Is that all?"

"You need a marketable look, Angus. You know, colored hair, nose ring, tattoo, creative piercing, whatever makes you look like a mass-marketable nonconformist." He shrugs. "It's all about marketing, Angus. Don't blame me; I don't make the rules."

"The rules," I repeat. "I forgot about the rules."

Nathan smiles and shrugs his shoulders but not for long.

The gun roars in my hand practically knocking me over while his knee-cap explodes in a spray of bone chunks and bloody pulp.

He writhes in agony, clutching his injured leg. "Why'd you do that?" he cries.

"Cause I wanted you to understand the true nature of honest, self-expression, Nathan. Did you forget about *self-expression*? About *feeling, passion, soul, honesty* and *sincerity*?"

"Oh, yeah," he says, groaning. "I guess I did forget."

I see a guitar leaning against the couch and as I pick it up, Lily comes in, saying, "Oh my, what a mess you boys have made," and she leaves the room, probably to go get some first aid.

I hand him the guitar and his eyes are wild with fear now. "Write a song, motherfucker. Express *yourself*. I'll be listening for feeling, passion, soul and sincerity. Oh yeah, and skill, theory and craftsmanship. You have five minutes you son-of-a-bitch, and if your song doesn't move me, I'm gonna spray paint your brains all over your wall. Now, *express* yourself!"

He takes the guitar, hands shaking. He's terrified. "I really don't know how to play guitar. I'm more of a horn man."

"No excuses, my expert friend. You got four-and-a-half minutes."

Lily comes in with a towel and throws it around his knee. "I just had the carpet steam cleaned," she scolds.

"Bring me another beer, Lily," Nathan commands her.

"Don't talk to her like that!" I scream.

"It's okay, Angus," she says. "Would you like more tea?"

"Sure." I am swooning with love and emotion. "Sorry about the mess. Do you think there's a chance we could ever be together again?"

"Look, Angus," she says, impatiently. "You've had *way* too much caffeine. I told you that I need space to explore my feelings for all of my past boyfriends."

I sigh as she leaves the room, then turn my attention back to my new friend. "Play me the song, Nathan. Move me. Make me cry. You have two minutes."

"I can't," he cries.

"Play something, man. Do it."

"I'm sorry I was so mean."

"Play the song, Nathan."

"I can't," he cries again. "Please don't kill me."

"Why shouldn't I kill you Nathan? You're a parasite. You and all of the promoters, booking agents, A&R people, publishers and club owners make money off of us while we starve. You live in a cubicle totally removed from reality making your proud, timeless declarations on what's good and bad music knowing you'll never be accountable to any one whose art you've trashed. Now play me a song you low-life egotistical moocher."

"I can't," he wimpers. "Don't kill me, man."

"You have a minute-and-a-half, Nathan. Why are you so afraid? You said there were millions of others just like you, so what would the world be missing?" The gun roars again and he screams while a pillow explodes next to him. The room is filled with feathers.

"I don't know how to play guitar," he sobs.

"Of course you can't, Nathan. How could you know of anything real living in your cush world of comp tickets and fancy dinners. You're just another face in the machine grinding dreamers into cynical, star-struck robots. You are part of the grand conspiracy to destroy those who play and think for themselves and for what? For profit? The profit motive can never co-exist with real art, Nathan. This is my manifesto. I have declared it so. Therefore, it is so." I point the gun directly at his head. "Now play me a song with feeling and sincerity or I must kill you."

"Please *don't!*" he wails.

"Come on, Nathan, play something. How about *Smoke On the Water?* At least play *Smoke on the Water* and I won't kill you."

He tries, but it's true. The loser can barely make a barre chord.

"Play the bass line. It's just one note. Do it."

He finally does, but it sounds so bad that the gun roars again while his other leg takes a slug. He falls back, screaming.

"Gosh, Nathan, I feel kind'a bad for you. You're having a rough day, aren't you? Too bad you have to die."

He stares back at me through tear-streaked terror.

"Tell you what, Nathan. Since you can't seem to express yourself in music, I'll let you have another shot at reviewing my tape. Any revisions?"

"You are the shit, man," he says, his voice begging for life. "Step aside Pete Townshend, Neil Young, U2, and Bob Dylan."

"Bruce Cockburn," I add, as I am now holding a rocket launcher trained on his tiny head.

"Bruce Cockburn," he repeats quickly. "Step aside because a new songwriter has just graced us with talent like the music world hasn't seen since The Beatles. His name is Angus Keegan and he has it all: the voice, the chops, the songs. And we out here in Bellingham are damn lucky and proud to call him one of our own."

"That's all right," I say. "That's actually pretty good. Except for one thing."

"What?" he weeps.

"You're *still* too insincere!" I cock the bazooka.

He holds up his hands. "I *swear*, you're the *best* singer, songwriter and guitarist I have *ever* heard. *I swear*. I'll tell the world man, I will. Please don't kill me...Bob Dylan is *shit* compared to you...Jimi Hendrix isn't *close* to as good as you. Carlos Santana isn't even in the same *league*...please don't kill me...I swear, you're the *best*!"

"Wow. Thanks Nathan. That makes me feel good about myself. Better than Santana, Dylan, and Hendrix? I don't think so, really. I do really appreciate your kind, encouraging words, though. It was very nice of you to say all of those kind things."

"It's all true," he sobs. I mean he's really crying and I do feel bad for him.

"Well, Nathan, I gotta go now. I wish I could stick around for another cup of tea but I have a few more visits to make. By the way, did you learn anything, tonight?"

"I did, and I'm sorry I hurt your feelings." He's a bloody mess and reeks of diarrhea.

"Hey, it's all right, man. Everyone makes mistakes. I forgive you." I pat him on the head and before I'm out the front door, I yell goodbye to Lily. She cheerfully calls back from the kitchen and tells me stop by again. I thank her for the tea and when I open the front door I am standing on the edge of an abyss, looking down on a crackling, infinite furnace, the wailing of the damned floating up to me on smoke and flames. Somewhere down there I hear the sound of a twangy guitar. I gently close the door and turn back to the living room. Nathan and Lily stare at me without saying a word. I plop down into a recliner, exhausted. "Mind if I hang out here for a while?"

Nine

It's past noon when we all emerge from Elvis after our first night out on the road. We pulled into Millersylvania State Park just south of Olympia at about three in the morning last night and now as I contemplate our 300-mile trip to the Oregon Country Fairgrounds, I'm glad we have an extra day to make it there easily. Our set isn't until tomorrow afternoon so there shouldn't be any problems. The plan is to take a leisurely swim in Deep Lake, shower, and then head south so as to get through Portland before rush hour. I try to shake the strange images still flitting about the periphery of my brain as I focus on the *only* thing that really matters: finding coffee. We all agree to go off on our own for a couple of hours before meeting back at the rig around three.

Of course when three o'clock rolls around, Ollie is nowhere to be found. We fan out on the network of trails surrounding the area and it is Angel who finds him wandering lost in a field, though Ollie claims he wasn't actually lost at all. We are finally on the road around four and are primed to hit maximum rush-hour traffic in Portland. We pass through Chehalis and the conversation centers on how cool the Oregon Country Fair will be. It's true, I think. I'm glad we're playing the main stage. That will be a perfect tune-up for our break-through show in the Redwoods.

We pass the Hamilton Farms billboard in Chehalis, nationally famous for it's demonic-looking Uncle Sam pointing at cars coming from both directions displaying it's right-wing thought for the day. Today it reads: You Can't Wipe Your Butt with a Spotted Owl!

"What a jerk," I say.

"I'm hungry," says Ollie in a sudden panic. "Is anyone else hungry?"

It is determined that while everyone isn't hungry, Zen does need to piss. After extolling on a guilt laden tirade about the evils of factory meat and how it is destroying so much good, arable land, Ollie convinces us to stop at a fast-food grease pit near the freeway. Ollie orders a few thirty-nine cent hamburgers and a milkshake and while he eats, Angel stares at him.

"Meat is dead, Ollie," she whispers. "Remember, meat is *dead!*"

Ollie mumbles apologies between bites and soon we're back on the freeway over-pass heading to the southbound on-ramp. As we make the turn and begin accelerating we see a tall, middle-aged Native-American male with short black hair wearing a Free Peltier shirt, a pair of jeans and some well-worn cowboy boots. At his feet is a paper bag and as we pass by him he smiles almost sadly, giving us a slow wave with his left hand.

"We should've picked him up," I yell.

"You can't trust hitchhikers these days," counters Ollie.

"I'm with Ollie," says Zen. "A guy pulled a knife on me one time."

"Yeah," says Star. "We're on a schedule, anyway."

"Exactly my sentiments," I say, as we're back up to speed on I-5. But something, and I'm not sure what, happens when we pass the next exit, and I find my arms wrenching the wheel toward a line of cars getting off.

"What are you doing?" yells Star.

"We're going back for him."

"Are you kidding?" Zen asks.

"I thought we were going to make decisions together," Star says, obviously angry.

It doesn't matter, anyway. It's as if my arms and wrists are under command from somewhere else. "Sorry, but we gotta pick him up." I'm at a loss to explain why.

Soon we're on the over-pass driving into the glare of the late afternoon sun and as we turn back onto the south-bound lanes, we see him, standing in the same place, though this time I swear his hair is longer. He sees us and begins laughing as Elvis comes to a halt. He picks up the paper bag and Ollie removes himself from the passenger seat. The door opens and as he climbs aboard a threshold of a different sort has been crossed. From this point on, our lives will never be the same.

~

"My name is Walter Simon," he says in a soft voice as he settles in the passenger seat. "Thanks for coming back for me." I find his facial features even more striking up close. His brown skin is weathered and leathery, with little crater-like acne scars. On his left cheek is an off-color faded scar that slopes vertically downward toward a large mouth with surprisingly beautiful white teeth, though one of the lower ones is missing. His eyes are like dark, black whirlpools, surrounded by pillowy wrinkles. The most striking feature is his large and bony nose, which makes him look like he could be a descendant of Sitting Bull. Then again, I'm always reading into things.

Introductions are a little awkward. Star is uncomfortable with his presence, while Angel's discomfort is over-ruled by her curiosity. As usual, it's hard to get a read on Zen.

"Where you going?" I ask as we're comfortably southbound again.

"Chemewah," he says, quietly.

"Where's Chemewah?" I ask.

"South of Portland about fifty miles."

"Never heard of it," I say.

"It's a boarding school." He smiles, and I feel a sadness in him.

"Where's Chemelia?" asks Ollie, suddenly.

"It's Chemewah, Ollie," I say, correcting him. "He just told us that it's in Oregon."

"Sorry, I've got my ear plugs in. They say that low-level, industrial, ambient noise is one of the greatest contributors to hearing loss."

"Eh shi men toe say no moro, Ollie," I say quietly.

"What did you just say?" yells Ollie again and Walter laughs loudly, while looking at me. "I can't hear with all the noise."

Now Angel and Zen are laughing, too, and Star smiles wistfully a bit. Ollie never figures it out.

"So what's your story?" asks Walter as things die down.

Ollie rambles on for the next half-hour about our big gigs coming up and how exciting it is to play drums for a band about to be signed. Somehow this monologue includes a reference to Desert Storm as well as the above-ground nuclear testing that took place in the Bikini Islands during World War II.

"So you're the drummer," Walter says, finally. He winks at me. "I love a good drum."

Before Ollie can continue with what might be an hour-long monologue about how he suffered through so many shitty bands before hooking up with The Cosmic Poets, I ask Walter where he's from.

"Why? Are you FBI?" he asks, smiling.

"Yeah," I say. "We saw your Peltier shirt from our satellite and decided we needed to check you out."

"You know Leonard Peltier?" Ollie asks.

"I met him at Wounded Knee right after I got back from 'Nam. I doubt he'd remember me."

"It's the greatest crime that he's in prison," says Ollie. "The whole COINTELPRO operation within the government makes me ashamed to be an American. I wouldn't blame you for not trusting us."

"He knows we're not with the FBI, Ollie," sighs Star.

"Where you from, Walter?" I ask.

"Rapid City, South Dakota though I grew up in Arctic Village, Alaska."

"Are you Lakota?" I ask.

"I'm half Lakota, half Gwich'in. I've been up in Alaska most of my life." He doesn't seem offended by our questions and I'm glad he isn't. He shouldn't be. We're just a bunch of dumb, suburban-bred whites out trying to get famous.

"Is that all of your stuff in the paper bag?" I ask.

"It's my lunch," he says, pulling out a couple of Tupperware containers. He opens them and hands me something. "Here, try this."

I take a brown dried strip of meat and tear off a chunk with my teeth. "What's this?" I ask.

"Dried caribou," he says. "Good, huh?"

"It's delicious."

The Poet Chronicles | 65

Soon even Angel and Star suspend their vegetarian leanings and everyone's chewing on a strip of meat. "This *is* good," says Angel. "Lots different than beef."

"I'm gonna have to get me a bow and arrow when I get back to Bellingham," says Star.

"That's the way it's done," he says. "We don't use guns up in Alaska. If you can't kill it with your bare hands, you don't deserve to eat."

"You don't use guns?" asks Ollie.

"No. We don't even live in houses," he says, winking at me. "We live in caribou skin huts. I really wish I did have some caribou."

"What?" asks Angel.

"Oh, this?" Walter says, pointing to the meat. "This is dried pork from a guy I know in Seattle. I'm kidding. It's really moose. Does it matter?"

"Well, this is better'n dried Elvis," says Zen, knowing he's found a soul mate.

Walter turns back and looks at Zen, strangely.

"Yeah," continues Zen. "Didn't they tell you I killed him?"

"You killed my hero?" asks Walter. "Why did you kill Elvis?"

"He was eating too much and I couldn't afford to keep him."

"He was staying at your house?"

"Yeah, he was," says Zen, taking a swig of beer.

"Did you play music together?"

"Sort of. He played percussion and danced."

"I didn't know Elvis played percussion. Was he good?"

"He was good until he bloated."

"What about the rumors of sightings?" Walter asks as Angel and Star shriek with laughter.

"All false," says Zen. "Actually, Walter, he killed himself. I was more of an enabler."

"What about his body?"

"We buried it up at my place. I would have eaten him, but we had to hit the road for this big tour."

"If you're still hungry," says Walter, smiling, "then try some of this." He passes the second container around and we all sample the best smoked salmon I have ever tasted. It's sweet, almost candy-like. Angel tells Walter that we've named our tour bus, Elvis, in memory of one great goat.

We are now paralleling the Columbia River and the ominous gray mass of the Trojan Nuclear Power Plant towers over the peaceful waters. Traffic is getting a bit more congested as we near Portland. The cozy confines of Bellingham seem more and more like a distant dream with each mile passed. Soon we are stop and go. *Thanks for getting lost again, Ollie.* This will put us behind schedule a bit, but still, we're in good shape.

"Walter," I say, "I know a bit about the Lakota from my readings, but I've never heard of the Gwich'in before."

Walter glances up again toward the sky. "Look at all the seagulls," he says.

Sure enough, far above the freeway, there is what seems like thousands of gulls spiraling gracefully above us with an infinite blue sky stretching beyond. They look like they're going so high that they could fly out of the atmosphere.

"The Gwich'in are the Caribou People," he says. "The last subsistence tribe left in North America. My father spent most of his life on a trap-line up the Porcupine River. Now the oil companies want to drill in the calving grounds of the Porcupine Caribou. If they do, we will fight." His proud voice trails off and I can tell he's taken with the scenery. I can also tell that he is particularly amused with Ollie. I sense tension between him and Star. Zen is now snoring and I'm glad he's having me do the driving on this tour.

Walter is comfortable with silence and though he's not shy, I do sense he is sad about something. It seems perfectly natural that a paper bag is his only visible possession. Ah the simple life of a renunciat, a wanderer.

For the next couple of hours the sun sets on a reluctant story about how being part of the Wounded Knee occupation in '73 got him on an FBI short list. He finally tells us of the Gwich'in resolve to keep the oil companies out of the Arctic National Wildlife Refuge and how he will fight to the death to stop them.

Ollie keeps interrupting him with questions, and each question triggers a lengthy, Ollie-like monologue ranging from Peltier, and the similarities to Nelson Mandela, to the Cuban Embargo, to The Who's *Live At Leeds Concert*. All this information expressed in one sentence would be an amazing feat for any individual; for Ollie, it's all in an hour's work. I think Walter appreciates having the attention diverted away from himself.

As we're passing Salem, it's now almost completely dark. Everyone but Ollie and Walter seems to be asleep. "Chemewah, next exit," I say, noting the sign. Walter seems like he's tensed up a lot. In fact, he seems frightened.

"You got a place to stay?" asks Ollie.

"I'll be fine."

We pull off the freeway at the Chemewah exit, and as we stop at the overpass, he says, "This is good."

"Right here?" I ask.

"The school's not far," he says. "I want to walk."

"Why are you going back to your old school, Walter?" I ask.

Walter smiles sadly. After a long moment he says, "I'm looking for my daughter." He then extends his hand to me and as I shake it I realize that he is handing me something warm and hard. "Thanks for the ride," he whispers before disappearing into the black night.

In my hand is a piece of bone, and as I rub my thumb over it, I can tell that it's been carved on. I look closely and see that it's an eagle totem.

"That was sure interesting," says Ollie as he climbs into the front. Everyone else still sleeps.

"Yeah, I learned a lot more about Pete Townshend's alcohol problem than I ever knew," I say, stuffing the totem deep in my front pocket.

"Sorry, I do babble on, don't I?"

"Ollie, babble isn't the word."

"I hope I didn't offend Walter. He seemed like a really neat guy."

"Yeah, he was, and quit apologizing all the time. It drives me nuts."

"I'm sorry," he says.

"That was neat about how he knew Leonard Peltier and all."

"Most Indians do, Ollie." I look over and see two fingers tapping on a coffee cup. "Let me guess. *Break on Through*."

"What?"

"The song you're playing. It's *Break on Through*, isn't it?"

"Oh...no...it's *Sky Pilot* by Eric Burdon. I hope he isn't freezing out there. He didn't even have a coat."

"Ollie, it's almost mid-July. Who needs a coat?"

"Say, Angus?" asks Ollie, nervously. "I really need to piss. I should've done it when we let Walter off. I'm sorry, but I need to piss right now."

"Will you quit apologizing, Ollie? It's okay that you have to piss."

We pull into the Talbot Rest Area and as Elvis shudders to a halt, Angel awakens and mumbles something about Walter before stumbling out of the door following Ollie toward the relief station. Star and Zen snore on and I grab the atlas to get our bearings. I actually consider parking here for the night. We're only about a hundred miles from the Elkton cutoff, which will take us to the Fairgrounds. A good night's sleep will do us good and we can make it there with ease in the morning.

Then an eighteen wheeler roars past me, gears grinding and clattering, and Elvis is flooded with lights. No way we're staying here. We need a quiet, side road in the country. If we can just get past Eugene we'll be in great shape. We'll get up in the morning, have coffee, and then proceed to the fair to rock the hippies.

The back side door of Elvis slides shut and I hear some hushed whispers and moans which tells me that Angel is back from the rest room. Ollie is another story, though. Finally, I see a shadowy figure racing across the lawn. "Sorry," he says, climbing in.

"What takes you so long to do simple things?" I ask as we're comfortably back on the freeway.

"I don't know," he says. "I got to talking with this guy from Reno, Nevada, named Bill Armond who's opening up a car dealership there and I told him that we were on a West Coast tour to get famous and he told me that he was looking for a band to play at his big grand opening. Reno's pretty far off the beaten path though, isn't it?"

"I don't want to play in the parking lot of some car dealership, Ollie. Get real; we're too good for that."

"He says lounge acts in Reno and Tahoe make a killing."

"Yeah, but I'm not Tom Jones, and you're not Jimmy Buffet. Damn, Ollie. How is it that you always get into these conversations with strange people in the weirdest times and places?"

"I really don't know, Angus."

We drive through Albany in silence.

"I'm sure glad you put up with me," Ollie says after some time. "I must drive everybody nuts."

"You do, Ollie," I say, honestly.

"I've been totally stressed over the divorce...I should've gotten a regular job when things were good. If I held up my end of the deal, things might have worked out.

"They still might," I say. "If we get signed, you'll be set."

"We are really good, aren't we?"

"You bet we are," I say.

"In spite of Angel's keyboard problems," he whispers.

"Shhhhh," I whisper back. "Don't feed the persecution complex. She thinks I have it in for her as it is."

"Actually, Angus, she's awesome."

"I know she is. She just needs to chill out a little."

"How many times have I been asked if we're on a label. I think we are gonna get signed."

"You just gotta believe, Ollie. You gotta believe."

"I should've cleaned out my room before we left."

"Don't worry about it Ollie; it wouldn't have mattered. I mean, you had your chance, but you found some really cool old magazines to bring on the trip."

"Did you know Janis Joplin was friends with Jim Morrison?"

"That doesn't surprise me."

"I once read where Morrison actually assaulted her after a party, and they never spoke again after that."

"That's sad, Ollie."

I can tell the big screen in his brain is lighting up. Ollie is a living paradox, and in his irony lies his greatness. In spite of his odd ways, Ollie has a detached, methodical logic and reason all his own. He is a pacer and a night person. He wanders the dark and rainy Bellingham streets long after practice is over, contemplating the impending divorce and, as a master film producer, he is constantly rewinding the film reels, pouring over the rough footage of his life, tormented by the two words that have become a mantra for his entire existence: "If only." If only he had gotten a real job when he got married instead of playing drums perhaps his marriage wouldn't be ending in disaster. If only he and his brother had given Jim Morrison a ride to

Vancouver, Canada on that strange summer day in early June of 1970. Damn…

~

For the next two hours Ollie tells me again of his encounter with The Doors' lead singer on a busy arterial east of Seattle. Ollie and his brother saw a man walking all alone down the street yelling at the traffic whizzing by. Ollie talked his brother into stopping the car and Ollie ran over to him. Sure enough, it was Jim Morrison—although it was only after being hassled by Ollie for several minutes that the man finally admitted it. At first he only admitted that he was Jim Morrison the poet and not Jim Morrison the singer. Then, after being pestered some more, he confessed that he was *the* Jim Morrison. "You happy now?" he asked.

Ollie stood back, stunned by the man's admission and was suddenly full of doubt. "No you're not," Ollie replied, his own voice shaking with rage. "You're *not* Jim Morrison."

Ollie describes how the man stared at him in disbelief while the color drained from his face. "I can't fucking believe it," he'd said. "People come up to me all the time asking me if I'm Jim Morrison. If I tell them yes, they don't believe me. If I tell them no, they don't believe me." Suddenly he whirled on his heel facing Ollie and screamed, "This *really* pisses me off, Ollie!" Then like a coiled snake, he struck Ollie, knocking him to the ground. Ollie recalled how the man's powerful voice seemed to echo forever off the distant buildings, kind of like Morrison's classic scream on *The End*. After a long awkward moment, the man helped him up and apologized for hitting him. He asked if Ollie could drive him to Canada for a gig that night. Just then a couple of star-struck girls in a psychedelic Volkswagen pulled over, screaming, "There he is!"

The man sighed with resignation. "Aw fuck, Ollie. Here they come."

Two young girls licked their lips and hurriedly touched up their hair as the driver jumped from the car and walked over to them. "Hi, Jim," she said with the familiarity of an old friend.

The man smiled and they began talking quietly. Ollie walked up to the other one who was still in the car. He recalled that she was blonde and rather cheap looking, and by the stench of incense and the way her eyes were all glittery, Ollie figured that she was stoned.

"Is that really Jim Morrison?" he whispered.

"Yeah, it sure is," the girl said dreamily, still touching up her make-up.

"How do you know?"

The girl turned to Ollie as if noticing him for the first time. She looked at him with contempt and scorn. "Because I saw him in concert last night you dumbshit!"

"Can you please cool it?" yelled the man. "He's just a kid."

"Sorry, Jim," she said, embarrassed. She looked at Ollie. "Sorry, kid."

"His name's, Ollie."

"Sorry, Ollie."

Ollie stood in their midst, basking in unspeakable glory. Perhaps, in some later interview, Morrison might recall this encounter. Ollie then saw himself behind a drum set in a dark arena, with a sea of lighters waving their approval. He decided at that very moment that he too was destined to become famous. Music was to become his life, success, and his dream. Someday he would be seen as a hero. He looked up in the cloudy, Northwest sky, and beyond the skyscrapers he saw a few sea gulls circling far above. The man said goodbye to Ollie, apologizing again for hitting him. Then he got into the girls' car and they drove away.

How different life could have been if Ollie and his brother had offered Morrison a ride that night. Maybe, somehow, Jim wouldn't have died three years later. But you almost never do the right thing when the opportunity presents itself. Ollie did get better on the drums, though. As he grew he pounded on them as if they were the heads of his invisible demons with rhythm his only force for good in an evil universe closing in around him. Now in his late thirties, with fame and fortune still hanging in an obscure limbo, he was well aware of the ticking clock, that time was quickly running out.

~

"It was really him; don't you think?" Ollie asks.

"I think whether or not it was, it's still a great story.

"But it *was* him."

"I think it was."

We drive in silence for awhile. A half an hour later finds us heading west on the Elkton cutoff, and the lights of Eugene are but a memory. "We need a place to park Elvis," I say to Ollie. "We're close to the fair."

"Why don't we just camp there?" asks Ollie.

"I hear it's too crazy. We wouldn't get any sleep."

But finding a side road isn't as easy as I thought it would be, and the concept of sleep suddenly becomes ridiculously irrelevant when a wide-awake Zen materializes from the back. His eyes are dark and fearful.

"Where's Angel?" he asks, quietly.

Ten

It takes a few minutes of carefully studying the atlas before I am able to determine that we're about one hundred and fifteen miles south of the rest area where we accidentally left Angel. "I was sure I heard her voice in the back before Ollie even got back himself," I whisper. "I was positive. I heard the door close."

"Well," says Zen, "I did get up to sneak a piss right outside the door at that stop. Maybe that's what you heard."

"Gosh," says Ollie. "This is serious."

"Don't wake Star," I say, contemplating the two-hour ride back up north. "I don't want to hear about it. We just gotta go back and get her. No big deal."

"I was kind of wondering if we didn't leave Angel back there," confesses Ollie.

"Why didn't you say something?"

He shrugs. "Oh, I don't know."

I look at Ollie and want to sock him one. But he wouldn't get it. And, even if he did, it wouldn't matter.

Going back is brutal. It really is. But I have to believe that in the end we'll all have a good laugh about it. Meanwhile I imagine Angel standing outside the rest room, cursing the day she ever joined The Cosmic Poets. *Angel, it was an accident. I swear it was. Hey, Angel, you wanna play more organ in the band*?

I know that there's nothing I could ever say now to win back her confidence. She'll never believe that it was an honest mistake. She wouldn't call Sunny, would she? I panic a little at the thought. Ollie nods off, and I'm getting really drowsy. Zen agrees to drive the rest of the way so I can sleep for a couple of hours. We pull over and in the atlas I show him where the rest area is.

As Zen takes over, I stretch out on the floor and it feels good. Star snores away while Ollie fidgets in the bunk next to me. It will all work out fine. We'll pick her up and once things are smoothed out, we'll spend the rest of the night there catching some sleep, leaving plenty of time to get to the fairgrounds for our 3:00 P.M. set. The dull monotony and vibrations of the moving vehicle soothe me, and I feel the drunkenness of sleep coming on fast...

I awaken to warm sun on my face and the sound of cars whizzing by and I have no idea where I am. Ever so slowly, the events of last night come into focus, and even then, they seem like a dream. Did we really lose Angel?

The first thing I notice is that Star's empty little cot next to the speakers. The next thing I notice is Ollie, lying on his back across from me, eyes closed and fingers twitching. As I stare out at the generic-looking rest area, it all looks very different than it did last night. Was this the spot we left Angel? Elvis's clock reads 7:56 A.M. Our set is seven hours away.

The door opens and in comes Star and Zen. "Smooth move, Angus," Star spits.

"She was gonna quit anyway," I say. "This just makes it easier."

Her glare tells me that she's not amused. "Should we call the cops?"

"I need coffee first," I say. "I can't think 'til I have coffee." I look around. "Zen, I don't remember those oak trees. This doesn't look like the right place."

"For crying out loud, Angus; it was 2:00 A.M."

I look out and see a sign that says Champoeg State Park. In a panic, I grab the atlas. After looking carefully at our location, my worst fears are confirmed. "Zen, we're north of Salem. The rest area where we stopped last night was at Talbot, about seventy five miles south of here."

"Are you sure?" He stares at me in disbelief.

"Damn right," I say, showing him where we are according to the atlas. "We're practically back in the Portland suburbs. How'd ya miss it, Zen?"

"I don't know," he says, looking queasy.

We are really up the creek now. Not only are we going in the wrong direction with our set at the Oregon Country Fair just hours away, we have also just wasted fifty dollars in gasoline which I really do not want to think about at this time. "Let's just high-tail it back down the freeway to Talbot and grab Angel. We're still not in bad shape. They probably have free coffee there, too."

"They do here," says Zen pointing toward a banner saying, "Free Coffee and Treats Courtesy of the Talbot Kiwanis Club." We tank up on the worst coffee in the world, and the packet of non-dairy coffee creamer only makes it worse. I lament not leaving it black.

We're southbound on I-5 again and Elvis's clock reads 8:23. Angel has been gone for almost eight hours.

"Are we gonna make it to the gig in time?" asks Star.

"No problem," I say. I hear Ollie mumbling something about how he was afraid that we had left her behind.

"Don't even talk about it Ollie. Just don't."

"Sorry."

"Quit saying you're sorry all the time," says Zen. "It drives me nuts."

"Sorry," says Ollie. Star just shakes her head.

"Actually, it's really my fault," I confess.

"No shit, Sherlock," says Star.

I try to imagine the upcoming scene at the rest area. Not only does leaving Angel behind play into her worst abandonment paranoia, it will certainly set the tone for the rest of the tour and place her squarely in the driver's seat for getting what she wants out of the band. Who could argue with her after what she had to endure? I'm gonna need a lot of coffee in me to deal with this one, and quite frankly, the Boyd's I'm drinking just isn't cutting it.

"I need a pile driver," I say as we're now cruising into Albany. Nobody argues as I pull off the freeway and up to an espresso stand.

We line up for our orders, and after a couple of sips, I feel the caffeine starting to work its magic.

Many of the world's finest rockers had drug addictions. For Kurt, Jimi and Janis it was heroin. Keith loved barbiturates and alcohol. In spite of the wackiness of my comrades, we're all pretty boring when it comes to drug abuse. Coffee and beer are about as far as we go.

I find a pay phone close by, and nervously dial Sunny's number. We'll be in deep shit if Angel called but I have to know. The phone rings about eight times before a sleepy voice answers.

"Hi," I say, full of dread.

"Angus?" She says, sounding a little more awake. "What are you doing calling so early? Is everything all right?"

"Everything's fine," I lie, relieved that Angel hasn't called. "I just called to check in with you."

"What time is it? Did you just call a few minutes ago?"

"No, I didn't just call. Everyone wanted me to tell you that we're having a blast. Sorry I'm calling so early."

"You're playing the Oregon Fair today, right?"

"Yeah, we sure are."

"Weren't you going to call me *after* the show?"

"I was, but I got excited I guess. You know, being the second day and all."

"There's a lot to be excited about, sweetheart. I left a message for you last night. Check it when you have time." She pauses, even more awake now. "Are you sure everything's okay?"

"Everything's fine," I say. I hear Peaches hacking in the background and I know it's time to sign off. I tell her that I'll call back later. The coffee has really kicked in, and I almost feel great. I fill the tank and once we're back on the road heading south, the mood is fairly upbeat. Yeah, Angel will be pissed. Yeah, it will be a scene. But it will be funny too. We'll shower her with kindness, pamper her, and maybe even offer her the chance to play a solo song or two in front of the big crowd today. Ollie's right, her organ playing actually has gotten a lot better.

Everything's going to be fine, and I'm now fully believing that we are a band of destiny and everybody who ever put us down will be very sorry. We'll be signed for sure by Christmas. I'll look a hell of a lot more attractive to Lily, too. That will be nice.

We pass through Albany and it's 9:22 A.M. I can't believe how far Zen overshot, but hey, we're The Cosmic Poets. Things like this are bound to happen to a band with a name like ours.

It's pushing 10:00 when I see the sign for the Talbot Rest Area coming up. "Here it is," I yell as we pull off the freeway. It does look different in the daylight. There are a few groups of people milling about as we pull in. We scan the place quickly but there is no sign of Angel, anywhere.

"Let's walk around," I say, feeling sick.

"I'll check the bathroom," says Star, somberly.

"I'll cover the dog walk area," says Ollie.

"Zen, would you mind sticking with Ollie? We don't need any more disasters today."

Ollie looks at me, offended. "I'm not gonna get lost."

"All right then, but do you understand why I worry about you?"

Zen and I head for the bathroom to relieve ourselves.

"What do you think?" I ask him, as we stand in front of our respective urinals.

"I think we lost her."

"Obviously, Zen, but what should we do?"

The man of few words sighs and zips up his pants. "Maybe we should call the cops."

"We don't want to get the cops in on this," I say, feeling a panic creeping up my legs. "She's gotta be okay. She probably caught a ride to the fair."

"Hey," says Zen, smiling. "You're probably right. We should just go there to try and find her."

"Yeah, and leave the cops out of it."

We emerge from the bathroom with a new plan, and after conferring with Star who has had no luck in the women's restroom, she is in agreement. No cops. Not yet.

Just then an Oregon State Trooper cruises slowly past and we all look down at our feet not wanting eye contact. I can tell he's staring at us long and hard, and I'm afraid I'll faint. There's no way in hell we're calling the cops to find Angel. They'll probably think I killed her or something. I can just picture her face on the back of a milk carton saying, "Last seen at the Talbot Rest Area..."

The cop is gone and I realize that our drummer is nowhere to be seen. "Where's Ollie?"

"I don't know," says Star, panicked.

"*Ollie*?" I scream. People are staring at us. Then I notice Star has succumbed to the curb, head in hands, shoulders shuddering as her body bucks and twitches with uncontrollable sobs.

"I can't believe this is happening to me!"she cries, as Zen puts his arm around her shoulders. She looks up at me, her light blue eyes brimming with tears. "How could you be so stupid?"

"Me?" I ask. "Angel is the one who got lost."

"It was *your* responsibility as the driver to keep track of *everybody.*"

"Sorry, you guys," says Ollie running up. "I met this guy over in the off-leash area who said he thought he saw a confused looking black-haired woman talking on the phone a few hours ago."

"That was her!" yells Star.

"Not so fast," says Ollie. "This woman was wearing a big, floppy, purple hat. Does Angel have a big, floppy, purple hat?"

"Yeah, she does," says Star. "But I'm not sure if it was purple."

"Did he say it was purple?"

"He did."

"Wait a minute," says Zen. "Would Angel wear her floppy hat in the middle of the night if she was just going to use the john in a rest area?"

"Good point, Zen," I say. "It probably wasn't her. Maybe I should check my phone messages in case she tried to call."

I walk over to the pay phone and dial the Bellingham voice-mail service. The robot voice tells me that I have four new messages.

First message left yesterday, at 3:10 P.M.: "Hi, Angus, it's Lily. I just wanted to say goodbye but I guess I missed you. And I do *miss* you. I hope the tour goes great and I think you guys are going to get signed. It's just a feeling I have. I don't know why I called. I know we need time apart, but I woke up thinking about you and I just want you to know that I really do love you. We need to spend time together when you get back. Quality time. Please don't think I'm too much of a flake. I'm working on myself. Things will get better...bye for now my love."

"*Yes!*" I holler joyously as I press the replay button, basking in the warmth of hope. Lily's voice is the best music to my ears. When I remain aloof and somewhat indifferent to her, she is always more attracted to me. Maybe it will work out. I mustn't try too hard.

Next message left yesterday at 6:03 P.M.: "Hi, sweetie, Sunny here. I talked to Frank tonight and he's very, very optimistic about things. He's trying to get some more of his contacts up to the Arcata deal, and to Rock City in Berkeley as well. I talked to my fortuneteller again and she says that huge events are about to take place in your lives. Peaches and I burned sage tonight and rubbed some Madrona sticks. I've got a great feeling about this. Bye for now."

How interesting, I think, contemplating the truth about Rock City. What is one to do?

Next message left today at 2:12 A.M.: "You fucking jerk! I just knew you were gonna pull some shit, Angus. How dare you leave me here you asshole! I'm fucking freezing!"

"She's alive," I yell joyously as everyone crowds around. Then things get weird.

"Angus? Angus, help me. Help me, Angus. There's somebody coming...Oh no...Oh my God, no...Please don't...Don't do *that*!" There is screaming and a great commotion..."*Get away!*" Then the line goes dead.

"Oh my God, Angel!" I collapse to the ground, still clutching the phone. "Angel's been abducted! It's all my fault!" Zen and Star bend over me while Ollie grabs the phone.

"What happened?" asks Star, panicked.

"Angel's been assaulted!" I cry. "We gotta call the cops."

Star explodes into screams of hysteria while Zen turns a pasty white. But, Ollie...Ollie is now laughing as he holds the phone to his ear.

"How can you laugh, Ollie?"

"Here, listen," he says handing the phone to me.

Fourth message left today at 8:45 A.M.: "I scared you didn't I you loser? You deserved it. After what you put me through...I'll never forget this one, Angus. You're gonna be really, really sorry you did this to me." I hear multiple voices in the background, laughing. "Did you think I was getting murdered? Good. In a way, you already have murdered me. But guess what, Angus? I've been resurrected. You'll see what I mean some day, soon. Bye for now, jerk!"

Her words have a strange, soothing effect on me. I lie there for some time as my strength slowly returns. Star is back under control, too, but we are all shaken. What has happened to Angel?

She's alive and seems to be okay. She also doesn't seem to be alone anymore. But where is she?

"She's alive and in prime form," I say, regaining some composure. "We've got a gig in five hours. Let's just go do it as a four-piece." I know that I must exert some semblance of leadership if we are going to survive our first potentially lethal blow of the tour. Angel must have caught a ride to the fair, and we'll just catch up with her there. Things will still work out, I tell myself. They always do. Now they have to, or all will be lost.

Eleven

We arrive at the fairgrounds at 1:33 P.M. and after checking in at the gate, we are driving through a sea of dreadlocks until we're finally shown a parking place. The warm, July sun brings me a new sense of peace and well being. Why Angel had to play such a mean joke is beyond me. In hindsight, Zen and Ollie thought it was hilarious and in perfect keeping with her good nature. I'm just glad she's alive. My immediate task is to find the manager of the main stage. I study the map given to me at the gate before proceeding off on my own.

The place is a zoo; groups of barefoot hippies playing hacky sack are everywhere, and kids are naked, running free. Jugglers, musicians, magicians, live theater, good vibes, happy people. The smell of sage, pot smoke, incense and body odor is heavy in the sultry air. In the distance, on what looks like the main stage, there is a reggae band playing some beautiful music. In front of it is a peaceful, hippie version of the mosh pit. More good vibes.

I wade through a sea of tie-dye and the crowd in a weird kind of way reminds me of eel grass, eel grass with a lot of colors. This will be a great audience to play for and Lord knows we need a great gig. A roar of approval ripples through the crowd as the band finishes the song and a dreadlocked dude yells, "Thank you!"

As I get closer to the side of the stage, I realize that the crowd is much bigger than I had originally thought. There are at least a thousand people and the odds of finding Angel, even if she is here, are slight at best. Finally I'm next to the stage, and find that the back stage area is cordoned off with rope. "Is Liberty around?" I ask a skinny dude who's standing at the gate looking malnourished.

"Why?"

"Because I'm playing with my band at 3:00 P.M. and I'm supposed to check in with him.

"Oh cool," he says with surprising respect. "Are you Sequoia?"

"What? My name's Angus."

"Just a second," he says, taking a long look at me before disappearing. In a few moments, he returns with a small, impish-looking guy with skateboard hair, a nose ring and a shirt that says, *Listen To the Children*.

"What can I do for you?" He is not smiling.

"My band plays at three, and I was told to check in with you."

"What's your name?"

"Angus Keegan. You're Liberty?"

"I am," he says absently as he flips through some papers. He then looks up at me with concern. "So, you're with Groovetribe?"

"Groovetribe?" I ask, suddenly feeling faint. "No, I'm with The Cosmic Poets." I envision Cheshire man back at the Ballard Firehouse writhing and reeling across the stage, drenched with sweat. I pull out my schedule that was mailed to me and read it. "Yeah," I say. "We're on at three. It says so right here."

He takes my copy and stares intently at it for a couple of moments. Then he breaks out into a big grin. "I see what's going on." He hands the paper back to me. "You're on the Shady Grove Acoustic Stage at 3:00. This is the Main Stage."

"I talked to Moonjewel two weeks ago before the final schedules were even mailed out and I *know* she said that we were playing the Main Stage."

"Look," says Liberty, "I didn't make the schedule. But I tell you, the Shady Grove Stage is great. There's a big crowd over there right now." He pauses, looking a little perplexed. "Funny though, they don't usually book full bands back there since no amplification is allowed."

"No amplification? Are you shitting me? We're a full band."

"Don't get mad at me," says Liberty. "I don't make the rules."

"Look, man," I say, desperately, "all I know is that we're supposed to play an electric set on the Main Stage at 3:00 P.M.

Saturday, July 11. I wrote on my application that we're a full rock band."

Liberty's face is turning red, and his nostrils flare a bit. "We don't tolerate attitudes here," he says. "This is an all-volunteer event and we're trying to accommodate everybody. This isn't just about you!"

"I know, I know," I say, trying to keep control. "This is all about trust-fund jam bands with names like Groovetribe, isn't it? Well, mister, we drove all the way down here from Bellingham to play at your stinkin' festival and now you're telling us we can't?"

"I didn't say you couldn't play. You just can't use amps, but since you've pushed it this far, you might as well pack your gear and go home."

"You're not nice," I say, trembling. "Why do you have to be so mean?"

"What are you talking about," he asks, staring at me with a flicker of fear in his eyes.

"You ought to be nicer to musicians," I continue, feeling a strange sense of sudden calm while my right hand shakes a little. "You never know who you're talking to, Liberty. For your information, we've got Frank Strong shopping us to labels, and we're on the doorstep of something major and I've got the most beautiful woman in the world in love with me, and you're gonna wish someday you were nicer!"

"You just don't get it, do you?" Liberty says with disdain.

"I do get it, Liberty, and I doubt very much that Frank's people showed up here today, anyway, and playing for you guys doesn't matter 'cause you're all too stoned to remember who we are! Have a nice day." I turn and begin to run.

I'm about halfway back through the crowd...the same crowd I had loved twenty minutes before when I trip and fall, landing in a pile of dreadlocks. As I stagger back to my feet, a surreal swirl of faces is now looking at me, some laughing. The reggae band kicks in again as the crowd sways to the vibe of universal peace, love and unity. I lurch through the sea of colored eel grass knowing that if we were preparing for our 3:00 P.M. main stage set this crowd would be the most beautiful thing in the world. But that didn't happen, so now I must hate and scorn them. The band finishes a song, and as the crowd noise dies down momentarily, I scream toward the stage, "*It's all yours, Angel!*" I blow a kiss in the direction of the stage and it seems like a thousand faces all turn to look at me. It occurs to me that what they've just heard is absolutely senseless. As I turn and run the rest of the way to the parking lot I hear what sounds like a roar of laughter coming from behind me, and my shaming is complete.

~

"What's the deal?" asks Star, afraid of her own question. Zen and Ollie stand by looking rather somber.

"We're screwed," I pant. "They put us on some acoustic stage with no amplification allowed, so I said forget it."

"You told them that we won't play on their acoustic stage?" Star asks, getting agitated.

"I'm sick of being jacked around," I say. "I was told in writing that the whole band would have a full set of music at the Oregon Country Fair's Main Stage at 3:00 P.M. on Saturday, July 11. Now they're telling me that Groovetribe has our spot. Screw it. We're doing this for free anyway, and quite frankly—"

"Groovetribe?" asks Zen, shocked. "That band of freaks from Seattle?"

"That's right, Zen," I say, bitterly.

"Will you *ever* take responsibility for anything?" asks Star. "It's always someone else's fault."

"In this case, it is."

"Yeah, just like losing Angel," she says, falling to the ground with a groan. "This isn't the way it's supposed to happen. What did I do to deserve this?"

"It's not just about you, Star."

"If only I pissed where Walter got out, we wouldn't have lost Angel," says Ollie.

"They wanted us to play un-amped?" asks Zen, ignoring Ollie's self-flagellation. "We might as well play naked."

"Well, Zen, that seems to be a common state of dress in these parts."

"I'm sorry," says Ollie, "but please clarify what was actually said."

"I told you, they wanted us to play un-amped on the Shady Grove All Acoustic Stage at 3:00 P.M."

"Drums are acoustic, Angus; you don't need to be so defensive. We need the gig."

"There's no way we can make it work. Besides, it's too late. I've offended everybody."

"I quit!" Star yells. "I've had it with you clowns."

"Go ahead and quit, then," I say, jumping to my feet. I climb into Elvis and grab my gig bag and guitar while my legs seem to have a mind of their own.

"Here's the keys, Zen," I say, once outside again. "Take these cry-babies back to Bellingham. I got a gig with Bonnie Raitt and Neil Young to save the Redwoods." I throw him the keys, taking an immense amount of satisfaction at Star's open mouth.

"You gonna hitchhike?" asks Zen, laughing.

"Why the hell not?" I say. "You babies have a nice day, now." I begin stomping toward the gate. *Star's got some nerve.* Before I'm even a hundred yards, I am drenched in sweat. Shit, I've got about four hundred miles to go.

As I hit the main road, heading east, I'm starting to feel better. Neil Young plays solo. Bruce Cockburn plays solo. Bob Dylan plays solo. Willie Nelson plays solo...My mind ponders the many artists who often sound better solo than with bands. It's gonna be fine. Wouldn't that be hilarious if I scored a record deal on my own? Boy, would they all be sorry.

In the distance, I hear a wall of percussion and the roar of the audience. "Namaste," someone screams over the mike. It's Groovetribe. They're playing our set. I can just see Sequoia with his sweaty dreads, writhing across the stage. Soon I hear a refrain, "We are all one, we are all one, dance to the beat of the drum, the rhythm of earth and sun, we are all one, we are all one..." Fucking Groovetribe. There is something strangely familiar in that refrain of voices and I hurry forward, trying to put some more distance between us.

Then I hear the sound of wheels crunching over gravel as Elvis pulls up behind me. "Want a ride to California you good looking Cosmic Poet?" Star asks, smiling. Zen's driving and both he and Ollie are laughing too.

"I know this is driving you nuts," says Ollie, "but you're gonna need a backup band at Redwood Summer."

"What makes you so sure of that?" I ask. I'm still not sure whether I'm glad to see them. "I like my solo career so far. It's a lot simpler."

"We're taking you to California," says Star. "We love you. We need you. We need each other."

"You don't need me. Guitar players and singers are a dime a dozen."

"But you're special, Angus."

"Thanks," I say sarcastically. Then, Ollie breaks into *Cherish*, and soon the whole band is singing along. I'm powerless to the spell and find myself climbing aboard. As I take my seat Zen guns the accelerator, sending a plume of dust and gravel high in the air. We're on our way to California.

Twelve

Being on tour is a perpetual ride on a roller coaster of emotion. An hour ago the band split up. Fourteen hours ago, we lost Angel. Five hours ago, I thought she had been murdered. Now we're heading back toward the freeway and the glory of California and the biggest gig of our lives looms directly beyond the three hundred and seventy-one miles we must travel to get there. Life is good again. To hell with the Country Fair. There weren't gonna be any label people there anyway. To hell with people who've got attitudes. We're The Cosmic Poets and things like this are bound to happen to a band with a name like ours. We're just paying our dues. Everybody's got to go through it. In the end, it will pay off and Liberty will be sorry.

"I-5, one hundred yards and closing," yells Zen.

"Fasten your seat-belts and prepare for take-off," yells Ollie.

We pull into a turn taking us up the on ramp when Zen sees him first. "There's Walter!"

Sure enough, standing on the on-ramp is Walter Simon. At first he doesn't seem to recognize us.

"Let's not pick him up," Star says.

"Are you serious?" I ask. "It's Walter!"

"We're on a schedule," she pleads.

"Aw, come on, Star," says Ollie. "We can't leave Walter."

"Pull over, Zen," I say as we've passed him and he is now looking at us with a mixture of confusion and dismay.

Zen pulls over and Star sighs loudly, letting everyone know that she's pissed.

"Walter, what are you doing?" I yell as Elvis comes to a halt.

"Going South," he says running up. "Got any room in there for an old Indian?"

"Hell, yes," I say as he climbs up. It's damn good to see him. "Got any more dried caribou?"

"I wish," he says, nodding to everyone as Star clears a place for him to sit.

"Hi, Walter," she says, quietly.

He looks at her and smiles.

"How was Chumwahalal?" asks Ollie.

"Chemewha?" asks Walter, perplexed. "Not very good."

"Did you find your daughter?"

"No."

"Is she all right?" Ollie asks, not caring that he's prying. I poke him hard.

"Good to see you, Walter," I say. "How long you been standing out here?"

"About five minutes," he says with a laugh.

"Really? How'd you get here?"

"Big Indian family from Warm Springs dropped me off. They were afraid to leave me stranded here in white man country."

"I don't blame you," says Ollie. "A black man was dragged to death behind a pickup full of Nazis down in Texas not too long ago."

"Let's talk about something a little more pleasant, okay?" I say. "Where are you going now, Walter?"

"San Francisco," he says. "I've got cousins down there."

"You're just going to San Francisco just to see some cousins?" asks Ollie.

"Look, Ollie," I say, exasperated. "Mind your goddamned business."

"I was just asking—"

"You ask too many questions. Sorry, Walter."

"That's okay," he says to me. Then he turns to Ollie and says, "Maybe some day I'll tell you all the story." For the briefest second, he looks as sad a person as I have ever seen.

~

"We've got a gig in Berkeley in three days," says Ollie. "That's really close to San Francisco."

"Yeah," I say. "We can take you there no problem."

"That's nice of you," he says. "But I only have ten dollars for gas. Maybe I can give you some old Indian wisdom, though. Sometimes that's worth more than money."

"Some wisdom might be great," I say, reflecting on the fact that we are now down to $106.64 in our travel fund. How far that will get us, who knows.

I force away thoughts of Rock City and the fact that we do not have nearly enough money to get back to the Northwest. Instead I think of Bonnie, Neil, and all the other nice people we're going to meet down there at Redwood Summer, and how it's going to be the biggest turning point in our careers with the A&R people watching us play in front of thousands of people. We've suffered enough and I'm through having to deal with head-trips and being yanked around.

"Where's the other Cosmic Poet?" asks Walter.

"We lost her," says Star matter-of-factly. She has calmed considerably and I'm glad. "We accidentally left her at a rest-area last night while she was out for a leak."

"That's funny," he says.

"Funny?" asks Star. "How can that be funny?"

Walter only smiles, shrugging his shoulders a little.

Star stares out the window saying nothing; yet for the first time, I'm seeing the chinks in her armor.

Meanwhile Ollie is blabbering away in the front about some run-in with Ian Eisner back in Bellingham, and how Ian had invited him over for some wine and porno, and how Ollie had balked at first before succumbing. Zen just sits there driving with an occasional nod of the head. I know he's listening intently. Listening intently to Ollie helps pass the time on long road trips like this.

Here we are on tour to get famous. It feels like we're going backwards. Sunny would pull the plug if she knew the true state of affairs, and I couldn't blame her, really. She's a pro and we're misfits. But the delusions of fame still beckon like a Twilight Zone zombie, and we're not about to toss in the towel.

Getting famous and presenting an image of what you want people to think you're like is a very exhausting undertaking. According to Sunny and Frank, it's really just about making one's self marketable. Your promo's got to show the world how cool you are and how you can manufacture an attitude for any occasion. Predictability is a virtue and if your sound is "new" or "different", it's still gotta sound like the happening sound. You're also advised to stay away from politics or social commentary. Music is the escape from what's going on. Nobody, especially Sony Records, gives a rat's ass what you think about the Zapitistas or The World Trade Organization. Meanwhile, the world is embroiled in famine, war and disease, while whole ecological systems are collapsing at a rate unprecedented in recorded history. Rain forests fall and burn while toxic and nuclear waste incinerates the air and poisons the water, but hey, this Bud's for you!

"We're coming into Grant's Pass. Should we stop for dinner?" asks Zen.

"Sounds good, Zen. I gotta call Sunny, anyway."

We pull off the freeway and into the parking lot of a homogenous, chain-style restaurant with soft, bland food and take a table while a young girl dressed in a Barvarian style skirt comes to take our order. I excuse myself to go find a phone. I'm nervous as hell again. Chances are that if Angel were to call Sunny, she would have done so already. If she's not above leaving a horrible message like the one that she left on my voice mail, she's certainly not above calling Sunny to rat on me.

"Hello?" she answers after the first ring. She sounds stressed.

"Hi, it's me."

"I'm glad you called."

"Really?"

"Are you ready for this?"

"I'm not sure," I say, my hands shaking.

"Peaches has lost his mind."

"That's *great* news, Sunny!"

"What?"

"I mean, I knew he was crazy from the start," I say, quickly.

"I never told you that he was a diagnosed schizophrenic, did I?" she asks.

"No, but you didn't need to. I could tell"

"I might need you to wire me some money."

"What?"

"I might need some money to move out on Peaches. Mr. Harvey threatened to kill me last night."

"Who's Mr. Harvey?"

"That's the scariest of all his personalities. He hasn't shown up in quite awhile. I thought he was gone for good. Then going into the bottom of the eighth inning of the Mariners and Yankees, there was Mr. Harvey, standing naked in the middle of the living room with a plastic vegetable bag over his head and a pair of rusty scissors in his hand, speaking in broken Mandarin. I think I might need to move."

"Geeze, Sunny," I say. "We're down to not much money, and I'm not sure we're gonna make it back to Washington as it is."

"You've got gigs all the way to Southern California. What are you talking about?"

"Right…well, the Oregon Country Fair, and Redwood Summer don't really pay. The money won't start rolling in until we hit Rock City in Berkeley."

"Oh, yeah," she says. "You got my message about Frank's friends from RCA showing up there?"

"I sure did. That's really exciting, Sunny."

"They'll be at the Redwood show, too. We're on our way, sweetheart."

"It sure seems that way, doesn't it?"

"How'd it go at the Country Fair?"

"Great."

"Were there a lot of people there?"

"Tons. They kind of reminded me of colored eel grass."

"Eel grass?"

"Never mind. It's hard to explain."

"Tell me about it."

"Well, our set was 3:00 P.M. on the main stage. I bet there were at least a couple of thousand people there. Sunny, we had 'em in the palm of our hands. The crowd absolutely went wild. They *loved* us. I only wish you and Frank could have been there. We went bam-bam-bam, one song into the next, no tuning breaks. Ollie was so *on.* During his drum solo it was like Keith Moon's ghost possessed him, and you know how much hippies love drums. One of our the best gigs, ever!"

"Really?" She giggles. "Frank will be excited to hear this. Angel's organ solos went okay?"

"Actually, they were border-line excellent. Her attitude's improved immensely, Sunny. Something about being on tour has really mellowed her out."

"That's great news," she says. "You know, Angus, I actually want to talk to her. Can you go get her for me?"

Shit. I know why she wants to talk to Angel. Angel has rich parents.

"You know, Sunny," I say trying to sound indifferent. "Something kind of interesting happened today."

"Yes?"

"Well, this dude who said he was from...I think it was Polygram. Yeah, Polygram. Well he comes up to me after our set...I don't know if I should tell you about this."

"*Tell* me," she whispers.

"He said he really liked us a lot and thought we sounded like no band he's ever heard and that he might be able to help us get our foot in the door."

"Did you tell him to call me?" she asks.

"I did tell him that I was under contract with you. He told me that he only wanted to deal with me."

There is a ringing silence. Trying hide her sense of panic she says, "I don't want you talking with him or anyone at all. All business regarding the band goes through me and you even talking to him is a breach of contract. Remember, the ocean is full of sharks and I'm here to protect you from them."

"Sunny," I say, proud of my bait and switch, "he was a really nice guy, and I resent the notion that I can't talk to anyone about our business affairs."

"Sweetie, it's called protocol and if you don't follow it, you and I are gonna have some big problems."

"But can't I talk to him about how he could help us all?"

"He's to talk to me!" she snaps. "That's all there is to it. You are not to talk to him at all! Do you understand me?"

"Yes," I say, quietly. "I understand perfectly well."

"Oh, come off your Gemini high horse. Did he leave you a card?"

"No," I say, dejectedly. "I gave him a tape. I guess if he calls me, I'll pass his information onto you."

"Always get a card," she says. "Polygram, huh? I bet he knows Frank, too. Anything else we need to talk about?"

"No, nothing else," I say, amazed at how real the lie has become. "You're the boss."

"Look," she says, "you have to trust me in these matters. I'm only trying to make you successful."

"Okay, Sunny."

"Call me tomorrow, sweetie."

"Sure, Sunny."

We hang up and I'm relieved that I've bought us more time. Right now, buying time is what it's all about. Besides, it's her fault for making me lie. Didn't she once tell me that I might have to do things I really don't want to do in order to be successful. It's all for the sake of the band and, once again, the promised land of record contract nirvana does not seem as far away as it did three hours ago.

When I get back to our table in the restaurant, Star says, "How did it go?"

"Pretty good," I say, sitting in front of my tuna melt and fries. "Except that Mr. Harvey is threatening to kill Sunny."

"What?" asks Ollie. "Who's Mr. Harvey?"

"From what I gather, Mr. Harvey is one of Peaches's many personalities."

"He's wacked, eh?" asks Zen as he munches a hamburger.

"He threatened to kill her?" asks Star.

"I couldn't tell if it was for real or not," I say. "Anybody got a thousand bucks to send her to help her move?"

They laugh, thinking I'm joking.

"Are you guys worried about Angel?" asks Star.

"You know, I'm not," I say.

"Yeah," says Ollie, "I get the feeling she's all right."

"You don't think she's dead, or anything like that."

"No, Star," says Zen. "Angel isn't dead. She's probably in better shape than we are."

Walter just stares down at his plate, not saying anything. He has the slightest smile betrayed on his lips. I wonder what he's thinking.

Thirteen

We let out a cheer as we cross the California border, heading through the Siskiyous. The sun is almost down and the sky looks like a Louis L'mour painting with red, torn clouds hanging below a pink sky that is basking the sparsely forested mountains in alpenglow. We pull onto a country road that follows the Kalamath River toward Eureka and soon we come across a small, unmaintained campground right near the river. It has a picnic table and a fire ring. Soon after stopping, Walter has a blazing crackling fire started in the traditional Gwich'in way with newspaper and a disposable lighter.

The river's sigh is soothing and only after sitting down in a lawn chair do I feel my torso begin to loosen. What a day. It seems like weeks since we lost Angel, and yesterday's departure from Bellingham seems like another lifetime. Life is getting better fast and, now that we're in California, the reality that we're going to play in front of the biggest crowd of our lives is just beginning to sink in.

The sweet fragrance of the forest, the smell of wood smoke, and the sounds of birds make life rich. What more could one want? Sure, performing before upwards of ten thousand people the day after tomorrow will be incredible. Signing that record contract and cashing that advance check will be a triumph and a thrill. Of course, paying all the bills and winning Lily back will be a once-in-a-lifetime event. Going on an arena tour to support the debut album will be very cool as well. But this? We're talking about Tolstoy's first condition of human happiness: a life under the open sky in communion with all living and non-living things. What could top this? A life of mindless materialism and shallow self-adulation all centered on imposing a phony image of ones self upon the world? It is all vanity. But not the pure rivers and gentle breezes, or the music of the spring runoff…They are not vain and they will not be traded.

I will never be corrupted. Ever. Just give me a simple, ten-bedroom beach house overlooking the ocean with a couple of humble Mercedes in front with a Lexus to boot, a private dock and float plane, some property in Chile, some river front in Tierra Del Fuego for fly fishing excursions, a three-story cabin in Alaska and a house in Malibu to alleviate those stressful ventures into Los Angeles when I must appear at all the shallow awards banquets I'll probably be invited to. That's all I really want. Oh, and a cabin in New Zealand, houses in Dublin and Madrid with a small private jet that could be converted into a cargo plane for humanitarian food drops in impoverished third-world countries when I'm not using it. I'll be doing my part to change the world. Peace, love and unity. Give it a chance. Give me a chance. I'll be different. I swear.

It is a very special night out here in the forest. For once Ollie isn't monopolizing the conversation. Instead we hear a story from Walter about a time when he was much younger and went on a hunting trip with some Gwich'in Athapaskan down in the Yukon Flats, and how he walked fifty miles back to Circle Hot Springs through a raging blizzard after getting separated from the party and left for dead.

Everyone was amazed that he not only survived, but was relatively unscathed. He attributed his good fortune to the spirit of the late owner of Circle Hot Springs, affectionately known in local circles as Emmet John Quake. Every time Walter was about to give up and throw in the towel, Emmet would appear to him through the blinding snow and Walter would fix his eyes on Emmet's orange hunting cap and red flannel shirt that he always wore when he was alive, beckoning Walter to keep moving by saying, "Free popcorn, Walter, remember the free popcorn."

Walter did keep going and survived. The new owners of the resort had kept up Emmet's tradition of providing free popcorn to the guests and the first thing Walter requested upon his safe return to the resort was a large bowl of popcorn!

Ollie prods him about his days in South Dakota and Walter reluctantly tells us that he was present at the Wounded Knee occupation.

"I went to Vietnam under orders from the government and I never questioned them, but when I came back and saw what the same government was doing to Indian people, I thought that maybe I could make up for some of the bad things I'd done by helping out." His eyes are dark and his hands tremble a bit as he recounts the tension-filled weeks at Wounded Knee surrounded by government paramilitary personnel.

"Man, you've seen a lot in your days," I say.

"My people have suffered," he says. "A lot of Indian people died during those years, but nobody can take your dignity unless you give it away and I will never. The past only has power over you if you let it. A lot of Indians become what they're expected to be. I used to be that way too, and blamed all the whites for those two dumb ones that ate from that tree of knowledge. They say we're all paying for their sins, but why should I pay anymore than I already have? My daughter was the only one who ever understood what I meant by that. When she left, I lost everything I ever cared about."

Star says nothing but spits quietly into the coals of the campfire. Zen and Ollie are silent.

"I'm not angry like I was," Walter continues. "The Elders taught me that everything you need is right here, in this very moment." The fire crackles and pops, and we sit in silence observing the changing colors of the coals. It's so good to have real conversation about real things. Matters of importance, some would say. The stars and night crickets evoke a childish longing in my spirit for something lasting.

Zen and Star break out their instruments and begin jamming as the heaviness of the story fades. Soon the night air is filled with Zen's acoustic blues guitar and Star's saxophone lines floating upwards to the heavens, carried on pillows of smoke and sparks. Walter is really into it. He can't keep his feet still as they pound it out. Star is delighted with the fact that Walter's into it. Ollie pounds his snare with his hands and they play late into the night while I listen with a soul filled with inspiration, hope and anguish. What could be better than Tolstoy's first condition of happiness? I can't imagine much. Of course he viewed fame and fortune as one of the great human follies, misfortunes, and tragedies. I'm not ready to deal with that just yet.

Fourteen

It's late. I have no idea what time it is, but Elvis is full of snores as I lie awake, contemplating my over-stressed bladder. It is time to piss. As I step into the night air, the first thing I notice is how far the new moon has moved across the sky. I find some bushes off of the path. As I'm relieving myself, I hear a strange, high-pitched sound, like the sound of a band saw coming from near the river close by. Curious, I stumble down the path toward the river while the sound is getting louder. I think that it must be a pack of coyotes, which isn't surprising given how wild this place seems. As I walk out onto the beach it is much louder, but now it doesn't sound like coyotes at all. That's when I see him.

Walter is hunched over, back to me, facing the water, and the combination of his beautiful saxophone playing and the moonlight sparkling off of the stream causes a slow chill to pass through me. First it sounds like a slow, mournful blues, then it becomes very indigenous, mimicking the sound of wolves, and I'm suddenly in the Alaskan wilderness, standing alone on the banks of the mighty Yukon River as a pack of ghostly canines slowly reveal themselves to me. It is clear that Walter has had training. Probably, by the sound of it, much training. *You son of a bitch*, I think as it occurs to me that I ought not to be here. Yet I can't pull myself away. Like metaphysical arrows, the notes penetrate the core of my being, the vibrations of music and river becoming one while I am suspended in a confusion of spontaneous ecstasy where joy and sorrow have lost all meaning.

The music stops and I hear the sound of his voice, though from where I stand, I gather no meaning. By the way his shoulders are shaking, I can tell he's laughing. The eastern horizon is now banded with golden light as the first rays of dawn settle upon the cool mist suspended over the river. I hear the saxophone start again, but my eyes are confused, for he still seems to be clutching his legs and that's when I slowly realize that what I'm actually hearing *are* coyotes from across the river. Then it occurs to me that he isn't laughing at all; he's crying, engaged in a tearful, unintelligible dialogue with the unknown.

I turn and slowly walk back to Elvis as my world is becoming more shallow and absurd by the minute. I lay in my little bunk feeling something wanting to shift, kind of like your back when it needs to crack. I await the morning with wide, fearful eyes.

Fifteen

The sun is high in the morning sky when I finally emerge from Elvis. I'm glad for the few hours of sleep I was able to catch and the smell of coffee gives me hope for a day of good, even temper.

"Morning, Angus," says Ollie, sheepishly. He's always sheepish, though.

"Morning," I say. The scene by the river last night seems like a dream as I see Star who's managing to make herself look perfect with lipstick and make-up while telling Walter how she once swelled up like a beach ball after getting stung by fifty hornets when she was a kid. He listens intently to every word; I'm glad she's warming up to him. Is this really the same person who was serenading the coyotes with Star's saxophone last night? Our eyes meet, and I look away.

"Arcata today and our date with destiny tomorrow, huh?" I ask, feigning humor.

"I'm ready to conquer!" says Star, emphatically stomping her boot into the dust. She looks at Walter who smiles back at her. "The crowd, that is," she mutters, looking away.

We finish breakfast, load the rig and are soon on our one hundred and seventy-five mile drive to Arcata on an enchanting country road. I relieve Zen at the wheel. Walter sits across from me while I try to think of something light to say. The longer the silence grows between us, the more awkward and obvious things become. Zen and Star talk quietly in the back while Ollie intently reads his magazines.

"I knew you were there," he says, his pupils dark and serious.

"I had no idea."

Leaning over, he asks, "Do the others know?"

"No," I say, looking in the rear-view mirror at my mates.

"Don't tell them, please."

"Why? You're incredible."

"Don't," he pleads.

"I won't, but why?"

"It's not what you think. Maybe some day I'll tell you a story, but not now. My music isn't for entertainment." His words just kind of fizzle into silence and I'm left confronting my own shallow ambitions. We drive the rest of the way to Arcata in silence.

~

A small, Northern California town nestled near the last of the giant coastal Redwoods, Arcata was once a laid-back haven for loggers and artists alike. While there was some tension and concern over the cutting of these giant trees, Pacific Lumber made her profits through selective and sustainable logging, serving as a progressive industry model. That was until the day they were purchased by Texas-based-corporate-slime-ball Charles Hurwitz whose Maxam Corporation's sole purpose was to liquidate these ancient forests as quickly as possible to pay off his bad junk bond debts on Wall Street. This action sparked the ultimate tragedy of the commons: with the Northern Spotted Owl destined for the Endangered Species List, there was a collective push on the part of all timber corporations to cut as much forest as possible, quickly, while there was still time.

The battle lines were drawn. In ten years, if cutting remained at the present pace, all the Redwoods left on public and private lands would be a distant memory. Now came the call to take a stand. After three months of organized and unorganized activism, Redwood Summer was born. In the midst of it all would be a giant concert with some of the biggest named artists in the world—along with a few not-so-big named bands and singers who had supported the cause over the long haul. And here we were, one of the little bands in a motor-home named Elvis, trying to find a place to park on a suddenly dangerous afternoon in mid-July.

There are cop cars all over the place; where there aren't, jacked-up four-wheelers and logging trucks, covered in mud, rumbled through the streets. Blue lights flash, horns blare and I'm scared shitless. My first mission is to find my born-again pagan buddy, Ken Johnson, whose self-appointed tribal name is now Raven Spirals Madly.

We do find a place to park and it's decided that I'll go find Fourth Corner Organic Teas and Coffees where Raven told me to check in. There would be someone there to page him when we arrived. Star, Walter, Zen and Ollie will be on their own to go get some late lunch and, in spite of the tension and feelings of danger, I know it will be good to be away from everyone for awhile. I'm glad for the plan, since finding a guy whose name reads like a Haiku poem in a town that's about to explode could be a tricky thing.

After saying goodbye to my mates and agreeing to check back at Elvis in an hour-and-a-half, I scan the crumpled note for instructions to the teashop. When I find that I'm only a couple of blocks away, I'm relieved. I wave at the occupants of a jacked up mud-wagon with a fully occupied rifle rack and when they all respond by flipping me off, I decide that it's time for me to get off the street as quickly as possible.

"You here for the big rally?" asks a young girl in a paisley dress.

"Yes, I am." My eyes adjust to the light while the door closes gently behind me. "We're actually playing at it."

"Really?" Her big, green eyes widen, reminding me of a timeless maiden from an Aesop Fable. My heart swells with love for her in her innocence and wonder. When she says, "That's *fucking* awesome," my projections about her are dashed in reality's rocky surf. "What's the name of your band?"

"The Cosmic Poets," I say. "We're from Bellingham, Washington."

"I love Bellingham," she says. "My brother went to Fairhaven College."

"Oh, yeah," I sigh. "I know Fairhaven."

"There was a tree sitter killed last week," she says, her eyes turning dark. "She was two hundred feet up a Redwood when a logger cut the tree down. Cops were standing there watching it happen. Didn't do a thing to stop it."

"Golly," I whisper.

"She was only nineteen," she says, starting to cry.

I find myself walking around the counter and taking her in my arms. I hold her as the full reality of what is happening hits me.

"There are a thousand cops with riot gear showing up from the Bay Area, today," she says, regaining a little composure.

"Was she a friend of yours?"

"Not really, I didn't know her very well at all."

"I'm really sorry," I say as she clings to me. I know if I was to tell her about how I was being dumped by Lily, she would somehow understand. I break our embrace, saying, "I'm actually looking for Raven Spirals Madly; he said I could page him from here."

"Oh, yeah. Raven's my boyfriend. I'm Katrina, by the way."

"Hi, Katrina, I'm Angus." A familiar dejection sweeps over me.

She pages him, leaving a message that I'm at the shop. Then she turns to me, saying, "He's got his hands into everything. He's even organizing mill workers."

"Yeah, Ken's a trooper," I say, recalling the day Ken and I along with a bunch of other unemployed creative-types got blasted with a fire-hose by the manager of the Mitsubishi Dealership in Bellingham. We were only there protesting Mitsubishi's destruction of the world's tropical rain forests. In spite of the good press for the cause, it was a little embarrassing to see our sopping bodies on the front page of *The Bellingham Herald*. I think that put Ken a little over the edge. Soon after he changed his name and moved to Northern California to work on saving the Redwoods.

"That's so cool that you guys are playing at the concert tomorrow. They're expecting twenty thousand people there."

"Twenty? I heard ten," I say, astonished.

"The latest figures are now upwards of twenty. That's what happens when Neil Young, Santana and Tracy Chapman sign on the bill. There are rumors that Pearl Jam are gonna be backing Neil up."

"No way. Really?" How will an unknown band like The Cosmic Poets fare with all the big guys? We'd be the first to get bumped from the line-up, or at least moved to the beginning. Oh well, even if our set gets trimmed back to half-an-hour, that's fifteen minutes more than allocated by Mr. Warhol.

"There's this other really awesome band coming down from the Northwest…"

"What's their name?" I ask dreamily as I'm jamming with Neil, while Crazy Horse is kicking it out behind us.

"It's Gr—"

Then the door swings open and here he is, my long-lost, hell-raising buddy, Raven Spirals Madly. His head is shaved and he's got a fresh nose ring, but other than looking exhausted, he's still the same. His eyes are blue and fiery, though his wire-framed glasses make him look a far cry from the raging, fungus-worshipping nature priest that he is.

"Angus," he says, grabbing me in a bear hug. "I hardly even recognized you."

"Me? Look at you!"

"I'm so glad you guys made it. Things have been heating up."

"So I hear. A woman got killed?"

"It's terrorism, Angus. Did Katrina tell you how they cut down the Redwood she was in?"

"She did," I say, horrified.

"This whole place is on the verge of a riot. It did put us in the national spotlight though and there's gonna be international media at the rally tomorrow."

We stand in respective silence for a few moments.

"So," says Raven, suddenly, "you pumped for the gig tomorrow?"

"Oh, Raven," I say, "what an honor."

"Yeah," he says, beaming. "Santana and Bruce Cockburn just signed on, and it looks like Jackson Browne is gonna show, too."

"Wow."

"I'm really excited for you guys. You should get some great exposure."

"How'd ya swing it Raven?" I ask as reality sinks in. "I can't believe we're playing such a killer gig for a great cause."

"You deserve it, man," he says, "and since I'm calling the shots, you're in."

"What time is our set?" Originally, he sent a fax stating that we were on right before Bonnie Raitt. My fingers are crossed.

"Originally we had you guys set to go on at 1:00 p.m., just before Bonnie, but we just added Tracy Chapman along with another band from up your way, a band that really kicks ass by the way, and you know I always say, the more the merrier. Anyway, Neil Young and Bruce Cockburn want to go on earlier, but Groovetribe's manager said that since they're on a really tight schedule coming in from a gig in Oregon, they could only go on after 1:00, so we switched you guys to 11:00."

"Groovetribe!?" I scream. "*Again*!?"

"What's the matter, Angus?" He and Katrina look at me, confused. "It'll be awesome, so don't sweat it. We're expecting twenty thousand people, and you'll be in front of 'em all."

"How long a set?" I ask, fighting for control.

"Everybody gets twenty minutes except Neil, Carlos, and Bonnie get forty-five. Even Bruce Cockburn and Jackson Browne are only taking twenty. It's gonna be great exposure and you guys and Groovetribe totally deserve it."

"Groovetribe…" I hear myself mutter, still stunned.

"You've heard them before?"

"Oh, yeah," I say, my legs feeling weak.

"Do you know Sequoia?"

"I met him briefly when I talked with their manager after our set. He told me that they were about to be signed."

"They should be," says Katrina. "They are *so* awesome."

"Wait 'til you hear The Cosmic Poets," says Raven to Katrina. "Both you guys deserve record deals, man."

"Thanks," I say, trying to be gracious. There's more than enough room in the world for Groovetribe and The Cosmic Poets. Twenty minutes…That's only three or four songs. We'll really have to hit 'em hard. "You think there'll be people there at 11:00 in the morning?"

"Dude, there's ten thousand people who are camping out on fourth street tonight. Don't worry about it."

"Sorry for the freak out, Raven. I'm just worried we might get bumped. You know, with Neil Young, Bonnie Raitt, and all the other big shots."

"No way, dude," says Raven. "All of those guys called *me* asking to play. This isn't about rich rock stars' egos. It's about saving the damn Redwoods. I feel very strongly that bands like you and Groovetribe are recognized."

"Thanks Raven," I say feeling ashamed for my self-centeredness. I have no right to judge Groovetribe, even if they are a bunch of arrogant, trust-fund phonies. Who am I to judge anyone? They are only trying to become famous just like we are and just because their manager Matt is one cocky, pretentious asshole, our manager isn't exactly Mother Theresa. "Who plays after us?" I ask finally.

"Neil Young," he says. "It's gonna be killer."

"I can handle opening up for Neil." My mind races. Who knows, maybe we could back him up on *Into the Black* or something. I see him lurking off stage after we finish our brief, hi-powered set. As we leave the stage, twenty thousand people cheering at the top of their lungs, he reaches out and grabs me. *"Great set!" he says. "You guys know* Hurricane *and* Into the Black*?"*

"Of course, Neil. You're one of our great influences."

As we walk back onto the stage for our encore, the crowd's intense cheering suddenly becomes a roar as I look back to see a disheveled Mr. Young cradling his red Les Paul…

"Yeah, Raven. That'll work for me. 11:00 kicks ass."

We spend a few more minutes reminiscing about old times before he asks me if I might be into playing some acoustic guitar at a pre-concert rally and open-mike tonight over in the Town Park. That sounds fabulous, I tell him. It would be a great honor, not to mention a good warm-up for our set tomorrow. We have finally reached the apex. Tomorrow the masses will be introduced to The Cosmic Poets and from there, who knows? If Frank has done his homework, we won't even need to worry about Rock City in Berkeley…

Sixteen

It takes a half-hour of arguing and explaining the circumstances before I'm able to convince the band that losing our set yet again to our nemesis, Groovetribe, may actually work in our favor since it places us squarely in front of Neil Young. In spite of how wonderful Bonnie is, with the exception of Star, we all feel we can relate to Neil a little more and that the chances of a personal connection are better.

Groovetribe Shmoovevibe…Ollie complains that they tend to rush the tempos on the songs. Star mumbles that their sound is rather hollow, and they're missing something like, perhaps, electric guitar and saxophone. Zen and Walter don't seem to have much to say at all.

At 6:45 we begin walking over to the park down Thomas Street. At the intersection of Thomas and Cedar, Bill Graham Presents is assembling a huge stage for the show tomorrow and just the size of the damn thing gives me goose bumps. There are eight semi-trucks parked, with engines running. The top of the stage facing east is ten feet off of the ground.

The streets are jammed with cop cars, hippie vans, mud wagons, logging trucks and paddy wagons. This isn't about music anymore; it's about people losing their jobs, owls going extinct, and the last of the Redwoods being cut while some Texas asshole who cares about nothing but money gets rich off of everybody.

We're not even three blocks from the park when the crowd is beginning to thicken. We pass a couple of pot-bellied forty-something vendors in lawn chairs selling T-shirts that read:

Spotted Owls Taste Like Chicken, and Earth First! (we'll log the other planets later). Somebody even has a barbecue set up advertising marinated spotted owl meat...

"You wanna buy a shirt, hippie?" asks a raspy voice. I look over and see a rather small man with a lumpy head looking at me. There is deadness in his blue eyes.

"No thanks," I say, trying to be polite.

"No thanks?" he repeats. "You fucking preservationists?"

"We're musicians," I say. Everyone, including Walter, hurries past me. "I really don't want to argue with you."

"You fucking preservationist," he yells at me after we've passed. "I'll see you again."

I hurry past him, and even after we're a block away he's still yelling at us. I'm now very worried about Elvis's security, but there's nothing we can do now except sing a song and go back. There are definitely more loggers than environmentalists here; in fact, it seems like of the couple of thousand people here, most are loggers. The look on my comrades' faces reveals the fact that they've considered the danger as well. Because there's only a straight microphone stand set up on stage with no monitors, I can't amplify my acoustic guitar, rendering it useless. I don't sing acappella either.

It's five to seven when a swarm of cops in riot gear come sweeping through, forming a human barrier between what's become two large groups assembled in front of the stage. Meanwhile a guy stands behind the stage talking with several people, writing furiously on a note pad. I manage to inform him that Raven has asked us to play and he only laughs. The guy is really stressed out. He asks me if I know *America the Beautiful*. I tell him that I kind of do, but Ollie definitely does. We're told to stand by. Evidently the cops are about to pull the plug as major violence is trembling in the air.

There is a roar out in front of the stage and, like the rage of a spring flood, the crowd surges together like a human whirlpool while somewhere in all that there are two people fighting and it's about to become more. Cops in helmets converge, clubs drawn, and in moments a bloodied-up skinny-looking guy is being led off in handcuffs to the paddy wagon while others scream something about police brutality. The cops are doing nothing to the flannel-shirted logger with a Charlie Chaplin mustache who seems to have done most of the damage.

"Wow," I say to Walter who is standing next to me.

"Reminds me of Wounded Knee," he says.

"Did you see what they did to that guy?" asks Ollie.

"Ollie, do you know *America the Beautiful*?" I ask.

"Of course," he says and immediately I hear singing behind me. It's Walter singing the song and his voice isn't half-bad.

The open-mic finally begins and a logger-dude is screaming about how he's losing everything he's ever worked for and he doesn't give a goddamn about some stupid bird that preservationists who've hardly ever set foot in his woods want to save and come Judgment Day there's gonna be hell to pay.

"Oh, come on," Star sighs, impatiently. She looks at the saxophone case in her hand. "I guess I won't be needing this." She casually puts it down and pulls out her can of chew.

Already feeling sick as it is, I move away from her so I won't have to smell it.

Quietly observing the whole thing, Zen pulls out a flask. After taking a shot, he passes it to me. Knowing him as I do, I'm sure this is far from what he had in mind when he agreed to fix up Elvis for The Cosmic Poets' epic tour.

The crowd lets out a loud cheer, yet I hear people jeering as well. The first guy is finished. Our nervous emcee, who seems to be in charge, mumbles something that I can't hear over the microphone while there is a rumble of laughter that ripples through the crowd. Comic relief. There should be much more comic relief in the world. People take their illusions of reality too damn seriously. But what do I know?

The next guy up has long hair pulled back in a ponytail and is dressed in camo-fatigues. Before he even says a word, the boos are raining down. People obviously know him. He begins by saying that it's unfortunate that the bearer of bad news is always the one blamed for it, but he's willing to accept it if people would only pay him enough respect to listen. This elicits even more catcalls and commotion and now the cops have formed a human barrier between both factions in front of the stage.

The earthy fellow finishes his rap about how neither side should get too self-righteous. He insists that there is not enough old growth left to be cut sustainably, and that he didn't blame the loggers as much as all of consumer society as well as companies like Maxam which leads him to conclude that it's time loggers and environmentalists got together to fight the common enemy: the large timber companies and assholes like Charles Hurwitz. He manages to get all this out in one incredibly long sentence, perhaps the longest sentence (aside from some of Ollie's) I've ever heard. As his powerful words are left ringing in the air, they are swallowed up in more jeers, while another fight breaks out in front, the two sides surging towards each other. It's starting to get really ugly when the emcee is standing before me. He asks very politely if someone from our group would sing *America the Beautiful* to calm things down a bit.

I notify Ollie of the request and he's on it right away. Hunter S. Thompson once said so truthfully: "When the going gets tough, the weird turn pro." Ollie is a pro, though I'm not sure why Walter's following him onto the stage, but just the sight of them both up there is comic relief, at least for me. Ollie does not look like the drummer of one of the world's great unknown bands with his frizzy, mad-scientist hair, dark glasses and droopy soldiers. He looks more like a Saturday Night Live extra. And Walter…He should be straddling a horse in *Dances with Wolves*.

Their voices blended in perfect unison: "Oh beautiful for spacious skies, for amber waves of grain…" As they sing, all the enviros, hippies and loggers face the flag at the south end of the street in perfect submission and respect, hands over hearts. No, there won't be any flag burnings today. In fact, as my mates belt out this homespun classic, I think I even notice a tear or two coming to some of the hippies' eyes and I swear, they're singing louder than the loggers are. I never knew hippies could be so patriotic.

If only Sunny and Frank could see us now. I'm giddy with adrenaline and proud of Ollie and Walter for having the courage to sing in front of such a large crowd. As the last notes ring out and Ollie and Walter leave the stage, a roar of approval slowly builds into an eruption as the crowd screams their appreciation. I know I have just witnessed one of Ollie's great life moments. They leave the stage just as another logger is ready to go on, but he stops to shake Ollie and Walter's hands really, really hard. The man then consults a pile of notes before approaching the microphone.

He studies the crowd for a long moment. "My grandfather was a logger here in Humboldt County at the turn of the century," he says at last. "My father was a logger and so am I. We've lost our jobs, but you know something? That's life. These people are right. We've cut too much, too fast, and there isn't enough to cut anymore. I want my grandkids to see what's left of those old trees. I want them to know that I gave a damn. I started planting trees this year, and there's a lot of work to do. I hope you're all willing to join me. We gotta quit pointing fingers and start cleanin' up this mess."

As he leaves the stage, it is very quiet out front. No boos, just a few murmurs as people shuffle about and at 7:22 P.M. the show's over—it's time to go home. It's as if all the pressure has been let out of a giant tire that was about to explode.

We walk back to Elvis and are relieved to find that he hasn't been tampered with. I'm spent. We load up, following Raven's written directions to the camping area along Route 23, about eight miles out of town. It's been a long and intense day, and it feels like we've been on tour for weeks. I find it hard to believe that it's only day three. I hear that's the way tours go. We need a really good night's sleep to harness enough good energy for tomorrow. I'm looking forward to meeting Neil Young. Doing a gig with him should be fun. In fact, if it wasn't for seeing the giant black stage that is being assembled in town, I don't know if this whole thing would even seem real. Even now, I'm not so sure it is.

Seventeen

You may call me nervous if you like. I am. This is a fact, but I am not alone. Star vomited loudly right outside the door last night. She claims that it wasn't nerves but that she accidentally swallowed some chew. The campground where we slept was buzzing with tension; there were people with walkie-talkies and flashlights everywhere as rumors of angry loggers showing up at night had everyone on edge.

No loggers ever did show up, but the threat of them was enough to keep us from getting much sleep—the incessant tapping of Ollie's fingers didn't help much either.

"I hardly slept at all," says Ollie during breakfast. "I kept thinking about the gig."

"Why did you make so much noise with your fingers, then?" asks Zen. Judging by the rings under his eyes, it's clear that he's sleep deprived.

"Sorry," says Ollie. "What a thrill it was to sing *America the Beautiful* to all of those people. You were great, too, Walter. Our voices worked really well together."

"One of my favorite songs," he says, sarcastically.

"You guys stopped a riot from happening," I say.

We conclude our breakfast of dry corn flakes and take coin-operated showers. In a half-hour's time the male contingency is ready. But no one has seen Star, and just when I'm about to really stress out, she slowly walks out from behind Elvis wearing black leather pants, a tight yellow silk shirt, and black platform boots. She looks like a character out of *Mad Max*.

"Are you ready to rock?" she whispers.

Walter, who has been very quiet, just stares at her with a hint of a smile. We load up Elvis, knowing nothing can stop us.

The campground is now buzzing with life as we roll slowly back to Route 23, which will take us back to Arcata and the biggest gig of our lives. "For the earth!" I scream as cheers explode throughout the area. We are on our way.

I wonder if playing in front of the big crowd will be as exciting as the anticipation of it is. I hope so. We know we have twenty minutes to send a crowd of twenty thousand swooning into ecstasy. Twenty minutes will put us in the driver's seat of our musical careers. I wonder how all the experts will like the taste of their own feet. Probably not very well. Then there's Lily; she doesn't even deserve me after all the bullshit I put up with. It would serve her right if I dumped her after we're signed. How would she like that? Maybe I will. The tables are turning. Change is in the air. Something big is about to finally happen.

If we thought Arcata was a zoo yesterday, it is absolute mayhem today. We hit a traffic jam on the outskirts of town and it takes us over an hour to drive a half a mile to the blocked-off street behind the giant stage. I'm glad we actually left enough time to deal with this. I show our pass to the guy at the gate and we're guided to our parking place. "Look at the size of that sound system, guys." We stare in awe at the back of the immense black speaker columns stretching upwards. There are at least thirty guys on the stage swarming like ants as they finish the final set-up.

We grab our instruments and begin marching down the long block toward the back of the stage that towers before us. Yellow tents line both sides of the street and each one has a white piece of paper with a name attached to it. Reality hits.

"Look, there's Neil Young's tent," Ollie gasps. "Bonnie Raitt's too."

Sure enough, the names are bigger than life. This surreal walk takes us past Tracy Chapman, Jackson Browne, Carlos Santana….

"Cockburn's here," I say, stunned when I see Bruce's name. Of course none of the stars themselves have arrived yet.

"Say Bruce," I think in my daydream. *"I've been trying to figure out the chords for* Rocket Launcher. *You got a minute?"*

"Sure, Angus. By the way, you guys were great. Your song-writing is fantastic."

"No way," I say blushing.

"Seriously. I'm looking for an opening act on my next North American tour this Autumn. Are you interested?"

"Well, Bruce," I'll say, "if you're really gonna twist my arm…"

The only thing that could make this even more complete would be an appearance by Nick Drake coming back from the dead. Of course, it's hard to imagine Nick playing to twenty thousand screaming people even if he were alive…

"There's Groovetribe's tent," snarls Star, breaking the spell.

Sure enough, it's true. It's even closer to the stage than the others are. This realization brings me spiraling down to Earth.

"We don't get a tent?" asks Ollie.

"We don't need a tent," I say.

"I didn't come here to go camping," says Zen. "I came here to rock!"

"These tents are but cheap rentals, anyway," I say.

I notice that we've reached the foot of the stage and are standing before a metal staircase as a big, friendly-looking guy with gray hair in a Bill Graham Presents shirt comes up and asks if we need anything.

"Yeah," I tell him, feeling very important. "We're The Cosmic Poets and we were told to meet Raven here at 10:15 to get set up and sound-checked. We're on at 11:00 A.M. sharp, right before Neil Young and it's really important that we get everything right."

"Oh, The Cosmic Poets?" he asks, reading down a list. "What a great name. Here it is. Yep, 11:00. Come on up." We follow him up the metal ladder while he informs us that the concert almost got canceled due to security concerns.

We're now on top of the biggest, baddest stage I've ever seen in my life and, for some reason, I'm reminded of the Mt. Everest disaster of '95. We're at least ten feet off of the ground, and I'm thinking an oxygen canister would sure be nice. Looking out beyond the front of the stage is an empty street that stretches for about three blocks until it meets a large barricade with several cops standing in front of it. Behind it looks like a crowd, but it's hard to tell how big since it bends away and out of sight to the north.

"Excuse me, but we're playing at 11:00," Zen says to a short guy in a ponytail whose cheeks are sweating. "Is it okay to for us to set up now?"

"I don't give a shit," he snaps. He then yells across the stage at a couple of others standing behind the monitor mixer. "Bruce, can you set these pricks up? They're playing at the beginning."

"That's not nice!" I yell. "Why are you so mean?"

"If it were up to me," he says with a scowl, "I wouldn't let green-horn bands like you come *near* this stage."

"Mike!" yells another dude at sweat-cheeks. "I need those half-inchers now."

"Fuck you, Bob," snarls sweat-cheeks before stomping away.

"Don't pay any attention to Mike," says Mr. Friendly. "His brother's a logger, and besides that this is our fourth show in five days and we were up all night at Shoreline breaking down after the Dylan concert."

"That's all right," I say, trying to mask my fury.

"We're really glad you guys are here to play; it should be wonderful."

"Thanks," I say, realizing that Ollie and Star have been spared that ugly little scene. Zen's face is dangerously white. He's pissed.

Mr. Friendly takes me over to a young fellow with blonde hair and blue eyes…A total and true California dude. "This is Randy," he says introducing me. "He'll be helping you with your monitors."

Randy extends his hand and says, "Nice to meet ya, dude."

"Nice to meet you," I reply, and as I reach for his hand, I realize that mine's shaking a little.

"Yep, Randy's the best. He'll take care of you."

"Thanks," I say. What I could really use is a beer but it's too damn early. "So, do you have a schedule?" I ask.

"Yeah," says Mr. Friendly taking out a piece of paper and handing it to me. I open it, heart pounding. There is our name in print. What? I hear myself groan as it reads:

Opening—11:00-11:10
The Cosmic Poets—11:15-11:25
Neil Young—11:30-12:15
Bruce Cockburn—12:20-12:55
Groovetribe—1:00-1:30

Bonnie Raitt—1:35-2:30
Jackson Browne—2:35-3:20
Santana—3:25-4:10
Tracy Chapman—4:15-4:45
Don Henley—4:50-5:50
Closing Circle—5:55-6:10

"Ten minutes? We only get ten minutes?" I ask Mr. Friendly. "And Groovetribe gets a half-hour?

"Sorry, guy," says Mr. Friendly. "I didn't make the schedule. I'll try to get you guys an extra five minutes or something."

I feel a big depression coming on. We've got two songs to grab them with. I hear Ollie getting yelled at by a roadie for messing with the ride cymbal, and it's 10:45 when Raven finally shows. Before I can ask him about our schedule, he informs me that some hippies just had their van tipped over and set on fire by some loggers and now the cops are trying to cancel the entire event. He isn't looking so good right now.

"Is it canceled?" I ask, feeling sick.

"Not yet," he says, "but the cops aren't letting anyone in until things chill out. This place is about to blow."

The empty street in front of the stage is making more sense. There are a lot of people crammed up against the barricade three blocks away, and they stretch out of sight to the north. I wish they'd let 'em in. This is cutting it close.

"Two songs is fine," I whisper as I begin bargaining with God. "Just let them in, please?" The show's supposed to start in fifteen minutes. Suddenly I hear the thundering of a kick drum pounding through the great speaker stacks as Ollie sits proudly behind the set of some beautiful Pearls. It's time for sound-check. Star is in a frantic scramble to finish setting up her array of effects while Zen tunes his bass. I pull out my guitars and place them on their stands and my hands are shaking like crazy.

Soon Ollie is playing the whole set and I hear a distant roar of approval from the crowd pressed up against the barricade far down the street. Ollie beams, alive in his power.

It's now 10:51. The show starts in nine minutes. I wish they'd let the crowd in. This is cutting it really close. *Come on you assholes, let them in. Just let them in.*

Randy the monitor man is standing before me and in a calm and gentle voice that seems to transcend all the chaos, he says, "How ya doing, dude?"

"Fine," I say. "I'm a bit nervous, really." It occurs to me that there is no sense of unity with the band right now. It's as if we're all in our own private struggle for survival, and again, I think of the Everest disaster. "You have an oxygen tank handy?" I ask.

"You guys are gonna do fine," Randy says. "Just take a deep breath."

"Thanks," I say, sucking furiously for air.

"Let's get your guitars set in the monitors and then we'll check the whole band." This guy isn't stressed in the least. He's nice, too.

"Cool." I plug in and when I strum the sound guitar is huge.

Within moments we're all plugged in and riffing and it sounds huge and powerful. Under the pretext of testing her gear, Star lets a screaming tirade of lead electric guitar fly. Far down the block, the crowd behind the barricade is going wild. When I yell, "Big sound, huh?" Star only smiles strangely in response.

At 10:57 there seems to be a lot of commotion and yelling from down the street. They still haven't opened the gates yet. I just wish they'd let the crowd in. This is cutting it too close. Then a disheveled-looking Raven is cursing at someone off stage while a cop with riot gear and a helmet approaches a microphone. He voice booms, "Please move back from the fence immediately! We will not open the gates until people move back from the fence! Move back from the fence! Please!"

His words are met with a chorus of boos from the distant mob. Now it's all chaos and confusion as people dart back and forth in dream-like arrow patterns. I seem to be invisible or maybe underwater. Nothing is making any sense—except our dreams of stardom held hostage in this endless breath, waiting to exhale, waiting for something…

"Everything sound okay?" asks Randy.

"Sure, Randy," I say. "Everything's fine. By the way, why aren't they letting people in?"

"Who knows?" he says almost sadly. "I guess because these cops are power-tripping jerks."

It's 10:59 when Mr. Friendly appears out of the chaos and asks, "How would you like me to introduce you guys?"

"Tell them we're The Cosmic Poets from Bellingham, Washington," I say, desperately, "and that Frank Strong says we've got a record deal cooking as we speak…"

He looks at me for a long moment. "Bellingham, huh? My sister-in-law's from there."

"Really?" I ask. "Seems like everyone I meet has a sister or brother-in-law from Bellingham."

It's 11:00 straight up, and now there is a megaphone piercing the chaos, trying to get people to back off from the barricade. I catch a whiff of sage and I hear someone yell, "Clear the stage!"

A Native American Troupe climbs up, all brilliantly dressed in their regalia as they begin pounding out the a song on a traditional drum. I look around for Walter, but don't see him.

"Why aren't they letting people in?" asks Star, panicked. She is just noticing this fact for the first time.

I tell her I have no idea, and ask if she's seen Walter lately. She hasn't.

When the troupe finishes the song with a mighty whap on the drum, we hear the roar of the crowd three blocks away. Raven comes up to the microphone looking really stressed. He pleads, "I've been told that this whole event is going to be canceled unless people back away from the fence and gate. Please friends, this is for the Redwoods!"

His words work a little magic as the crowd withdraws and given that they're coming in from a right angle to the main street, I cannot see them at all anymore—though rumor has it they're backed up for several city blocks. Then they're back again, pressed against the fence. It's out of control.

"I'd like to thank all the musicians for showing up today in support of the Redwoods! Especially, Bonnie Raitt, Neil Young, Santana, and Groovetribe…" As each of the names is read, there is a roar of approval from blocks away.

"…and I've been told that we're gonna start the music regardless of whether or not you back off from the gate but the sooner you do, the better. We have an incredible show for you!" He walks away from the microphone looking at me forlornly. Then he wheels on his heel and stomps back to the microphone screaming, "Come on! Let them in!" He then leaves the stage shaking his head. The Native American drummers are gone, and Mr. Friendly materializes again.

"You're on in one minute," he says.

"Aren't we gonna wait till they let people in?" I ask, feeling weak.

"We run these things down to the second," he says. "It's not for you to worry about. I got you an extra five minutes, which gives you fifteen. That's the best I can do." He looks at his watch. "Thirty seconds."

"Oh man, thirty seconds? Where's Ollie?" Zen and Star stare at me, confused.

All is panic. Ollie is gone. "...ten seconds..."

I hear the voice over the PA saying, "From Bellingham, Washington!" And then the pick goes flying out of my hand, and though this time I find it right away, I end up pushing it around the hardwood stage like a little hockey puck, trying to get a grip on it... Trying to get a grip...

"I'm gonna strangle you, Ollie," Star says calmly to Ollie who's now back behind the drum set, wearing different pants. He just glances at her, his head cocked sideways, and now he's my whole world because I cannot look at the empty street in front of the stage to which we'll be playing. But eventually I *must* turn to face the great Void. The great Nothing. I do, and begin strumming my guitar as Ollie, Star and Zen dutifully kick it in.

Ah, the silence of living underwater where no one can hear each other. Only the sound of bubbles. Refuge from the years of living on the edge of failure's great abyss, held there by the taunting dream that some big break will finish the mental script that we've started beginning something like, "I never doubted that I'd make it..." or, "...To my detractors and all those who never believed in me..." and suddenly, when everything falls away, it all makes sense. We're just driven by the sheer terror of irrelevancy and indifference.

I want to cry for Ollie. I want to tell him to keep dreaming even though dreams die, because dreams are what keep you alive when nothing else will, and nothing is ever as good as you hope it will be. I picture Lily smiling sadly to me in our last goodbye, and I want to go fly fishing by myself up the Queets River, or maybe take a twenty mile walk along the North Coast of Washington so

I can figure some things out. It sure would beat camping out in a motor-home named Elvis with a bunch of neurotic people and one really interesting Indian. Somewhere, I hear people cheering.

My goodness. We have a gig. We must play our hearts out…and we do…we really do…and the first song is over before I can believe it. Even though the street is empty save for the fifty or so security people in yellow coats who seem to be going wild over our music, we can clearly hear the roar of twenty thousand or so potential fans in the distance, tucked carefully away from our line of sight.

"It's a great honor to be here!" I scream into the microphone, but as I look at my mates, I'm filled with sadness at their bewildered expressions. Whoever said the show must go on? I introduce the next song, and in moments we're grooving along. But alas, like bad sex, it's very mechanical and cerebral with no real joy—just an awkward, rapid-fire function with one objective: to get it over with. I never could beat Star in a race and in this gig, I have no chance. The electric guitar is out of control, drowning and drenching everything—her strange musical SOS to the Fates who have, yet again, set us up for bittersweet agony.

But the security guards absolutely love us and their cheering is drowned out in the dull roar from far away. The last song finishes in a blur, and as we leave we leave the stage, spent and stricken by this bizarre twist, I read the devastation in the eyes of my mates and feel a shame sweep over me. Yet I also feel strangely triumphant—though I do not know why. The whole thing is now passing like a dream.

"Great set," says Mr. Friendly as I pass him by.

"Thanks."

"You guys were awesome," says Randy the monitor man. "Bummer about the crowd."

"Yeah, it sure is."

As we pack our gear off the stage I think of Sunny, Peaches and Frank. Somehow, I think it's their fault. I notice Star staring at me, shaking her head as she wipes her eyes. I hear a dull but growing roar behind me and turn to witness the source of her tears.

I laugh aloud as I witness twenty thousand people running up the street toward us in a giant flood of color. At last the gates have opened. This could have been huge. It should have been, and I dread the thought of hearing Ollie telling me this for the rest of my life.

Then a tall, hunched over, crusty-looking dude with wild eyes and an acoustic guitar slung over his shoulders materializes before me, walking slowly toward the now screaming crowd. Mr. Young seems to acknowledge me in a callous, aloof fashion, but that's all right. The sight of him is a thrill and temporarily takes me out of my despair. I see Ollie and Zen mesmerized as well. Star looks at him, too, but I can tell she doesn't recognize him.

"Ladies and gentlemen: Neil Young!" yells Mr. Friendly, and the crowd goes crazy. What a great job it must be introducing famous rock stars and hearing the crowd cheer. I bet that's a satisfying job, making people so happy.

"I'm down, man," says a yellow coat to me as I stand shell-shocked back stage.

"Yeah, I'm down too." I say, honestly.

"No, I mean I'm *down*," says the guy, smiling.

"I can relate, man," I say, getting more irritated.

"No, I'm *down*," he says.

"Then why are you in my face?" I explode.

"Dude," he says, shocked, "chill out. I said I'm down. So down with you guys."

"I can't help you, man. We're all really down."

Another dude comes up laughing and says, "He means he really likes your music."

"Oh," I say, absently. "Sorry I yelled at you."

"It's chill," he says, happily. "I'm so down."

Neil's beautiful guitar chimes out the tranquil notes of *Comes a Time* and we all turn to watch the master himself. Though I'm completely taken by the song, it doesn't escape me that I'm just watching a guy playing a guitar in front of a crowd. He could be anybody, and suddenly I realize that in spite of stardom, we're all the same. We eat, shit, fuck and love—suffering for all of it.

I notice that Ollie is in a deep conversation with some guy with dark glasses, and Star just stands near me, staring forlornly at Neil's back.

"Can you believe it?" I ask.

"Figures," she says.

"Should we leave?" I ask, having no idea where we might go.

"I really wanna meet Jackson Browne." She has tears welling up in her clear blue eyes. "Boy, Angus, you really fucked up."

"Me?" I ask in a whirl of fury. Before I can defend myself, she waves me off and walks away. We're stuck for now. I'm worried about Walter. I haven't seen him since we got here. I head down the ladder thinking that I might as well catch some of the music from out in front.

As I pass through the security gate another yellow-coat taps me on the shoulder saying, "Great set, man. Where'd you guys say you were from?"

"Bellingham."

"Oh, my Aunt Marie lives in Bellingham," he says with a smile.

"Cool," I say. "I'm down with that." I pass through the gate and disappear into the seething mass of humanity.

I might not be more than twenty or thirty feet out in front of the stage, but it might as well be a hundred, since it's so difficult to move in this throng. Neil's working the crowd on his old organ, doing a beautiful rendition of *After the Gold Rush* and I find myself swooning away with the masses, my pain momentarily forgotten. The rest of his set flies past and he finishes with *Into the Black*, while I scream the words aloud. People around me seem to stare.

He leaves the stage while Cockburn's waiting in the wings, getting set to play. I'm startled by a voice behind me that asks, "Who was that first band that played?"

"I don't know," says another, "but they were killer."

"I really wish I knew who they were. Their lead guitarist is incredible."

"I hear they're from Bellingham."

"Bellingham, Washington? What a great town. My step-father's from there."

"Bellingham's a very nice town," I say as I turn back to the voices, trying to mask my bitterness with a smile. "The name of the band was The Cosmic Poets. They were good, weren't they?"

"Amazing," says a youngish girl. "I wish I could have actually *seen* them."

"Yeah, it's a real bummer." I turn back to the stage.

Cockburn's up and plugged in, ready to go. Man, they really do run these things down to the wire. As the opening chords of *If I had a Rocket Launcher* pierce the early afternoon air the crowd ripples violently. Someone has thrown a bunch of roses onto the stage at his feet and when the song is over, he bends over and picks them up, smiling shyly at the person who presented this gift. *Would people ever smile and pass me roses?*

His set is over in a flash and he leaves the stage waving and smiling awkwardly in his usual brilliant and humble way. I wonder if I should be back-stage right now. Maybe I could meet some of these guys. But the sound's so much better out here and I'm not in a very social mood right now. Besides, celebrities are more in Ollie's department. Wondering who's up next, I fish for the crumpled and sweaty schedule in my pocket. I read the fine print and laugh.

Sure enough, I can already see Cheshire man off to the left of the stage as Groovetribe assembles for their pretension parade. They're in our time slot, but I can't think about that. My sour-grapes soul is filled with loathing as Mr. Friendly introduces them as "…An amazing group from the Pacific Northwest who has been on tour to support the saving of our natural heritage: the Redwoods!"

As a couple of hippies pound out a tribal groove, Sequoia, dressed like the mythical Adam, wanders out onto the stage. The massive crowd begins to sway—they're into it.

"Namaste!" says Sequoia in his baritone. "We call upon the spirits of our ancestors, the Great Grandfather, and our Earth Mother!" The crowd ripples at his words as I send hate and death vibes his way. The rest of the percussion ensemble walks out in single file to their respective instruments. In moments the air is alive with the sound of drums and percussion. There is a strange ringing in my ears that's growing louder and louder…

Yet nothing in the world could prepare me for what happens next: *I am back underwater where I can only hear the sound of bubbles…Peaceful little bubbles. It is nice down here and I would like to stay for a good, long while. But my lungs are burning and I must rise for air. I must, but I won't…I must…I do. I blast to the surface, gasping. The ringing is now unbearable as I'm being swallowed up in the maddening chaos. "It's her! It's her!" my mind is screaming. "Somebody do something!"*

People around me turn. They do not understand, even though I keep pointing my finger toward the stage, trying to explain to them that the black-haired woman with the purple hat who is gracefully walking out and waving to the crowd really is Angel. It doesn't matter. As she makes her grand entrance, I notice that there is a keyboard set up on the stage, a newer model than the one still stashed in Elvis. Wow. It really *is* Angel, and she's alive.

~

"Welcome to the garden, baby!" Angel's voice is rich and the crowd goes wild. I have never seen her so powerful and beautiful. As the tears of shock and disbelief fade a bit, a new, insanely confused, awestruck jealousy fills my soul.

Groovetribe's bass player, a skin-headed Dali Lama-type dude starts thumping away while the tribal drumming intensifies.

Angel says, "I'm talkin' about the Redwood garden, baby…" The beat picks up behind her. "For our children's children's children…" Her voice is powerful and sexy. "Talkin' bout our *mama*, baby…" She is now behind the keyboard they've supplied her and the sound of organ creeps into the mix as the mossy Aphrodite named Sequoia writhes away in the early afternoon sun, sweat glistening off his rama-tofu and spicy-peanut nourished frame.

"Do you *love* your mother!?" Angel screams. The crowd erupts enthusiastically. "I said: do you *love* your mother!?"

"YES!" the crowd screams, and now Angel is ripping out one of the most kick-ass organ solos I've ever heard. The place rocks and swelters. "*Groovetribe!*" screams a star-struck fan.

What was ever wrong with me? Was I deaf? She *is* the true artist. She rocks, harder than I ever could have imagined and I was the control freak, not her. I cannot believe that I'm witnessing Angel in absolute control of twenty thousand people who are fixated on her stunning beauty, charm and charisma. How the hell did she get such a big role in the band in such a short time? And how did she hook up with them to begin with? Were they the ones I heard in the background of her terrible phone message? I wonder…

"It was all my fault!" I scream. "She was right all along! It was all my fault!" Tears of bitter joy are falling from my eyes.

Groovetribe sails through the rest of their set like seasoned pros, not in the least bit nervous and always in control of their sound. The final dagger comes as Angel introduces their last song.

"This song is for a man I once loved who very recently passed away. I'd like to call for a moment of silence for my soul mate. Angus, though you've passed out of this life as we know it, I know you're here with us today. I'll always love you." The place becomes eerily quiet while Angel and the rest of the Groovetribe bow their heads. All I hear is the sound of my own sobbing and some girl puts her hand on my shoulder, saying, "You knew him, didn't you?"

"I did," I weep.

Then the song begins while her beautiful voice fills the air, "Come down off your throne, and leave your body alone…" It's *Can't Find My Way Home*, by Steve Winwood. My goodness…Am I really dead? I'm not sure, anymore. As the song progresses the crowd is still deathly quiet. Angel cups her hand over her ear as if to better hear herself in the monitor: "You are the reason I've been waiting so long…Somebody must change." As the words fall from her lips I feel a chill sweep over me as I realize she seems to be staring right into my eyes. Her lips betray the slightest smile and, as she pauses for a moment, I swear that I see her stick her tongue out at me, but when I look again it's gone. What I do see, however, are the fingers that were moments ago curved around her ear now flipping me the bird. Me, out of twenty thousand people.

People around me do not know why I laugh but I do not care to explain anymore. They say that laughter is the best medicine and I need lots of medicine now. Our back-up singer has defected to our arch nemesis and it's likely, given the looks of things, that she's on her way to stardom. The Cosmic Poets, on the other hand, are in a slow, smoky spiral downwards as I try desperately to figure out a way to restart the engine during this free fall to our deaths. So I laugh. And I ask those around me to laugh, too. Please laugh with me, I say, but they only look at me as if I've lost my mind. Perhaps I have.

Eighteen

The first thing I notice backstage is that Ollie is still talking to the poor guy with the dark glasses, who I can tell wants to break away. Sequoia is talking with Neil Young and Jackson Browne. He seems right at home there. Angel, Star and Zen are conversing together, and when Ollie sees me approaching he finally lets the guy with dark shades go. I notice the guy shaking his head as he walks off.

"Who was that, Ollie?" I ask as we converge.

"That was Jackson Browne's guitar tech."

"How interesting." Angel now sees us approaching. I am full of dread, though glad she still lives.

"Hey, Angel," I say. "You were fabulously awesome up there. I couldn't believe how great you sounded."

"Yeah," says Ollie. "You were really good."

"Awesome," says Zen. Star smiles, but says nothing.

"You're all saying that now," Angel replies. "You seem so surprised. I've never doubted what I could do when I was supported by people who *believed* in me. But it doesn't matter anymore. I need to get my keyboard out of Elvis."

"Grab your keyboard?" I ask in shock.

"Well, duh, Angus."

"You mean you quit the band?"

"Do you think I'm gonna stick around after what you put me through?" she asks.

"What about Sunny, Frank and the major labels?" I ask as I hear Bonnie Raitt and band take the stage to the roaring delight of thousands. Her bluesy notes pierce the mid-afternoon summer air. The crowd goes even wilder.

"Groovetribe offered me a full-time spot playing keyboards and singing in the band. I'm having the time of my life, and these guys really *are* on the verge of a record deal."

"No shit," laughs Star, bitterly. Zen and Ollie are uncomfortably quiet.

"Sunny and Frank are blowing smoke," says Angel with a little more compassion. "It takes years of touring and building a name for yourself before there's even a hope of getting signed—like these guys have. It's my chance of a lifetime."

"I'm sorry we left you at the Talbot rest area," I say as our dreams of success and stardom unravel like Star after a bad gig. "I didn't know you got out when Ollie went to piss. You didn't have to read my obituary from stage, though. Plus that terrible phone message…"

Angel smiles, finding it all very amusing.

"Yeah, Angel, it's really my fault that we left you behind," says Ollie, sheepishly.

"No, it's not, Ollie. Angus has never wanted me in this band in the first place. It's his fault."

I have nothing more to say as we all stand behind the giant speaker stacks watching Bonnie woo the masses. Success is thirty feet away. Stardom, a stone's throw. As Bonnie Raitt and band crank out John Prine's classic hit *Angel From Montgomery*, Angel tells the story of what happened after we left the rest area, and how she hooked up with Groovetribe.

~

When Angel emerged from the rest-room of Oregon's I-5 Talbot Rest Area and found us gone, she thought it was a joke—although she wasn't at all amused. It was a bit on the chilly side and she was still groggy from sleep. After twenty minutes or so, she realized it was no joke. Because it was beyond even her wildest imagination that I could be so stupid as to drive off without her, she assumed that I had orchestrated it to look like an accident since I had long conspired against her.

She actually did call Sunny, but hung up when Peaches answered. At that point, she was afraid she might freeze to death, and when a trucker offered her a cup of coffee inside his rig, she gratefully joined him. They drank coffee and smoked cigarettes for an hour or so, but she had to leave after he proposed marriage to her, promising her a beautiful New Mexico Ranch on five hundred acres. There's something creepy about middle-aged truck drivers with ranches in places like New Mexico. She politely excused herself and resumed freezing and cursing my family name and the day I was born. It was about 8:45 A.M. when she decided to call Sunny again, but just as the phone started to ring she saw a psychedelic coach liner pull up with the hand painted *Groovetribe* logo scrawled on the side of it. She hung up and walked over to it, remembering Groovetribe's performance at the Ballard Firehouse and asked the driver if by chance they were headed toward the Oregon Country Fair. The rest was history.

Sequoia told her right off that everything happens for a reason, and that he had a vision about her in a dream a few nights back. In the four-hour bus trip she learned eight songs, and after a sage burning, chanting and an aura-sharing ritual, she was inducted into Groovetribe as a full-time member. She thought for sure that she would see us at the Oregon Country Fair. But, alas, we never showed up.

"We did show up," says Star, "but Angus freaked."

"Yeah, no offense, Angus," says Ollie, "but, you really need to control yourself more. I would've loved to play on the Shady Grove stage."

"They didn't allow amps, Ollie," sighs Zen. "Just let it go."

"I don't want to talk about it anymore," I say, truthfully.

"Does anyone know the story about the White Buffalo Calf Woman?" asks Angel, changing the subject.

"Why?"

"Because Groovetribe keeps talking about me like I'm part of that story."

"White Buffalo Calf Woman was the virgin keeper of the Sacred Pipe for the Lakota People," I say. "I doubt that there's a connection."

Angel glares at me.

"So you're quitting the band," says Star, getting to the bottom of it.

"I guess I am," says Angel, smiling again.

"I'm really happy for you, Angel," I say. "You sounded so good up there. Great rendition of the Winwood song, too."

"Yeah," Zen says. "You fit in really well with Groovetribe."

"Better than us, actually," Ollie adds.

"Good luck, Angel," Star concludes. "It's all for the best."

Angel's eyes have grown dark and her face is red. "You mean, you *want* me to quit?" she asks, quietly.

"Absolutely," I say.

"I can't *fucking* believe it," she snarls. "I gave up the best years of my life for this group. We go on tour to get signed and you leave me in a fucking rest area where I could've been murdered and now *this*?" She walks over to me and slaps me hard. "You ungrateful jerk!"

"I'm sorry you feel this way, Angel," I say, gently touching my stinging face. "You're quitting anyway so what's the big deal?"

"Hey, Angus, are you sure you wanna do this with the major labels looking at us?" Ollie says, reconsidering. "Remember, Sunny said no line-up changes for four months."

"You just don't get it, do you, Ollie!" I stare at Angel as I speak. "Angel has got the chance of a lifetime to get signed to a major label with a band that's letting her play organ. If I were she, I'd bail too."

"Her," says Ollie, coldly.

"What?"

"Her…If I were *her*, I'd bail too."

"No, it's she," I snap.

"It's *her* you goddamned moron," says Star, shoving me hard.

"Give me the keys to Elvis," says Angel, suddenly. "We're heading to Berkeley for a gig, and I wanna get my keyboard."

"We'll go together," I say.

"Why?" she asks. "You don't trust me?"

"About as far as I could throw a cheesecake underwater," I say, recalling how Angel was arrested a year ago in Bellingham for slashing her ex-boyfriend David's truck tires.

"I'm the one who got left at a rest area in the middle of the night and you don't trust *me*?" she screams.

Now Sequoia is standing in our midst and we stand awkwardly in his presence. One might expect him to be a bit sheepish, given the fact that he has just stolen one of our band mates, but no. Not even close. "Is everything all right, Angel?" he asks.

"It's okay," says Angel, blushing a bit. "It's a very emotional time for me."

Sequoia stares at me like he knows all about what a loser I really am. Manager Matt walks up and stands there quietly.

"You guys just got signed, huh?" I ask, trying to be cheerful, but he doesn't acknowledge me at all.

"You guys sounded fantastic," says Star. "There's just one thing missing in your sound. You ever thought of sax? I could bring a lot of sax to your group."

Sequoia looks at her for a long moment. "I love sax," he says, slinking over to her and embracing her in a slow, methodical hug, pulling her close to his saturnalian loins. After a few moments, she wriggles away. Her face reveals mild disgust with the slightest hint of amusement.

"I should get your number," he whispers.

With that, we begin migrating back down the block toward Elvis. I then realize that someone now very important in my life is missing and I can't believe that no one has noticed until now. "Has anyone seen Walter?"

The transfer of Angel's keyboard plus a few other belongings into the belly of the Groovetribe coach-liner is as uneventful as could be hoped for, though there is great concern as to Walter's whereabouts. Hugs, condolences and regrets are passed along, though I can tell it bothers Angel greatly that we're happy for her. We learn that Groovetribe, like us, will be playing at the Battle of Seattle at the Showbox in a little over a week to wrap up the mini-tour. We joke about how funny it will be to compete against each other, though privately my stomach churns.

It's funny how we haven't even seen one A&R dude yet, and I'm starting to wonder if they even exist. It doesn't matter anymore. I must soon make my big confession to the group, and I shudder at the thought. I'm not thinking about dreams anymore; I'm just wondering where the truth might lead.

We're pulling out of the parking lot and I'm trying to figure out how to tell them all that the tour's over because I had big dreams and had to lie to make them real and how I only want to drive back to Bellingham to break it off with Lily before disappearing into the mountains where I can contemplate the the love, hope and idealism of yesterday. I realize that I'm trying like hell to keep it together, but it wouldn't matter anyway because nobody's talking and it's only after I pull a right onto Fredrick Street that I see Walter. He's wearing a torn, scuffed-up shirt, standing there like he's been waiting for us to show up. His eyes are sunken and dark. He is not smiling.

Nineteen

We are all very glad to see him, though he's in fairly rough shape. The thing that hurts the most is how he won't talk at all about what happened. It appears that he's been beaten. His left cheek is torn and swollen. Nonetheless, he serves as a welcome distraction from our own pain as first-aid and comforting words are shared; with cold packs and tender words, Star in particular seems to have an interest in comforting him. Ironically, this buys me some time to decide how to break the bad news. The thought of accepting defeat after working so hard causes my stomach to knot up like never before, though I can't stop thinking about the truth now. It's too late.

We drive south, dazed and shaken, and about forty-five minutes out of Arcata, it occurs to me that I have no idea where in the hell we're going. Nobody asks, either. Ollie is now babbling about where he's gonna spend next Christmas after the divorce, and that depresses me even more. I tell the crew that I've got to check in with Sunny and there is no opposition as I pull off the highway at a country store and gas station. Elvis is thirsty, too. After putting twenty-three bucks in his bottomless tank and paying the cashier, I head for the pay phone outside, not wanting to count the few loose bills left in my wallet. It's time to spill the beans.

"Hello?"

"Hi," I whisper, knowing she's onto me.

"Oh, hi, how's it going?" she says, trying to sound laid-back and my gut feeling is that she's not alone.

"Good. I got a really good feeling about things this time."

"Yeah?" she says, sounding interested. "What's going on?"

"Well, for one thing, we just played a killer gig with Bonnie Raitt and Neil Young in front of twenty thousand people and they loved us. There's a good chance there were label people there too, and Sunny says we've already had a couple of bites. I got a good feeling."

"Good," she says. "I'm happy for you."

"Look, Lily, we're talking big. Really big. I mean, Frank Strong was the past president of RCA Records and Sunny says we are the luckiest band in the world to have him on our side. It's only a matter of time before…"

"It's been raining like crazy up here," she says. Now I know for sure that she's not alone. "How's the weather been down your way?"

"Hot," I say, just realizing this fact. My shirt is soaked with sweat. "How's Nathan doing?"

She hesitates for a second. "Oh…fine. He actually just stopped by and we're on our way out the door to go get some dinner."

I'm choking up, but manage to say, "I know I really blew it, but don't you think we can give it another shot?"

"Can we talk later about all this stuff? You're doing what you need to be doing and so am I. Let's just see where we land in all of this."

Don't punish me for loving you, Lily. "Sure we can talk later, but can I just ask you a hypothetical question?"

"Go ahead."

"Where would you and I stand if I scored a record deal?"

"I can't say," she says, gently. "I wouldn't love you any more or less because of it, but you do know I want stability in my life."

"Lily," I plead, "I can't emphasize enough how close we are. To have Frank Strong on our side, well, Sunny said she's never heard of a band as lucky—"

"You already told me that."

"Yeah, but you gotta believe. I really, really love you and you're the only woman I'll ever be with."

"Call me in a few more days," she whispers. "We need time apart, remember?"

"Okay, but I just want you know that we're close to a deal."

"I'm sure you are."

"Say hi to Nathan for me." I imagine him lying naked next to her, smoking a cigarette. I hear her giggle something to him.

"He says, hi to you too," she purrs. Then her voice turns quiet as she whispers into the receiver, "Don't bum out, it'll all work out for the best."

"Damn it, Lily," I say, wanting to tell her that my dreams have died and that I would now consider getting a real job like delivering Chinese food. "There are a lot of other things I can do besides play guitar and pull weeds at pre-fabricated condominiums…"

"You are very talented," she says. "But do what you want to do. Don't worry about me." We say goodbye and I replace the phone in its cradle. Should I fight for her? Maybe I really need to lay it all out there for her to see. Maybe she needs to see my rage and my resolve. How's Nathan any better than me? Just because he has a steady gig? There are millions of people in the world with steady gigs. So what? Who's willing to risk all and put everything on the line to survive on one's art? The Cosmic Poets were, and I'm not going to hang my head because we gambled big and came up short. I tried my damnedest to score; we all did. If Lily can't see the value in that, why should she even deserve me? Why must the story come to an end in such a way that lets people say, "See, that's what happens when you put all your eggs in one basket. Angus never did understand the value of practicality and how hard it is to really make it in the arts. It's arrogant of him to even try." A fire is starting to burn within me in a strange, new way. To hell with Lily, Nathan, and the naysayers back in the land of the sheltered and ignorant. I'm not quitting yet. It's not over. I swear it's not.

~

"Hello?"

"It's me."

"Sweetie, I'm so glad you called." Sunny sounds upbeat. "How'd it go?"

"Great. There were over 20,000 people there." I imagine the crowd choking four city blocks, tucked neatly out of sight from us. "It was quite a thrill, really."

"Anybody talk to you afterwards?"

Yeah, a few nice security guards in yellow jackets talked to us. "Nobody from labels if that's what you mean."

"Bob and June from RCA told Frank they tried to get in to see you, but there was some sort of barricade in the way. They missed your set."

"Really? They were there?"

"Yeah, but don't you even worry about it, sweetie, because I have some really *big* news."

"Yeah?"

"RCA absolutely *loves* you guys—your demo is a smash!"

"For real?"

"For real, sweetie," she says, excitedly. "Bob Stills postponed his vacation to Puerto Rico so he and June Farrow from marketing can come to your show at Rock City down in Berkeley. They think you'll be a really good match for them. Isn't that exciting?"

"Oh my God…!" I gasp.

"Are you okay?"

"Yeah, Sunny…That's huge news…The best ever."

"The way Frank's talking, you'll be signed by Labor Day. I told you, didn't I?"

"Told me what?"

"That you were gonna be huge."

"You sure did," I sigh. It seems so simple now. We play the gig with our two RCA friends there, and boom…record deal. But how?

"In the meantime, I need your help," she says, turning pensive.

"What can I do?"

"I gotta move out of here before Peaches kills me. I need to borrow some money."

"Sunny, I'm flat broke, and we're gonna be lucky to make it back to the Northwest as it is on what we got."

"You told me you have a credit card, right?"

"Yeah, I do, but it's only for emergencies."

"My friend, this *is* an emergency." She's suddenly hysterical and I listen to her sob uncontrollably for a few moments. "Peaches has really gone over the edge and I gotta get out of here before something real bad happens. Mr. Harvey showed up with a butcher knife last night when I was sleeping. He was just standing over me waving that thing with his head covered in plastic."

"Geeze, is he on crack or something?"

"Who knows? I swear I saw horns on his head. He's never acted so strange. I really need some money now. I'm afraid for my life."

"I can't do that, Sunny," I say, trembling.

"What do you mean, you can't!" she cries. "When *you* want something, you expect everyone else in the world to bail you out. This isn't just about *you*! We are at the most critical point of your entire musical career, but you seem to have no idea how close you are to the big time, and you seem to have forgotten that I'm only working for *you*, and just because I'm asking for a little help, you're acting like *you're* being abused, but you know something? If anything happens to me it's *your* fault!"

Her words are ringing in my ear across the miles. She's right. It would be my fault if something happened to her. I would have known there was a danger and my inaction would be seen as inexcusable. "So you need some money." My stomach is sick.

"Tell you what, Angus," she says, still panicky. "You wire me a thousand dollars on your credit card and I'll pay you back in a few weeks out of my share of the advance money plus double the interest you're paying now, plus your three thousand dollar deposit. You'll be in fat shape."

"Oh my goodness," I hear myself say as a plan is starting to form in my mind about how we might pull off a gig at Rock City. We've come this far and if anything did happen to Sunny it would be my fault. The stakes have been raised significantly, but there is now a realistic shot at the jackpot. I mean, if the A&R people are flipping out about our demo, imagine what they'll think when they see us live. It's all about timing and playing to win. Suddenly, Redwood Summer doesn't seem like such a disaster… "Sure, Sunny, I'll wire you a thousand dollars on my credit card."

"God bless you, sweetie," she snorts. "I wouldn't even ask this if I wasn't sure that you'd be getting signed. You'll get it all back plus interest in a few short weeks."

"I know I will." I feel like I'm floating. What'll Lily think now? I smile as my plan to get us a gig at Rock City crystallizes in my mind. When you've got a big fish on the line, you need to get it in the boat as quickly as possible because big fish can get away.

As I take my place behind the steering wheel I inform my mates that our fortunes have changed for the better and that our breakthrough gig is now going to happen at a club called Rock City. Walter is sleeping, and I feel bad that I'm not there for him, though it doesn't seem to matter. Our cash situation isn't good. We have enough to fill Elvis's tank perhaps once, if we're lucky. Rock City now looms as the biggest gig of our lives, and as we're back on the highway heading south again, I wonder who's the biggest fish of all…

Twenty

We pull into the Berkeley suburbs about 11:00 P.M. that night, and thanks to some good luck, we find a quiet pre-fabricated housing development with a cul-de-sac in which we can hunker down for the night. It's amazing how easy it is these days to find pre-fabricated housing developments with cul-de-sacs where you can camp.

Several hours earlier I had stopped at a Western Union to max out my credit card with a fifteen hundred dollar cash withdrawal, a thousand of which I immediately wired to Sunny to help save her life. I'm confident that I'll see it all back in a few weeks plus interest, just like she said, not to mention the likelihood that we'll be rolling in advance money, anyway. Redwood Summer was a good learning experience. It's actually kind of funny now. Ollie and Walter's rendition of *America the Beautiful* was the high point, and Angel's appearance on stage with Groovetribe a close second.

I have decided to hold off telling the band that we're not booked at Rock City and that we have no other California dates on this tour. Truth can wait and the truth is I'm feeling great. I know that when it's all over they'll understand why I did what I did and how it was all for the band. I even buy a twelve-pack of microbrews to celebrate our up-coming success. Within minutes, the beer is just about gone. Things like getting bumped at the Country Fair and screwed over at the Redwood gig are bound to happen to a band called the Cosmic Poets. Star is in a much better mind set, and Walter, though tired, seems to be feeling better, too—though he still won't talk about much of anything. We now have $35.54 left in our tour fund, but if things go according to plan that figure may soon be three hundred and fifty thousand times that amount. We shall see...

~

We arrive at Rock City at 5:00 P.M. and I cannot believe my eyes as I stare at the marquee out in front. None of us can, for that matter.

"They got our name wrong," sighs Star as the rest of us stare in silence. The marquee reads: Rock City Welcomes The Caustic Poets with Special Guests Groovetribe 8:00 P.M.

"Yeah, but at least Groovetribe is warming up for us this time," says Ollie. "Did you know they were opening for us?"

"No, I didn't," I say, trying not to act too surprised. Groovetribe again? I now recall Angel saying they were headed for a gig in Berkeley. What a bizarre coincidence that the headliners are a group of Poets, caustic as they are. "I kind of like the name, caustic," I say. "Don't you guys?"

"Who cares," says Zen. "At least we got a cool gig. Good job."

"Thanks, Zen," I say. "Serves Groovetribe right, anyway, after what happened in Arcata and all." My mind races. "Say, why don't we get a bite to eat before load in? I saw a Mexican place a block and a half away."

Walter quietly explains to me that he is out of money. He is still in obvious pain, though he looks much better then yesterday. I ask him what happened and he says he couldn't explain, even if he wanted to.

"No problem, Walter," I say. "Dinner is on us."

We head back to the restaurant and in moments we are sitting in a dark, air-conditioned room with baskets of chips and salsa placed before us. Ollie is going off about how Neil Young kept rushing the tempo on *Sedan Delivery* and how even the best musicians in the world have tempo inconsistencies.

"It's amazing how you notice those things when nobody else does," says Zen.

"Well, Zen, you were actually rushing yourself on the second chorus of..."

His voice fades as I momentarily excuse myself from the group; in a moment I am running full speed down the block through the sultry, evening air, headed for Rock City, hoping for a date with a small miracle.

The inside of Rock City is dark and smells like millions of cigarettes have been smoked there over the years. The stench seems to hang on everything, yet there is something rather fresh and charming about the club as well. A signed portrait of Phish hangs on one wall and, given the history of this place, it's a thrill to even be standing here. It's smaller than I expected. As my eyes adjust I see a few shadowy figures on the stage setting up for the night's show. I do recognize one of the percussion players from Groovetribe as I jump up on the stage.

"How's it going?" he asks a little nervously.

"You guys were awesome up at Arcata," I say, sucking up to him. "We're all happy for Angel."

"Hey, man, I hope there's no hard feelings. She's so bomb."

"Oh yeah. I'm down. So very down."

"That's chill, dude. I'm very down with you guys, too."

A little guy with red hair and a Padres cap hauls an amp in and asks, "Where you want this?"

"Right over there, thanks," says the Groovetriber, pointing to the corner of the stage. I come to know him as Kimta. He is a very friendly guy and I feel bad for all the nasty things I've thought about his band. There is a steady stream of equipment being hauled to the stage by various people, but I feel like nobody even notices me. Being invisible can, at times, be good.

"Say," I ask him. "I've got a huge favor to ask you guys. I was wondering if we could play a short set to kick things off tonight. We really need a gig here tonight and we'll do it for free."

He looks at me for a long moment. His face is soft, with compassionate, laughing eyes. "The Cosmic Poets, Groovetribe, and The Caustic Poets…That sounds like the total literary bomb to me. I'd be down with that, but you'll have to clear it with Matt."

I know he's thinking it would be cool because it would put the tribers on later and in front of more people. "Where's Matt?" I ask, dreading the thought of having to be phony nice to him.

"He's out in back, by the trucks."

I wade through the equipment and as I emerge on the back loading dock, I see him and Sequoia smoking cigarettes and talking. "Hi, you guys," I say as they turn to me in shock.

"Angus," says Sequoia, bristling, "if you've come for Angel, she's not interested."

"Look, it's not about that at all," I say. "I thought you guys were killer up at Arcata yesterday and we're all real happy for Angel."

"I remember you from the Big Brother show," says manager Matt, and now he's a little friendlier. "You guys are from Bellingham, right?"

"Yeah," I say. "I'm surprised Angel hasn't told you."

"Maybe it's something she's trying to get over," Sequoia says and they both laugh loudly. "What do you want?"

"Can we please play a brief set in front of you guys for no money, please?" I try not to sound desperate.

They look at each other, puzzled by my strange request. "Why?" asks Matt.

At great risk, I spill my guts to them telling them about the labels, the struggle to get real gigs and the mandate by Sunny that led to this tour to begin with. I do not tell them that they've become our arch-nemesis and that we hate them greatly because they are a bunch of phony, neo-pagan hippies and that their bus is as pretentious as their music, nor that they are the reason we got bumped back to a shitty time slot at Redwood Summer and missed the Oregon Country Fair…I do not tell them any of that. Instead, I praise their superb talents.

"As long as you keep it short and do it for free, I don't have a problem with it," says Matt at last. "We all gotta help each other out sometimes, ya know?"

"Yeah, I guess I don't mind either," says Sequoia. I know they must be excited at the prospect of playing in front of our label contacts.

"But you still gotta clear it with The Caustic Poets' manager first," says Matt as I can barely contain my elation.

"Can't we just clear it with you?"

"We're the opener, too," he says. "I'm sure it will be cool, but I don't have the final say."

"Where is he?" I say, nervous again.

"Right over there," Matt says, pointing to a group of guys standing behind the tailgate of a white pick-up truck. "His name's Kevin."

"Which one?"

"Right there," says Matt, singling out the short guy with the Padres cap and a red tank top hauling a Marshall half stack up the ramp.

I wait until he finishes his errand before I introduce myself. When he reappears on the dock, I walk up to him. "Hi, are you Kevin, the manager of The Caustic Poets?"

"I'm the Boss," he says boldly, and with a surprisingly disarming smile. His eyes are bright and the heavy, red freckles spattering his face make him appear much younger than he probably is. "What can I do for you?"

"I got a big favor to ask of you."

"What's up?"

I explain to him our situation; I even tell him how I lied about our whole tour to keep Sunny and Frank from pulling the plug on us, how we now have the chance of a lifetime with two dudes from RCA Records coming out to hear us, how it could benefit them as well. He seems intent on everything I tell him. The way his face lightens up as I finish my story, I know it's going to be cool. That's why I'm shocked when he says firmly, "No, we can't do that."

"Why?" I ask, stunned.

"Because, for one thing I've never heard of you guys before and my guys here have worked really hard to get where we are. A lot of people want to play with us, and to be honest, we usually only allow Bay Area bands the opportunity. Groovetribe is totally the exception. Sorry about that."

What a hard-ass. I hate managers like this. They listen to everything you say, then act like it's nothing to shit all over you. "Sorry? You're sorry? Look man, we need this gig. One half-hour set is all we want. RCA is coming to hear us tonight. Please. Just one half-hour?"

"I don't mean to be a hard-ass," he says, "but it won't work. Send me some promo and maybe we'll do it another time."

"No," I whimper as the time has come for a last act of desperation. I was hoping to God that it wasn't going to come to this. I reach into my pocket, knowing I've reached my limit and have been pushed far enough. My fingers curl around the root of all violence and evil in the world, and as I slowly pull my hand out he watches with fear and fascination. *You low-life bastard* I think as I deliberately point my loaded hand toward him and open it slowly. I show him five, brand-spanking new one hundred dollar bills fresh from Western Union where I drained my credit card account. He looks at the money—then at me. "Will this make a difference?" I whisper.

"Are you serious?" I notice that his eyes have changed.

"We need the gig."

He takes the cash. "All right. But a half-hour is all you get."

My impulse is to grab him and kiss him, but I don't. I hate him too much. Instead, I say thanks, and in seconds I am off and running back to the restaurant to meet my band to tell them the good news.

Back at the restaurant, Ollie is still engaged in a monologue with Zen. While everyone else's plates are empty, Ollie's is still full of rice, enchiladas and beans. He's hardly taken a bite. I sit next to him and Star asks me where I've been.

"Just down at the club checking in," I say.

"Everything all right?" she asks.

"Everything's great," I say.

"Cool. Did you see Angel?"

"No, she wasn't there yet." I begin eating Ollie's dinner and he doesn't even seem to notice.

"Who's gonna be there?" Ollie asks, suddenly.

"Two dudes from RCA," I say. "They've been freaking out about the tape. They absolutely love us. Now eat your dinner before I do," I say.

"Sorry," he says.

"I know I told you guys that Redwood Summer was the biggest gig yet, but I am now without a doubt convinced that this will be the biggest gig, ever. All we've ever asked for was a shot. A chance to show those bastards what we can really do, live. My friends, this is it." Now comes the tricky part. "It's been arranged so that we can go on first which I think is great because we'll stand out more, and we'll hit 'em hard and be done with it. I like our chances."

"First?" questions Star, after a long silence. "We're going first, *again*?"

"Look, I know I said it didn't matter up in Arcata when it turned out that it really did, but I swear, this time I know for sure—"

"*First*?" repeats Star again, hardly noticing what I've just said. "You sold us out again?"

"Star," reasons Ollie, "isn't that a bit harsh? Angus's been trying his hardest to—"

"I could really use a pinch of that," I interrupt as Star's expression suddenly waxes wistful and she smiles as she hands me the can. Within seconds of putting some chew in my mouth, I'm dizzy as hell and spitting madly in a cup. I hear far away laughter. "How do you chew this stuff?" I ask. I go to the bathroom and wash out my mouth, taking a deep breath before looking in the mirror. The face looking back at me is a stranger. He's older, and the eyes are different too.

~

There are far more people at Rock City when we get back, and the first thing I notice is that all of Groovetribe's percussion gear is carefully arranged on stage. I wonder if we'll get a sound-check, too. Probably not, but that will be okay. We begin hauling our gear to the foot of the stage and in a few minutes, we have accumulated quite a pile.

"What are you doing?" It's Matt, his voice heavy with concern.

"We get a sound-check, don't we?" I ask. "We also wanted to know if Ollie can use your drummer's trap set?"

"What are you talking about?" he asks, looking at me strangely. Why is he acting so weird? "I told you that you had to clear playing tonight with The Caustic's manager, Kevin."

"But I did."

"You *did*?" he asks, puzzled.

"Yeah, I sure did," I reply, feeling a big nausea coming on.

He says to wait, then disappears into the smoky crowd gathered near the bar. In a few moments he returns with a tall, lanky surfer-dude with a bony face. "This is Kevin Johnson, manager of The Caustic Poets," he says, introducing me to a guy I've never seen before.

"We never talked about you guys opening the show," the guy says as he softly shakes my limp and trembling hand.

"I know." I'm confused. I turn to Matt. "You told me that short guy with freckles was Kevin the manager."

"Short guy with freckles?" asks Matt.

Suddenly Kevin laughs out loud. "You mean the Boss? You talked to the Boss?"

"Yeah," I say, panicked. "He said he was the boss. I assumed that he was you."

"Oh, man." Kevin shakes his head. "The Boss is an honorary groupie of The Caustic Poets. We let him come to our shows for free 'cause he helps us haul gear."

"He's not the manager?" I gasp.

"Dude, the guy's homeless. He's lived on the street for years. He got fucked up in 'Nam pretty bad, I guess. He's always giving us advice about what we need to do to break out of the Bay Area. He sure loves our music, too. Says it relaxes him, and as long has he's willing to help us haul gear, he's welcome at our shows. Rumor has it he's a brilliant poet."

"No way," I hear myself say. "Have you seen him lately?"

"Not since load-in," says Kevin. "Which is kind of strange, really. He usually hangs pretty close by."

"Look, I'm trying really, really hard not to lose it." They both look at me with concern as I explain to Kevin about our agent Sunny and how she and Frank Strong have arranged for record company people to come out and see us tonight and how I had to lie to them about Rock City and the whole tour for that matter to keep them from pulling the plug and how Groovetribe has gotten all the breaks while we've got nothing but misery so far but we've worked hard for this opportunity and if he could find it in him to let us play a brief set to kick things off I would be forever indebted to him and that perhaps our label contacts could help them because after all aren't musicians all in the same boat anyway and isn't helping each other what it's really all about?

"Sorry," he says, "but, we can't." He goes on to explain that the time and technical constraints won't allow it, and how it's hard enough having Groovetribe play as it is. There's no way we can play. Not even for a half-hour. "Why don't you send me some promo; maybe we can do it another time."

I realize that Ollie, Zen and Star have gathered in a quiet semi-circle around us; everything is starting to fall away. "Look, Kevin, you don't understand what's at stake. I gave the Boss five hundred-dollars in order to play this set. I thought he was *you*. Please, can't we play?" I see horror in Ollie and Star's eyes, and I'm forced to look away.

"You gave the Boss five hundred dollars?" asks Kevin in astonishment. "Well, we won't be seeing him for awhile."

Manager Matt just shakes his head in disbelief.

"Hi, you guys," says Angel, suddenly appearing before us. "I'm so glad you're here for our show." She turns to Matt. "Can we put them on the guest list?"

"Sure," he says, sadly. "It's the least we can do."

"And the most," says Kevin walking away. "I'd be down for some promo; maybe we can hook up another time."

I try to hold back. I really do. But I can't.

"Why are you all staring at me?" I ask. There's a large crowd that has now gathered around me. "Where's Walter? Did we ever find him, Ollie?" I ask.

Ollie nods his head, but he looks really sad. Why does everyone look so sad? A half-hour won't take too long. "Let's set up." I grab my guitar and amp and climbing up onto the stage. "Come on, we don't have much time; the labels will be here any minute."

Angel stares at me with horror in her eyes.

"What are you staring at, Angel?" I scream. "I thought you got murdered back in Talbot!"

I hear a far away voice say, "You're in no shape to play music, man." I look and it's Sequoia. He gently escorts me down from the stage and suddenly I'm flashing sweat and everything is really bright and screaming like there's a B-52 in my head and I'm running for the bathroom and the first thing that crosses my mind after vomiting is that I wish I'd held off on the jalapenos. They rarely agree with me anyway. I lament wasting Ollie's enchiladas which still don't taste half-bad traveling in high speed reverse though my mouth and throat burn like hell and my brain feels like it's been hanging out in a microwave oven. Oh well, we can always stop for a bite to eat later on if we're hungry.

"Well, guys," I say, feeling very upbeat as I return from my glorious upheaval. "Let's pack it up and drive back to Bellingham." I clap my hands in mock enthusiasm. People are whispering, but they always do. Angel is gone, and I'm glad. It's quiet as we pack our gear out of the club, but it's damn near full of people and I wonder if our friends from RCA have shown up yet. Probably, but who cares anymore. Life has become an absurdity. Or maybe it has always been so, but only now am I starting to see the truth.

Twenty-one

Elvis is quiet and it's starting to rain. Zen is behind the wheel now since I'm in no condition to drive. We're all just as silent as Walter, and that is a good thing. It's over. Finished. I've been unmasked as the smoke-and-mirrors man behind the curtain in the city of Oz. The curtains have fallen and I'm exposed, naked to the world, or at least to the band. Nothing matters anymore. It's kind of nice having it all quiet like this. Rock bottom isn't so bad, really. I inform everybody in a very casual way that the whole tour was my own fabrication and that we have no more gigs until Seattle. My words are met with more silence.

We've been driving about an hour-and-a-half and nobody has said a word. About ten miles west of Sacramento, shit hits the fan. It starts with the sound of weeping. I look over and see Star huddled in back all by herself. "I can't believe this is happening to me," she says.

Yeah, well you're not fifteen hundred bucks in the red on a credit card advance, I think.

"It's not just about you Star," says Ollie. "I'm sick of you feeling sorry about yourself."

"Fuck you, Ollie," she says. "You all made a fool out of me."

"That's a nice thing to say," he mutters and I can tell things are about to unravel. I don't have the will to stop it. "You are so absolutely clueless I can't believe it."

"Fuck you, dipshit!" she snaps. "Where were you before we went on stage up in Arcata, out spankin' the noodle?"

"I spilled coffee all over my crotch and had to get out of my white pants you spoiled little bitch."

"Bitch? I'll kick your ass, Ollie. I have never in my *life* been so humiliated! How did you think you could get away with lying about a whole tour, Angus? I feel like I've been living a lie!"

"Don't blame me for living a lie," I shoot back. "You're just in this band to get famous and I'm sick of being a rung in your ladder. All I've heard from you is: 'I can't believe this is happening to me!' Like you're the only one that matters. What about us? What about me?"

"Don't forget, Angus," says Ollie. "You *did* lie about everything, and for someone who's always praising Tolstoy in his relentless pursuit of truth, isn't it slightly ironic, not to mention hypocritical, that we're even in this situation? You set us up."

"We were set up the day we listened to Sunny and her freaky friend from Florida!" I shout. "It wasn't just me; you all wanted out of Bellingham. It was about getting famous together. I swear I tried to get gigs; I really did. You guys don't know the humiliation of calling these arrogant music people and just asking them to please take a little time out of their lives to listen to our demo, and not just the first thirty seconds, either. 'I just wanna play music,' you say. But you're the first to complain when things don't go right. You'd like to think that good art and music or anything that's sincere will get an audience, some consideration for *something*, but it's just the opposite, 'cause if you don't talk to these shallow jerks like you're the hottest shit in the world they won't even give you the time of day. And when you call them back you don't know if demo made it into their player or is sitting in the bottom of a wastebasket covered with cold coffee grounds! Fuck them! I can't even talk to those people without feeling like I wanna throw up. I'm just a stupid musician who wanted to get famous for all the wrong reasons. I tried to make it work and I'm sorry I lied about the tour, but you know what? Everybody lied by caring more about glory than music and the real crime is that I let myself become a part of it!"

"Oh, come off your high-horse!" Star shouts. "Nobody made you become a phony and liar." She bursts into more tears.

"You're calling *me* a phony?" I ask as Ollie positions himself between us. She won't look at me. "Look at me, Star!"

"Yeah, Star, you gotta lot of nerve calling him a phony," Ollie says. "You and your warrior-girl armor. Sure, Angus lied about the tour, but what are *we* when we buy into all the image stuff? Why don't you *try* just being a musician for once?"

There is silence again, save for the bumping of the road and the hum of the engine, but I know there's a wicked storm brewing and it begins as a low pitched whining kind of like a big cat but it's growing fast and then it erupts as I see dark silhouettes, scuffling, yelling, and screaming and I know Ollie might be in trouble when I hear his muffled voice crying, "Let go! Ouch! Come on!" Star has him in a headlock on the floor rubbing his face in the carpet and her eyes are all wild and laughing while the strand of drool falling from her mouth onto Ollie's head seems intentional.

"Bitch, huh?" she says, wrenching his head back.

"*Owwwww!*" he screams.

"Stop it, Star!" I yell but she doesn't hear me and I'm afraid she might accidentally kill him.

"You got a lot of nerve calling me a bitch when you know damn well that I can break your neck any day of the week you little punk!"

There is a strange laughter filling Elvis's interior. I first think it's Zen, but Zen's driving and not laughing at all. I realize that it's coming from Walter who's doubled over, shaking his head. He seems to want to say something but each time he's about to, he bursts into more hysteria, and now I'm beginning to feel a bit offended. I hear a painful groan as Star releases Ollie from the clutches of her death grip and I wonder if he knows how lucky he might be.

"Pull over." Walter comes forward, his tear-streaked and beat-up face even more menacing. "There's enough bullshit here to fill a long house. You never learn, do you?"

"You can't just walk away," I say. "It's raining and we don't even know where the hell we are."

"The hell I can't," he says, now looking deadly. "I'm through being your mascot." He clears his throat while we all stare. "Here's some advice. Don't let the past have power over you. We Indians survive by finding the power in the present. Everything you've ever needed is right here." Saying this, he disappears into the night. I jump out to try to stop him, but he's gone and I can't see much of anything in the pouring rain and thick darkness. It's as if he just vanished very suddenly, leaving us to contemplate the naked truth about ourselves while wondering if he ever really existed at all.

~

It must be an hour or two later when Zen pulls Elvis off onto a gravel road, and I notice a Forest Service sign that says: Welcome to the Lake Tahoe National Forest. One spark is all it takes.

It's okay to maul the whole damn thing with chain saws, but for God's sake, don't you dare light a match. I can relate to that.

"Where the hell is Tahoe?" asks Zen, and I describe the general location. Star hasn't said a word since the big fight. Ollie has been pretty quiet, too—although he didn't want to leave Walter in the rain and darkness and insisted that we spend an hour driving back and forth looking for him. Walter's absence leave my guts in a knot, though the scene back at Rock City now seems hilarious—as does everything else.

"I guess I overshot I-5," says Zen, looking at the atlas.

"To say the least," says Ollie.

"We're not talking about the past anymore, remember?" I actually find a spark of joy in my joke. This could be good practice. None of us discuss the evening's events during and after Rock City, but I sense we're better off than we were a few hours ago.

We get ready for sleep and I do a quick cash inventory, immediately wishing I hadn't. We're down to twelve dollars and seven cents and now my fifteen hundred dollar debt on my credit card weighs rather heavily. I wonder what the Boss is up to right now. Probably checked into some high-rise motel and having the time of his life. In a strange way, I'm happy for him. You never know when the breaks will come.

Twenty-two

*In my exhausted slumber, I dream. I am walking through the gray
downtown on a busy street in some big city. In my arms, I carry a couple
of boxes of half-inch, analog tapes, probably masters. I am suddenly
moving very quickly through the lobby as if I'm on some sort of conveyor
belt and as I pass the receptionist's desk, it seems perfectly natural to see
Sunny sitting there filing her long red finger nails.*

"I want to see someone about my tapes." It feels like I'm talking
underwater.

She gets on her phone and calls someone and then says to me
momentarily, "Mr. Sorenson's in a meeting. Would you like to
leave those with me?"

"Why?" I ask. "They're my tapes, not yours."

"They're all mine," she laughs, her voice dripping with evil.

"No, I want Mr. Sorenson."

She gets back on the phone and I'm swept away and onto an
elevator that morphs into his office. I'm looking way down
through clear windows at the streets far below. Mr. Sorenson's
face is crystal clear and the first thing that overwhelms me is his
remarkable human appearance. Two brown eyes, two nostrils,
one nose, thin lips and a large Adam's apple.

"So, you're an A&R rep," I say.

"I am," he replies in English. "What do you want?"

"I'm here to negotiate my advance money," I say.

"Do you have something for me?" he asks.

I pull a tape from its box and give it to him. He takes out a pair
of latex rubber gloves and picks it up, examining it carefully and

holding it a distance away from his face. Then he's on the phone mumbling something to…Frank…Frank Strong from Florida, and suddenly Frank, Sunny and a bunch of suits are standing around his desk looking at my reel to reels.

Mr. Sorenson puts the tape on and the sound coming out of the two-inch speakers sitting on his desk is warbly and transistorized. It's terrible. Before I can say anything they are all laughing, and when I try to speak over them, my mouth feels like it's full of peanut butter. My words are thick and awkward which makes them only laugh harder.

"What's wrong?" I scream.

"Where are the hooks?" Mr. Sorenson yells in a very scolding voice and this makes them laugh even harder.

"Yeah, where are the hooks?" laughs Frank Strong, whom until now, I've never seen. He looks strangely human, too.

"Where are the hooks?" screams Sunny. Her pale, laughing face swirls by in a strange, river-like way. They're all laughing at me and I look down into my arms. I'm not holding tapes anymore; it's an AK-47 assault rifle with Charlton Heston's laughing face embedded on the stock.

"Here's a hook, motherfucker!" I scream as I blow out the plate glass window behind Mr. Sorenson's head. Immediately they're all very quiet. "Got your attention now?"

They say nothing, but only smile politely. I like this powerful feeling. "You're A&R people, but you resemble human beings. Do you shit like humans?" I scream again and blow out another plate glass.

They cower amongst themselves, still smiling politely to me, but it seems as though they might be starting to take me a little more seriously. That is until Mr. Sorenson opens his mouth again. "Your songs need hooks and they need to be shorter. Not one has clocked in under six minutes so far."

"Suck on *this* hook, you bastard," I say, pointing the barrel of the gun at his head and squeezing the trigger. The gun explodes and the air is filled with snowflakes falling gently everywhere. No, it's Styrofoam. His head was made of Styrofoam.

The rest of them converse quietly amongst themselves, still smiling politely to me. Frank Strong speaks.

"Look, Angus, even if you blow all of our heads off, your songs will still need hooks. It's only reasonable for us to make this request. If you don't have hooks, you can't tour."

"Well then, Frank, take this." I pull the trigger, his head floats gracefully high in the air, tumbling in slow motion and then lands, bouncing lightly on the table, still smiling with flickering eyes. His head is Styrofoam too.

"You're all worthless!" I yell. "You don't even know what art is! You think it's all about making everyone sound and look the same!" I train the gun on another dude and, in a blue-hot flash, the air is filled again with floating, feather-like chunks of Styrofoam.

But they're all still laughing and one dude in a suit says, "You can't kill us, you idiot."

"Why not?" I scream.

"We were never alive to begin with!" he screams back, but I shoot him just the same, before yelling to Sunny to give me my advance money.

She walks up to me all business-like and opens this briefcase. In it there are a few pennies, dimes, and nickels rolling around.

"What's this?" I ask.

"Your share!" She shrieks, laughing with her remaining colleagues. She hands me a giant piece of paper that says: *Record Contract*, *Sign Here…*

"You're very funny." My gun roars again, but now there is more laughter and I see Angel and all the Groovetribe members along with manager Matt and Lily who seems to be holding Sequoia's hand and they're all laughing at me with condescending eyes. I'm suddenly very frightened, though not too surprised that they're all made out of Styrofoam, and here's Ollie holding me down with Star and Zen, and I'm hollering, but now it's all dark and I realize I've been dreaming but I can't explain it to them because they wouldn't understand. I spend the rest of the night wide-awake and loathing what I've let myself become.

Twenty-three

The sun's probably been up a few hours when we arise. I can already feel something is going to be different from this day, though I still can't for the life of me understand why The Caustic Poets wouldn't let us play a stupid one half-hour set. Our opportunity of a lifetime on a dark night in Berkeley is becoming a strange and fleeting memory. I want to believe that Sunny was full of shit about the A&R reps coming out to hear us, but I know she wasn't. We were close. I think of the Boss: he probably had the time of his life last night.

All we can scrape up for breakfast are a couple of over-ripe bananas that Ollie found under the passenger seat plus a green pepper with half a bag of old, blue corn tortilla chips we got back in Oregon. But no coffee. Things can always be worse. I walk down the gravel road to practice living in the moment and, as I walk, I relish the sound of wind tickling the high branches of the firs and the hush of the creek. I breathe deep and exhale slowly, suddenly aching for Walter and the fact that he had to leave us. His words drift through my mind. I begin to tremble inside which makes me think of the Styrofoam people. So what if the big fish got away. Don't they always get away?

Far up the valley the road bends to the left, disappearing from sight. Beyond lay granite sculpted foothills speckled with trees, and the way the wind blows warm with everything so quiet, I decide that I just want to stay here for awhile.

"It sure is gorgeous, huh?" Star asks, startling me.

"Yeah," I say, not really wanting to talk.

"Bummer about the fifteen hundred bucks," she says. I notice that she is quite beautiful without the goddess armor on.

"Yeah, that was really stupid of me to do that."

"Do you think Sunny will pay you back?"

"It was going to come out of her share of the advance money plus interest, so I'm not counting on it. It all probably went up her nose."

"Yuck!"

"Them's the breaks." We stand in silence for a few moments, but she won't leave. Instead she pulls out the can and offers me a chew, which I wave off.

"I didn't like what Ollie and you said about me being in it just for myself."

"You know, Star? I think we can stop playing roles. None of us have anything to prove anymore, and I'm really sorry I lied about the tour."

"I had a feeling you were hiding something," she says. "I didn't know what, though. I do like the music. I'm not just in it for myself. In a weird kind of way, I'm gonna miss you guys, even Ollie."

"You're quitting?"

"Yeah, I wanna go home and beat the shit out of my ex-boyfriend before I start my life over. I'm thinking about forming a heavy metal bluegrass band, and Bellingham's the place to do it."

"You're probably right. Sorry it didn't work out for you."

"It's not entirely your fault, Angus. I mean, I kind of bought into your bullshit, too. I'm just glad Walter's out of the picture. The nerve of that asshole after all we did for him."

I stare at her in shock. "Does the truth hurt?"

"I really don't have time for guilt trips," she says, spitting into the grass at her feet.

"I honestly don't think you get what's going on here, Star." I leave her standing in the road as I wander up a faint trail.

~

I guess I've been climbing for hours and it seems there's a meadow coming up that's bathed in golden sunlight and even though there are old silvery stumps in it from being logged years ago, it is nice.

The distant whine of an airplane causes some irritation as I try to push Lily from my mind. She keeps explaining why she must say goodbye. Why does there always have to be an explanation? Why not just be done with it? Explanations only confuse things. I know why, anyway. I was a character in her script and she grew tired with the revisions. I'm sorry I wasn't there for you, Lily. I know that I helped make you colder, wanting to blame you for that, too. It's all so confusing, such a waste. What do I really need? I could always hire someone to tell me. But how much would it cost to hear the truth?

Far up on the ridge, I see a person walking away from me. It's Walter. He carries nothing with him. He lives like the lilies of the field.

"Walter!" I yell. "What are you doing up here?"

He won't turn back to me, though I do hear his laughter echoing off the hills. He seems to be walking toward the sun and I'm overwhelmed with sadness as I realize my path leads back into the shadows of the valley.

The sun is fading fast as I descend the last set of switchbacks to the road and as I round the last bend before the straightaway that leads out towards the main highway, I can tell they're gone—in spite of the fact that Elvis is still parked in the same place. That's all right with me. I mean, I didn't tell them that I was going to climb a mountain and be gone for eight hours. It doesn't matter now. Elvis is unlocked, and on the table inside there is a note by Ollie that reads:

Angus—

It's not all your fault that things turned out so bad, but Star and Zen decided at about 12:08 P.M. that they were going to try to hitchhike back to Bellingham together and last I saw them, they were heading east on Route 50. At 2:47 P.M. I decided that I should follow them though I was, and am kind of worried about you, too, but there's only one of you to get lost while there's two of them, but you know, it could be more dangerous for you out there in bear country though I read in *People Magazine* about a pair of hitchhikers who were clubbed to death by some psycho and then cooked and eaten in a kind of stew, and I think it actually happened somewhere in North Central California but now I'm really torn because Star said that you took off by yourself. Shit! I'm following them toward a small town called Twin Bridges and likely beyond, and the keys to Elvis are under the seat, and we left a few chips there for you too though they're pretty gross. God, I hope you're okay. See you back in Bellingham. (I assume the Battle of the Band's gig at the Showbox is off since Star quit the group and all, and I get the feeling that Zen did too. Hey, maybe I won't go find them…It's confusing, what to do and all…I'm sorry, I guess I feel like it's all my fault somehow and if I hadn't gone for a leak at the Talbot Rest Area, we might still be together although maybe it wouldn't have mattered since you lied about the gigs but I don't really blame you; Sunny can be quite overbearing at times although she was right about a lot of things as well which makes me wonder if we shouldn't call her and Peaches before we set anything in stone? After all, Frank did have some good bites. Well, good luck Angus and I hope to see you really soon.

Your friend, Ollie.

P.S. I'm sorry about everything…It's all my fault, really. Someday I hope I can make it up to everyone.

Alone again (naturally) as Gilbert O' Sullivan said in a song he recorded what feels like about a million years ago. Yes, everything does seem strangely natural—if not exceptionally numb. How odd to feel nothing. No anger, bitterness or sorrow.

I pick up my acoustic guitar because I know it's time to play. I have no one to play for but the creek rushing through the evening shadows close by, and that is a good thing. The creek is neutral; the creek will not condemn. The creek will listen. I can finally be myself. I walk down a small trail with no plan and no purpose anymore. I know not who or why I am, nor why a band called The Cosmic Poets who wanted only to get famous like ninety-nine percent of all the bands in the world embarked on a tour that began with high hopes and ended in disaster. At least I got to talk to the Boss—and he scored big!

Out of respect for nature, I decide to play an original. The stream is flowing silver in the moonlight, and the crickets chatter. As I walk onto the little beach, I wish I'd brought a sweater. The stars are starting to pop out above me though dusk casts a pale swath across the fading sky. And I wonder, as I always do, why I still remain after so many others have passed on from such an indifferent day.

I play a song to the creek and when I'm done I smash my guitar on the river rocks, though I swear, I'm not feeling sorry for myself and I am not a victim. I just want to hear the sound of wood groan and splinter with the sound of discordant strings vibrating, and I couldn't stop now, even if I wanted to. Afterwards I build a fire, offering up the remains of my once beautiful instrument—still strangely beautiful in its new form, the enamel and finish bubbling, hissing. It's warmth comforts me. Walter is right; there is power in the moment, and you shouldn't get caught up in a lot of bullshit. All you need is a small, nameless stream on a late July summer night somewhere in California when you're all depressed 'cause things didn't go right after Sunny and the Boss scammed fifteen hundred bucks you didn't have to spare as you tried to make your band the next big thing and were so close you could taste it though bands like Groovetribe will always be there to steal the glory at the very end despite the fact that I swear I'm not a victim anymore and things like this are bound to happen to a band with a name like The Cosmic Poets.

Twenty-four

A stew…Some creep ate hitchhikers after he cooked them in a stew? I ponder this gruesome thought as I pull into the Twin Bridges Cafe. I'm hungry as hell, and I don't know how far I'll even be able to drive tonight. Stew actually sounds pretty good right now, though the contingency of logging trucks parked outside makes me a little concerned. But I'm just a fool named Angus driving a motor-home named Elvis back to Bellingham. A fool like me needs a good meal from time to time.

Besides the milky cloud of tobacco smoke and grease smothering me, the first thing I notice when I walk through the door is the sound of very familiar laughter. The place is about half full, though most of the locals who are gathered here are standing in a large group at the far end of the bar, away from the food tables. I scan the room for a place to sit. When I see Ollie, Star and Zen, huddled around a few beers and a giant plate of fries, I do not even feel surprised.

"How's it going, Angus?" asks Zen as I approach. Star seems engaged by a story Ollie is telling and hardly acknowledges me as I pull up a chair.

"Not bad," I say in stride. "I went for a really cool hike today."

"So I hear," he says. "Sorry we split, but we didn't know how long you were gonna be gone, and we wanted to get on back to Bellingham." He seems so casual. So does everybody.

"Did you have a good climb?" asks Star.

"It was okay," I say. "I think I figured some things out."

"I think we all have," she says.

I do, indeed, order some homemade stew and Zen pours me a beer. Nobody seems angry with each other. It's as if we're back in Bellingham before handing over the reigns to Sunny. We chug cheap beer, eat fries and laugh, just like old times. I haven't felt this relaxed in a long time. There are more people starting to show up, though they're not here to eat. They're gathering at the far end of the dark, rectangular room where someone is decorating it with cheap Christmas lights. I notice signs that say: Live Music Most Saturday Nites and Spotted Owl Tastes Like Chicken. I notice that the folks standing around are all wearing yellow arm bands—which makes me nervous. I'm hoping this isn't a logger's rally.

"What do you think's going on?" I ask.

"Who knows," says Star. "They don't seem to be a very friendly bunch, do they?"

"Let's just eat and get the hell out of here, then," I say interrupting him while wondering for the first time how we're going to pay for the food and beer. I lack the energy to find out how the three of them ended up here, and why they're all getting along so well, but that's the case with most band blow-outs. Any insult is fair game during battle; afterwards, especially with Star, it's like water off a duck's back. I'm just glad she isn't packing heat or half the band would be dead by now for sure.

I find myself in a slow downward spiral again, and the table conversation grows more distant. I know Lily's with Nathan and, with no hope of a record deal, there's nothing I can do. "I'll be right back." Zen just looks at me.

The phone booth is back near the pool tables, and I have to walk through the gathering crowd, who all seem to be wearing black. People just kind of stare at me while talking amongst themselves. People always do, and it doesn't bother me half as much as the knot in my stomach. With no hope left in my heart, I know I won't be able to bear the sound of her voice—but it doesn't matter. I must call.

The phone booth is filthy with imaginative, highly-intelligent graffiti and I really do want to get the hell out of here. I've got a bad feeling about this place. The phone rings once before she picks it up.

"Hi."

"It's me," I say.

"I knew it would be," she giggles. "I think I'm psychic."

"I've always thought you were," I say, weary of the game.

"How's everything going?" she asks.

"Terrible," I say. "How about with you?"

"Really, really wonderful."

"That's nice."

"What's so terrible?" she sighs. "How'd the gig go?"

"It didn't," I say, feeling the floodgates starting to burst. "What I mean is that we never were on the bill at Rock City, though Sunny and Frank thought we were and they even had a couple of A&R reps from RCA come out to hear us there. I tried to bribe the manager of a band named The Caustic Poets into letting us warm up for them and I even gave him five hundred dollars off of a credit card advance, but it turned out that he wasn't the manager but just a homeless, ex-Vietnam vet-groupie known locally as the Boss, and of course he split with the cash before the whole thing got really funny, even though it wasn't funny at all, and afterward Walter, our Indian friend told us that the past has no real power over you unless you let it, so I'm just calling to say goodbye and to tell you that I want to forget that I ever loved you."

"You are so *funny!*" she says.

"Funny?" I ask. "Why is that funny?"

"You're such a tradgedian," she giggles. "Everything is either wonderfully beautiful or intensely tragic. You are so far out of balance. Why must everything be black and white with you?"

"Are we still together?"

"You see? There you go. Black and white. Why can't you just let it be gray for awhile?"

"So we're *not* together."

"I didn't say that, either, but if you need to move on, then move on."

"Well, the band split up, and at first I thought it was a horrible thing, but now I see that it's good so why not just say goodbye to you?"

"Do what you need to do Angus," she says. "You really should read *Zen and the Art of Motorcycle Maintenance*, though. I think it could really help you. You can have my copy when you get home."

"You know what, Lily?" I say as a curious sense of calm sweeps over me. "I don't want your stupid book. You've always got some book for me to read about making myself better, like if I just understand my problems somehow I'll be good enough for you. I'm not an engine rebuild project in your metaphysical auto shop. Find someone else to work on."

"Get a life," she says, slamming the receiver down in my ear. I hold the phone away from my head feeling dizzy, then the slow warmth and tingle as blood begins flooding my system and my heart starts back up again. It's all about guilt with her, but if she gets angry enough she *will* gloss over her own infidelity. And I, as usual, provided her an easy out. This time, it's okay. This time it's over. For real.

One down, one to go. The phone rings. Peaches answers.

"Hey, Peaches. It's me."

"Oh, how ya doin' maaan," he snorts, sounding like he's got a bad cold.

"Oh, we're doing just great," I say.

I hear Sunny groan next to him, whispering angrily, "Give me the goddamned phone, you idiot." Peaches slurs a goodbye.

"I'm so glad you called." I imagine her lying there with Peaches in a depressed, coked-out funk and for all I know he's probably blowing a line as I speak.

"Did you get the thousand bucks?"

"I did, and you saved my life," she says with a sniffle. "I can't really talk right now."

"My, you sure sound congested, Sunny. You catch a cold or something?"

"Oh, it's just my allergies," she says, quickly.

"Yeah, Mr. Harvey sounds like he's having an attack too."

"Mr. Harvey? Oh yeah. Right. You know I just talked with Frank a little while ago. They sure loved you guys."

"What?"

"Didn't they talk with you?"

"Who?"

"Bob and June from RCA. They were at Rock City. They didn't talk with you?"

"Nobody talked with us, Sunny."

"It doesn't matter; Frank's flying into town in a few days to catch your gig at the Showbox. Funny, though, he made it sound like you guys made contact. They *loved* you guys, and the only question they have is why you didn't play anything off of your demo. Remember, I told you to stick with the familiar."

"Sunny, the oldies get boring," I say, playing along. In the back of my mind, horror has a new name. I push the thought back. That would be a little too much to believe.

"You also need to make sure that when you play, the club spells your name right on the marquee though the name Caustic Poets does seem to fit you guys pretty good. Mistakes like these can turn into gold mines. I swear, this time you're on the doorstep."

It *is* true! The record people were there and they thought we were The Caustic Poets. Damn.

"They also really liked your opening act, Groovevibe. Did you know that they're playing the Battle of Seattle with you?"

"It's Groove*tribe*, Sunny," I say coldly, gently placing the phone receiver in its cradle.

The crowd has grown by a third as I make my way back to the table, and everything looks and feels different. For some reason the fact that the band is splitting up doesn't bother me in the least. In fact, it seems very funny to me, as does the fact that I gave Sunny a thousand dollars to party up a storm with Mr. Harvey.

"What do you think's going on?" I ask the crew, still immersed in grease and cheap beer.

"There's been a tragedy," says Ollie, shaken. "Two loggers were killed yesterday. There's a memorial for them here tonight."

"That's heavy," I sigh. The whole world's going to hell and I think I have problems. Suddenly there's a high-pitched squeal of feedback and the sound of tapping.

A crumbly, transistorized voice says, "Testing: one-two-three." It seems that during all of the commotion, they've managed to set up a small PA system, and people quiet down quickly. "Hi, everybody, my name's Jess and I'll be the emcee tonight." From the corner of my eye I see Zen ordering another pitcher of beer for us.

When he gets back, I say, "You guys wanna get out of here? We're about seventy five miles east of I-5 and we should get a jump on things."

"I just bought more beer," garbles Zen.

"Sounds good, Zen." Weariness has overwhelmed me—beneath it, a melancholy peace.

Our barmaid brings the pitcher and we consume beer and listen. I wonder how Zen thinks we're gonna pay for it, but I do like this living in the moment business. I'll worry about it later.

The emcee is named Jess and he thanks everyone for showing up tonight to celebrate the lives of John Morgan and Phil Williams. Both were hard working loggers who were alive yesterday morning and dead by afternoon. John was evidently more of the philosopher type who read a lot, while Phil was a party animal. Neither could withstand a four-hundred-year-old fir rolling over them.

As I ponder this somber reality, I notice near the entrance of the restaurant, a table of six or seven crusty, logger types who seem to be staring at me. I don't look back at the table directly because I do not want to make eye contact. Making eye contact with logger types who are staring at you can be a risky thing, especially in small towns near the Sierra foothills. They might think you want to start a fight or something stupid like that. I can't imagine they'd be all that frightened of us, except for Star that is. Maybe it's Star they're staring at. I'm not sure, but they're making me very nervous.

The speakers crackle again and Jess's voice introduces a friend of John's family who wanted to open things with a prayer. An older, silver-haired minister-type with a white collar and weary eyes takes the stage and offers his condolences. I notice the crusty logger types occupying the table behind us are talking amongst themselves, one guy still staring at me like he might know me from somewhere.

When the minister is finished, he leaves the stage and the place is quiet except for a little talking coming from the back. Jess takes the microphone again and introduces a friend of John's who wants to share a song with the crowd. As he walks toward the stage, guitar in hand, his nervous eyes make him seem less menacing than he probably would if he were to come across you with chainsaw in hand after you had fastened yourself to an old growth tree that he had been thinking about cutting.

"Thank you, sir." He takes his place, slouching on a stool while Jess slaps a microphone on his guitar and another one for his voice. "I didn't exactly write this one, but it was one of John's favorites." His voice breaks and his words falter. "Is this thing on?" Jess nods to him as he takes his place stage right behind a little mixer. "I guess I'll give it a try."

"Go, Jim!" a woman from the audience screams and the place is cheering.

He smiles, turning red, his rugged face betrayed by his vulnerability. He strums a minor chord and the guitar is significantly out of tune; he improves it enough that, shaky as it is, I recognize the opening chords to *Knockin' On Heaven's Door*. His hands seem way too thick and fat for the guitar. As his off-key voice fills the room, it occurs to me that this is probably the first time he has ever played in front of an audience.

Hearing the way people sing the words with him, hanging on to every line like it's some kind of cosmic life jacket, reminds me that a good song that means something to someone is always a good thing.

Star, Zen and Ollie are into it as well. It is good to be into things like this. As long as guys like Jim have the courage to approach the microphone with fear and trepidation, there is hope for the world. He finishes the song while the room explodes in cheering, and he's got tears rolling down his cheeks.

"Play another," yells a woman. "Play the crow song."

"I don't know," he says shyly. "I always liked crows. They seem a lot smarter than people like me." He pauses, taking a long chug of ice water, looking more comfortable. "One time when we was kids, me and John were out huntin' pigeons and we scared up a flock of crows, and John got real excited as they were flyin' over our heads. He plugged one with his 4-10 and it fell, I mean, like a rock out of the sky, and we went over to look at it, and it wasn't dead or nothin' and John, I mean, he felt terrible. He was gonna shoot it 'cause it's wing was all mangled-like. But he couldn't do that either and I sure as hell couldn't 'cause if you ever looked at a crow in the eye, they're real smart birds and they look back at you like they know something about you, and having some bird knowing something about me can be more information than I care to have out there, if you know what I mean. That crow put up an awful fuss, but John wrapped it in his coat and we took it home and healed it up. It never could fly, but it made a good pet and John became a vegetarian after that, never shot his gun again. He told me the crow made him make that promise. He was the smartest damn bird you ever saw 'til John's cat got him one day. John was really sorry about that. He even cried a bit. He said the crow was like his guardian angel and now that it was gone, he'd have a rough time of things. John liked to plant things; he didn't even like logging much…" Jim's losing it and leaves the stage carrying the guitar by the neck like he doesn't want it to touch his body.

As if on cue, Star turns to me and says, "Let's get the hell out of here; this is too much."

Zen seems to wobble a bit as he stands up.

"You're in no shape to hitch-hike, Zen."

He laughs, telling us that he's buying the dinner and beer with the last of his cash.

It is a good thing, too, since I'm down to twelve dollars. We all thank him and when we settle at the counter, I look at the table by the entrance and it's empty and already cleaned off. I feel much relief. The creepy logger types are gone and now we're ready to head west as a group back to I-5 and north toward Bellingham to figure out what happened, what we're going do with the rest of our lives.

We step through the door into the warm July evening. Already the stars are flooding the sky with shimmering veins of cosmic glory. Life may once again be good. The evening air refreshes, though there is the faintest odor of tobacco smoke. It's only when we're well across the gravel lot nearing Elvis that things suddenly feel weird. Somebody coughs close by; the cigarette smoke is stronger. A voice with crystal clear familiarity startles me as it says, "You sure you don't wanna buy one of my shirts, hippie?"

Twenty-five

They say when you're face to face with a grizzly bear, you never want to look her in the eye or she will interpret it as a challenge. Instead you're supposed to talk to her gently while looking at the ground, slowly backing away until you're able to move quickly away from the area without provoking a charge.

"Do I know you from somewhere?" I ask, staring at my shoes. A quick glance up shows me that the man who has materialized from the shadows with four other shadowy hulking figures is the bitter-looking dude with the lumpy head from Arcata. Ollie, Star and Zen are now standing very close to me.

"You're preservationists, aren't cha?" he sneers. "Never do forget a face, you worthless fucks."

I'm sweating like a televangelist at St. Peter's Gate. "I've never seen you before, man. We don't want trouble. We've had a really rough tour and just want to go back to Bellingham and get on with our lives."

"Bellingham?" he snarls. "Where the fuck is Bellingham?"

"Up by the Canadian Border," says a shadowy guy behind him. "I got a cousin who lives up there."

"Bellingham's a nice town," says Ollie suddenly. "Did you know that it was actually three towns just seventy five years ago. Squalicum to the north, Fairhaven to the south, and right in the middle, good old Bellingham. I've been there about fifteen years and have seen a lot of changes—not all good mind you—but nobody wants to change, really, though when you think about it, the past only has power over you if you let it."

Lumpy head seems to have trouble following him, but politely lets him finish. He says, "I heard you sing *America the Beautiful*, but you can't fool me you tree-huggin' piece of shit. Far as I'm concerned, you just put us out of jobs." Suddenly we're surrounded, all of them moving in closer.

"We're only musicians," says Star. "We've been on tour to keep a buzz going."

"Jack knows about keeping a buzz going," says another shadowy guy and they all laugh. They're slowly closing in.

"Look, I really just want to go home, now," mumbles Zen.

"Oh, you do, huh?" says lumpy head, as he turns to a shadow his left. "You wanna escort this gentleman to his car?"

"Why, I most certainly would." With mock kindness, the shadow walks over to Zen and holds out his hand. "Name's Jack Williams," he says in a super-friendly tone.

"Zen Goodman," Zen says. "Nice to meet you."

"Nice to meet you, too," says Jack, smiling as he looks at his buddies. He's flexing his hands, which is not a good sign. "That your rig over there?" He points to Elvis.

"Yeah, it sure is," says Zen. "I kind of need to lie down in it. I'm not feeling so good."

"What's the problem, Zen?" asks Jack. "Our food doesn't sit well with ya?" Zen holds his head down and the shadow bends over to look up at him; he stands just inches away. "You don't look so good."

"I don't?" Zen asks before Jack slams him hard in the gut, the blow lifting him a foot off the ground. In a loud "*Hoooaaah!*" Zen reciprocates by sending a coffee-colored stream of partially digested French fries in a frothy bath of warm beer right back in Jack's face. Soaking wet and fizzing, steam pours off him. If I wasn't scared shitless I'd be laughing like hell. Zen collapses in a heap while Star screams. Puke-soaked Jack runs off spitting and swearing; soon he, too, is retching somewhere out there in the dark.

The other shadows are laughing hard at their friend, but there's big trouble brewing. The only question is who's gonna get it the worst, and that's when I notice for the first time that Star doesn't seem so cocky. Although her face remains calm, her eyes are dark with fear. She pulls out her can of chew and begins tapping it.

Lumpy head and the three other shadows stop laughing and one bums a chew off Star as if it's the most natural thing in the world, and while the shadow spits the others just stare, and in a way that tells me that she might be in some serious danger. Lumpy head says, "A guy could really have some fun with a good looking, tree-hugger like you."

Star just works the chew under her lip, staring at him. There is a hint of a smile on her lips, but she says nothing.

Lumpy head moves a little closer toward us and while looking at me, he asks, "This your bitch?"

"Am I his *bitch*!?" she asks, astonished. "Come on you wussy motherfuckers, I'll take you *all* on!"

"You're pretty spunky, there girl," he whispers. "Careful for what you wish for."

This triggers an Ollie monologue involving the story of how Star almost broke his neck during an argument after I tried to buy our way onto a bill down in Berkeley and that they are ill advised to be messing with her, given how crazy she can be even on a good day. But lumpy head's hardly listening. He just kind of smiles and stares at her.

Then there is a sound like a sack of flour being thumped. Zen is collapsed in a heap with the shadow named Jack kicking him. Before I can move to help him my arms are wrestled back by strong, unseen hands and my shoulders feel like they're being ripped out of the sockets. I hear a weird sound and turn in time to see Ollie being wrestled to the ground and everywhere is the sound of laughter and yelling. Star is backing up as the shadows descend upon her, her face white like I've never seen. I really can't believe this is happening until something crashes into the side of my head and everything becomes all slow-motion and warm-like.

The side of my face burns and I wonder if I've just been shot, and I think what a terrible way to end a tour. There is more screaming but it's not Star because she's still slowly backing up, lumpy head and his shadow friends following her. I holler for her to run but she doesn't and lumpy head turns to me laughing all psycho-like and I can't believe there's nobody else around.

"Run, Star!" someone screams, and it's me, but she doesn't listen. She's still backing up, stress lines formed around her mouth like when she's going off on some crazy solo.

"Leave her alone!" someone screams, and it's not me. It's Star. She makes her third person command again and the shadows look at her a bit strangely.

Then a weird singing fills the night air and the billions of stars lend a strange peacefulness to this rapidly deteriorating night. It sounds like a pack of coyotes.

The chaos has stopped and there is only the sound of wind in the trees and the distant chorus of laughter or clapping coming from the restaurant. The coyotes have stopped singing. Though unseen arms still hold me tightly, I sense the shadows are clearly spooked. Something tells me not to struggle.

When the coyotes start up again they sound closer. Lumpy head turns. "What the...?" But it's not coyotes. It's something else, coming from behind a wild juniper adjacent to Elvis. I notice that Elvis' door is ajar. Did I leave it open?

The night is flooded with a fury of lights as a red Camaro comes flying across the lot toward us. There is a horrible screech as a door opens. I turn to see Star squirming between two of the shadows who have picked her up by the arms and are trying to force her into the car. I kick and struggle with the arms holding me, while panic and nausea wash over me.

Star's scream sounds nothing like I've ever heard. She pleads for them to stop, shaking her head back and forth wildly while her long legs whip those hard-heeled boots outward, trying desperately to connect with a leg, a shin...anything.

But the shadows are too strong; they almost have her in the car. I scream for help, but a fat hand covers my mouth and a quick glance tells me Ollie is in the same position. "We'll see you up at the falls," says lumpy head to the other shadows.

Star has now managed to force her legs against the outer edges of the door; her exertion is weirdly muffled due the leathery hand over her mouth. It's like we're all drowning and the horror is so great that I'm starting to float above the scene, thinking I'm at the movies. Then I'm back in reality, though screaming underwater where no one can hear me.

The sound of coyotes is back and getting louder. But it isn't coyotes. The sound now is clearly a saxophone, and I know it's Walter even before he comes walking around the side of Elvis, hunched over the instrument like a musical shaman, gliding evenly on his legs, staring at us all wild-eyed, though with an unbelievable calm about him. The shadows stand motionless while he circles us very slowly playing something so haunting it could never be described. The scene rivals any fable ever told about snake charmers in India. The music has stopped the action. When an Indian playing beautiful saxophone music shows up as a woman is about to be raped, it kind of goes without saying that no one knows what to do.

It's the Camaro driver who finally decides what to do. He guns the engine sending a torrent of gravel and dust high in the air while the car careens wildly across the lot and onto highway 50 westbound.

Walter plays and continues circling slowly and I feel the steel hands pinching me slowly relax as I am able to step away from my captor. I think I hear him crying, but I'm not sure. The saxophone wails, rising and falling in pitch and I think of Rembrandt contemplating the last painting he left on earth, something about a prodigal son and I realize that I'm numb and stunned and just want to go back to Bellingham. I can make no sense out of this turn of events except that we've somehow got to get out of here fast. And the opportunity is now.

As Walter circles, I go over to Zen, and slowly pick his sack-of-flour body up off of the gravel and brush him off a bit before half carrying him to Elvis and up the welcoming steps. When I go back to get the others I notice that they're all frozen like we're in some sort of mime play or trance. Even Star, who was just moments away from horrors unknown, is watching Walter. Though the tears are pouring down her face, she makes no sound.

Meanwhile Ollie has been released as well and he's white-faced and silent. I try to take Star's arm, but for some reason she won't move—probably shock. Ollie, however, responds when I touch him, and after leading him back to Elvis, I go to get Star. The shadows are fully focused on Walter and they don't look so evil anymore. Now I see their faces, taut and sunken, their eyes betraying a deep shame. They almost look human again. As long as Walter keeps playing they don't seem able to move. We've been given an opportunity to get out of here and we've got to go fast before they come to their senses and realize what cruel assholes they truly are.

Walter looks at me and as our eyes connect, I feel something ancient stir in my soul. When I try to pull Star gently toward Elvis, she snaps out of her trance and walks over to lumpy head. Though it looks like she only touches him on the neck, he screams, grabbing his head as he falls to the gravel.

"I told you not to fuck with the goddess," she hisses, finishing him off with a lightening karate kick to the face. He writhes in the dust, groaning and twitching.

Then it's all commotion again and we're running with Walter toward Elvis and we do make it aboard before our assailants have come to their senses. I'm searching frantically for the keys as fists rain down on Elvis's sides. He fires up, but when I jam my foot on the accelerator to peel out, he dies. I fumble with the key. The engine catches. I jam it in drive and we're on our way.

Cruising madly across the lot toward Route 50, I notice a few people finally coming out of the restaurant—though no one seems to know what just happened. As we begin climbing up the highway, I see headlights coming up behind us fast and I know it's not over yet.

I wish like hell we were back in Bellingham, chilling out at La Pinata, and that we'd never signed that stupid contract with Sunny because staying local is okay, even if guys like Jed were still tuning my guitars because even hands covered with greasy venison are way better than those hands that had me around my throat and now I miss Angel immensely, not because the babe can sing like no other, but because in spite of all the conspiracies that plague her, she is and will always be my sister from Bellingham. Just being from Bellingham somehow makes up for everything and we're not victims anyway; we're just The Cosmic Poets, and things like this are bound to happen to a band with a name like ours.

Twenty-six

On tour…the home stretch. Perhaps we'll be the first band ever to do a West Coast tour without playing a gig. The black pick-up has turned away after following us for a few miles. No Hollywood drama on a steep mountain highway with Elvis being run off the road. No big chase scene with guys hanging onto the outside before plunging thousands of feet to their deaths as we careen around a corner. No lumpy-headed antagonists in a final showdown between good and evil. No, nothing like that. The punks are gone leaving us shattered and alone, limping slowly up an empty California highway in the middle of the night.

Things have calmed a little. Ollie is babbling on about having a weird feeling about those guys sitting at that table. Star's black silhouette is isolated and unmoving in the back though I'm sure she's still crying. The rage of being assaulted is all we can deal with for now. But one fact of life to which we are all intimately bound is that Walter has mysteriously appeared back into our lives, saving us from horrors unknown. He is now in the back with Star, talking with her quietly. Zen is sobering up and Ollie retells the story of Zen puking all over the guy who punched him and how Star blinded her assailant with a bull's eye shot of spit right in the eyes. Now I can't stop laughing, though my hands are shaking worse than at the Ballard Firehouse when I couldn't find that stupid guitar pick. Though I fear that we're not out of danger, I pull over on the deserted highway under a silver, inverse carpet of stars. We all get out and hold each other. We could have lost everything back there, but right now the people I'm standing with are real human beings. As Walter joins our circle, Star turns to him and puts her arm around his neck, squeezing him lightly. She says nothing.

We got off easy, and now everything is absurd. And why bother with explanations anyway; better save one's breath and write it down later. Even the earth's landscape has become ridiculously altered: clear cut scars slashing everywhere across her, obscured from space by a brown sheen as millions of people hurry everywhere quickly to get nowhere fast. And art, the organ of life in all cultures, the one constant that shows up even in places like the Twin Bridges Logger's Memorial, is tainted by bitter people so full of hate that even Bellingham doesn't seem far enough away. Oh well, we'll be one less band choking the airwaves and that's all right with me; Walter's music is what's powerful. At least somebody in the world gets it. There's no point in calling the cops, either.

Elvis is getting low on gas and when I see the sign for Lake Tahoe, I realize that we took a wrong turn as we were being chased out of the parking lot and now that we're about forty miles east of Twin Bridges, we might as well keep going.

"We're on our way to Tahoe," I inform the crew. "It doesn't make sense to turn back now."

"You mean, we're going the wrong way?" asks Zen. "I want to go back to Bellingham."

"We'll drop down to Reno and then drive north," I say, unable to break it to them that the twelve dollars I have left will probably get us a little North of Reno, but that's it. The rest will have to take care of itself. Only one thing matters now and that's finding another side road that feels safe enough to park for the night and as if the cosmos hears my plea, I see a turn off on Crystal Creek Road, #253. I pull onto it and we take it almost a mile, winding through forests interspersed with open areas, which are probably clear cuts. I find another side spur road, which winds away and out of sight, dead-ending in a parking place under some dark pines. This will have to do for the night. There is much to reflect upon. Much to figure out. One thing is for sure. Things have changed. Come tomorrow things will be different and now Walter's past words about history having no control of one's destiny ring true, and I wish I could apologize to Star for all of the creeps who've ever lived. Instead I silently bed down, trying not to think about what a whore I've become during this big push. I do not want to face the shallowness in myself. Tomorrow's a new day. I'll figure it all out tomorrow.

Twenty-seven

Once upon a time, a guy named Larry lived in Bellingham. He had frizzy, long hair, a Jean jacket and pants that he never changed. He also had a whole bunch of amplifiers and guitars, including his prized Les Paul that he carried everywhere with him. Day or night, you'd see him walking the streets of Bellingham carrying that damn guitar like he had some important place to be, some gig or something, but you'd know he never did. He'd just show up at the end of shows and ask real quietly if he could plug his guitar into an amp and play. I'd always tell him it was okay as long as he didn't turn it on, and he never did. It was enough for him just plugging in, and when he did, he would get so into it that he'd break into a big sweat. I knew in his mind the crowd was going wild. He seemed to be happy during those moments, and it's a good thing to make a guy like Larry happy whenever you can.

Most people, if they even noticed a guy like Larry, could never understand him. He didn't talk much, though he did seem to like it when people stopped by his apartment to borrow his gear. It made him feel useful, I guess. One time I stopped by and he was cooking some canned beans over a can of Sterno. I was amazed at all the instruments and amps scattered everywhere and as we sat in the midst of all the garbage and newspapers, he offered to split his dinner with me. I said, "No thanks, Larry." That was the only time I ever saw him smile. It was a rather sad smile that I remember.

~

I am alone. The arena is dark and everyone has gone home. I stand stage right, contemplating my naked guitar in its stand. Twenty yards away a wasteland of empty plastic cups and other garbage is scattered carelessly across the stage. My heart pounds loudly in my ears; I've anticipated this moment all of my life. How could it be so…empty? The people must be out there in the dark, somewhere.

Alone, white light emanating from a naked bulb hanging from the darkness above illuminating my guitar, I know it is my time. I walk forward. The great audition, the great arrival. There is no thundering introduction over the giant sound system, probably because the emcee has gone home, too. After all, it's late. The show's over and it's my turn.

Looking out at the dark stage I see Larry appear. He motions me towards my guitar, helping me with the strap. I plug in and strum, but there is no sound. The sound crew has gone home, too. There have to be some people out there. I begin playing to the void before me and the song is over in seconds. As the notes ring out into the emptiness, there is no clapping—though I'm hearing some quiet voices. There are people here, thank goodness. I try another song, this one kind of quiet. It's over right away too—still nobody clapping, still some people talking. In fact, it sounds like more people are showing up. This may be an okay gig after all.

I try another song, one I'm sure will win somebody over, but when it ends, same result, though it now sounds like there's quite a crowd milling about in front of me. I can't see them yet. I'm not sure if they can see me, either. They almost certainly can't hear me.

"Hey, how are you guys doing tonight," I say. There is no response, but I know I'm supposed to keep playing. The talking is getting louder and this is getting unreasonable.

"What do you guys want?" I ask the void. "Something fast or slow?"

A purple light shining down from behind me illuminates an individual wearing black leather, chains and a Mohawk. He stands up quickly as he realizes that the spotlight's on him. "Fast!" he snipes.

"Shut up. I'll play what I like."

"How about some folk music," says an older fellow nearer to the front. "That's good stuff, you know."

"You shut up, too. I'll play what I want to play."

"Play bluegrass, man," says a hippie. "That's real music."

"How about the first song I ever wrote?" I ask. "Don't you remember how I used to play it all the time and how it kept me from blowing my brains out?"

"Fuck your brains!" yells a punk in a Bull's shirt.

"Fuck *your* brains!" I yell back as I begin strumming, but there's no sound coming from the speaker stacks. "What's the problem Larry?" I ask.

Larry's not listening. He's hunched over a can of Sterno cooking baked beans and singing to himself.

"Does anybody hear me?" I feel a cold wind on me and it's because I'm wearing no clothes.

"Nobody hears you," says a guy sitting in the front row. "You need a genre."

"What's that?"

"It's a ticket to an exclusive club."

"Can I get in?"

"Not the way you're dressed, man. You need clothes and an image. Preferably angry, but indifferent will do. Sorry pal, you're too…too plain. At least get your nose pierced."

"Yeah, but if I did that I'd look like every one else."

"That's the idea, Angus. Now play us some music."

Now a dude dressed in a black trench coat reveals an Uzi and whispers loudly, "Gangsta, homey."

This is, without question, the most diverse crowd I've ever played in front of—I hate them all.

"How 'bout some real stuff like Phil Ochs, or Nick Drake?"

"Angus, Frank Strong here," says a tiny, dwarf-like guy standing up in the front row. "Don't waste my time with that mellow stuff. I'm talkin' to the big fish, and the big fish like the big sound. Know what I mean, pal?"

"Hey, Angus," says Angel looking dangerously pale. "No decent person with any integrity would have treated his worst enemy the way you've treated me…And after all I've given to you."

"How 'bout some Floyd?" asks a fat guy in the front row. Wow, there are actually a lot of people showing up here. If I could just play them a song.

"Here's a song that really means a lot to me," I say. There are several thousand people now sitting in the seats and I see the lighters coming on. "See, I wrote this after my girlfriend dumped me for her softball coach, and I wasn't feeling so good. I wandered around Bellingham for days, trying to understand why she—"

A bottle lands on the stage, shattering in a thousand pieces. Larry's all over it, sweeping it up. I hear Angel somewhere out there, laughing.

"Don't you even care that I can't remember whether or not the flowers blossomed one spring?" I plead, but the crowd is now booing me.

"Get a genre!" someone yells.

"Sting, man. Play something good!"

"Why are you all so mean?" I strum the guitar, but there is no sound, and when I look over at Larry, he's changed. He's laughing at me and his head is lumpy. "How come you never bought one of my shirts hippie?" His face is gray and mottled with large purplish slabs of skin sloughing off. The stench of decomposing flesh wallops me like a hot desert wind and I scream and hands are grabbing me from behind and I'm thrown to the floor with people climbing on top of me and I can't breathe…

I hear Ollie and Star in the distance, yelling, and I know they're trying to save me, but it may be too late.

"Wake up, wake up," I hear Star say, and now she's on top of me and she's crying as I open my eyes, understanding that I've been dreaming, though things will never again be the same and that it may be a good thing 'cause you can only be phony for so long before you start wishing for a simple life in your home town where everybody is a hero just for being alive. I hold Star and she cries herself back to sleep, and soon I hear others sleeping as well and I'm feeling a great relief. I fall into a deep and dreamless sleep, knowing that starting all over again will be a good thing. It always is.

Twenty-eight

It seems like we've been climbing for hours when another horn sounds from behind us. "Shit." I pull off onto the shoulder while a stream of thirty cars that had been backed up behind us for a mile whiz past, some honking and shooting us the bird. I smile and wave back. It's good to be alive.

We are nearing Lake Tahoe and are in a weird, alpine condo-land with strip malls and ski resorts, and soon when we cross the Nevada State Line we'll be in casinoville as well. Star is having a great time retelling the story of how she floored lumpy head with her death grip, and insists that she wasn't really even that scared since she knew the Force would protect her and, besides, they were all wussies and she could have killed a couple of them if she really wanted. Of course Walter's timing wasn't half-bad, and by the way, he had a lot of nerve holding out on us with his saxophone playing and all.

Zen insists that it was his well-timed vomiting that threw them all off and that his older sister had taught him how to spontaneously regurgitate at any time, a ploy he used to go home sick from grade school.

People's spirits are surprisingly strong, and I'm feeling a weird giddiness, yet struck by a deep sense of tragedy. Walter's presence is welcomed and there is a kindness that has returned, though no one dares verbalize what happened and what was said during that bitter blow out. Finally, when Star asks Walter how he cultivated such amazing musical talents, Walter decides it's time for us to hear his story…

Walter Simon was born in Fort Yukon, Alaska on June 12, 1952 to Rita and Dennis Simon. Dennis's blood lines were Lakota while Rita was a full-blooded Gwich'in from Arctic Village, sixty air miles north of Fort Yukon.

When she was only nine, Rita's father was killed in a bush plane accident and despite the protests of the Gwich'in Elders from Arctic Village, Rita was forced into a white foster home. Eventually she would find herself at the Chemewah Indian Boarding School in central Oregon where she would meet her future husband, Dennis.

They both moved back to Fort Yukon to get married. Dennis fell deep into an alcohol-induced despondency shortly after Walter's second sister was born. Eventually Dennis would commit suicide, leaving Rita to fend for the children. But the seven-hundred-dollar-a-month welfare check from the government wasn't cutting it, and she too fell deep into alcoholism and despair. Eventually the Government intervened, forcing the children into white foster homes, one of which would take Walter south to Anchorage where, at age eleven, he moved in with the Jones family.

They lived in a cul-de-sac in a suburban Anchorage housing development and Walter was enrolled at St. Francis Catholic School. Though he became a bit of a loner and was very shy, Walter was smart and knew how to play the game, cultivating an image of himself that would draw the least attention. His foster parents were nice to him and took care of his basic needs, but Walter missed his mother terribly. He learned to hide his feelings well.

It was his music teacher, Samuel Brennan who sparked Walter's interest and curiosity in music—namely, his interest in the saxophone. In fact, Samuel was very flattered at Walter's requests to attend the Anchorage Jazz Society rehearsals, which Samuel directed. Walter also became a good friend with Samuel's son, Bill, who, like Walter, was kind of shy. Samuel eventually started giving Walter private lessons twice a week for the two years prior to Walter's forced departure to the Chemewah Boarding School.

Samuel was astounded at Walter's natural musical instincts and abilities, but was concerned that Walter lacked the discipline to take his ambitions very far. This was partially due to the fact that Walter began getting into trouble and was arrested at age thirteen for burglary.

Walter wondered to this day why they assumed that he had no discipline when the only love and sanity in his life was music. "I actually got pretty good by the time I was fourteen. Not everything came easy for me, but for some reason music did."

After being sent to Chemewah, things only got worse for him, and soon he was a full-blown drug and alcohol addict. After a couple of years he ran away, and over a year's time of drifting and living on the streets of Portland and Seattle, he found himself back in Anchorage.

One day while Walter was panhandling downtown, Samuel Brennan passed him by complete coincidence. This serendipitous occurrence almost happened without either recognizing the other. Walter had gained weight, and his clothes were ragged and worn. Samuel had aged. He seemed heavy hearted and weary. It was he who recognized Walter after Walter had asked him for some spare change. Samuel broke down, crying. He told Walter the sad news that his son, Bill, Walter's one-time friend, had died in an accident earlier that winter. While snowmobiling with a buddy, they ran out of gas, dying of exposure. Alcohol was a contributing factor. "Don't kill yourself, too," Samuel had told Walter with tears in his eyes.

Walter described how upon hearing this, he felt something awaken in his own spirit. He sobered up. A few days later, Samuel approached him again, and handed him a saxophone case with the instrument inside. "This was Bill's," he had said. "It was custom made by Roy McCallister in Seattle. Bill would have wanted you to have it." And after saying this, Samuel just walked away and that was the last Walter ever saw of him.

He did keep the saxophone. In fact, he kept it for two years and as he began playing it, he got active in Alcoholics Anonymous. He also busked on the downtown sidewalks for quite awhile, earning good money. Then one day when he was feeling particularly good, he skipped his daily meeting and went out to The Igloo Bar and Grill for a few drinks. He ran into Kip Vandeman who had just scored some outrageously strong black tar heroin.

The next day Walter sold Bill's custom made saxophone to a pawnshop for seventy-seven dollars.

"It was worth a hell of a lot more than that, I tell you," he says, sadly.

"How much?" I ask, wondering if I really want to know.

"A saxophone made by Roy might go for twenty grand. It wasn't just the money, either."

"No shit?" says Star, astonished. "You sold it for seventy-seven dollars?"

"Yeah, just the price of a hangover, and a good shot of black tar. I've never forgiven myself for that one." He pauses. "When the country called for 'Nam, I was ready. I just kind of hoped that I'd go over there and die, really. When I got back and found myself still alive, I had to figure out all over again what I was going to do with my life. I didn't want to live, and I didn't care what happened to me."

He got even more heavily into drugs and alcohol and tried to take his life a couple of times, messing up each attempt. He opted for the slow slide into drug and alcohol oblivion. Eventually, he moved down to Seattle and after reading about some of the riots over fishing rights down at Frank's Landing in Thurston County, he decided to get involved. That's when he decided to sober up. For the time being, at least, he had some purpose in his life. At a Pow Wow, he met his future wife Victoria La Cruz, a Hispanic and Chippewa from Southern New Mexico, and they got married and moved back to South Dakota so that Walter could be closer to his relatives. In a span of five years, she bore twin girls. One died at age six. Walter started drinking again and within a year he was on his own. Victoria had left him, taking his daughter with her.

"I haven't seen them since," he says, sadly. "I was teaching the little one to play the cello. She was gonna be good too, I could tell."

Walter had spent that night he left us wandering through a dark, dripping forest, and later had a vision that we were about to have some major trouble. He caught a ride east but it was only by the greatest coincidence that he found us by noticing Elvis parked in the back of the lot of the Twin Bridges Cafe with her side door wide open.

Did I leave it open? I really doubt it. Walter asked the fellow giving him a ride to let him out. He was just going to climb in and catch some sleep before surprising us. Then he heard the commotion.

He joked that even when Star was being forced toward the car, he really felt sorry for the punks who were abducting her.

Star smiles and praises his eloquent saxophone skills, stating that she had never in her life heard music as powerful as his, and the moment she heard it, she knew that divine powers were interceding on our behalf and things would turn out okay. But when Star asks Walter what happened to him back in Arcata, he only shakes his head, saying, "What's done is done. The past has no more power."

We have decided to try and make Reno by evening, to possibly drive north from there before finding a deserted side road to bed down. I am now completely out of money as the twelve bucks have gone into Elvis's tank. But it's one mile at a time and anything's possible. I know that I'll have to call Sunny later and tell her what's really going on. I don't care what she says anymore. I just hope I get all my money back. When I think of Lily, a dullness sweeps over me. I ache for her, but know it's for the best that she's out of the picture.

Another muffled horn blares from behind and I turn into a pullout so we can all take a urine break. Afterwards Zen sits in the passenger seat next to me and we cross the Nevada State Line, climbing through a surreal, alpine suburbia toward the pass after which we will descend several thousand feet down into the desert, and on to Reno.

Twenty-nine

Weren't you just scared shitless?"

Zen just looks at me, eyes gray with sadness. We drive on for awhile longer in silence.

"Seems I've hardly talked to you at all lately," I finally say. "Isn't that weird?"

"I don't know." He sounds like he's deep in thought, too. "Maybe it isn't weird. You seem to avoid talking to me for some reason."

It's true. There's a quietness about him that reminds me of myself, the ever-changing chameleon. It's easy to project a warm ambivalence while those around you carry on without knowing you're observing them. You leave them with a false comfort that you're just kind of simple; they think you don't notice the little things.

"I guess I do, Zen," I sigh. "I'm always afraid that if I ask you what you're thinking, you'll tell me that you're going to quit the band and the fact is you're my favorite musician. What the hell you were thinking about last night as you were getting your head kicked in?"

He looks at me, and I notice his lower lip is puffed out. Star's got him hooked. He spits into a paper cup and looks at me and he's smiling. "I was amazed at how full of shit everybody is. That's about it, really. Oh, and how I wish I would have had my pistol handy; those bastards would've been really sorry."

"You pack heat?" I asked, shocked.

"Yeah, but who would've thought it would be needed on our West Coast Tour."

"Some tour, eh?"

"Hey, it looked good on paper. You shouldn't have lied to us about it, though."

"I know. I really thought Sunny and Frank were gonna pull off a miracle."

"I doubt Frank Strong even exists."

"It's funny you say that, Zen. I didn't tell you that I talked to Sunny on the phone back at Twin Bridges and she claimed that there were A&R people at Rock City who absolutely loved us. They're flying out with Frank to the Battle of Seattle at the Showbox."

"See? She's full of shit."

"Not so fast. Sunny said that they thought *we* were The Caustic Poets. She even brought up the name, not me. That means they were there. And to further the humiliation, Sunny said that they liked Groovetribe a lot."

He looks at me in wonder. "Really?"

"I kid you not, Zen. Sunny even asked why we didn't play anything off the demo. Turns out it didn't matter but still, that kind of proves it, doesn't it?

"That's incredible." Zen sighs. "Just figures with our luck, too. Time to move on to other things, I guess."

"But the Showbox gig…It's in four days. Shouldn't we show up and play? At least see what happens with the labels there?"

"Do we really even have a gig there?" asks Zen. "No offense, but after lying about the tour and all."

"We really do, Zen. Sorry for leading you guys on before."

"It almost got me killed. I know you did it for the band, but I gotta be honest: there's too much fighting. I just want a simple country life with Linda and the goats."

"You're really lucky to have a good woman," I say. "Good goats, too."

"You're still hanging onto Lily, aren't you?"

"I guess I am." *Perhaps I was too harsh on her. I do miss her terribly and who knows, maybe a Pirsig self-help novel might do me some good. Maybe if she knew how serious I was about changing myself.* "We should do the Showbox gig, Zen; it may be our last chance."

"You gotta let go of it all," says Zen, true to his name. "You've got no control over anything, anyway. This Battle of Seattle sounds like a bunch of competition crap. We should do music for the love of it. You're always trying to win the prize, Mr. Nonconformist. Don't you think you're being a tad ironic?"

"We've got four days to think it over," I say, wanting to avoid the question. "It's not about competition anymore. It's about completion and closure."

"And then what?" says Zen, suddenly angry. "A few more bones tossed our way, stringing us along? A few more hopes to be dashed? The odds of breaking things wide open are minuscule. The music's good but people don't want to hear the truth. People want to be distracted. You're too heavy. Just look at your idol, Nick Drake. He never made a dime off his music. It's all about marketing, Angus. You know that."

I'm stunned. I think I might take what he's saying as a compliment, but I'm not sure if I should. Suddenly I'm back in a dark arena arguing with nameless drones from the void.

"Remember Larry?" I ask. He immediately laughs. There was only one Larry back in Bellingham worthy of remembrance.

"What ever happened to him? He was a pretty wild dude."

"I had a dream about him last night. It was the strangest thing. He was the stage manager for this big arena gig. But there was hardly anybody there."

"Sound's like our gig at Arcata," laughs Zen.

"Think about the Showbox, Zen. I have a feeling it may turn out differently than we think."

"You're hanging on to the bitter end, aren't you?" he shrugs. "We'll see what happens." But I know he's only saying this for my benefit.

~

Down, down, down we descend the asphalt switchbacks toward Reno, shimmering in the late afternoon desert sun like a piece of fake, plastic jewelry. Nonetheless, it serves as a beacon from which we'll turn northward back to Bellingham and now that there's a mountain range between us and trouble, things are looking better. That is until I look at Elvis's gas gauge that is barely hovering above empty. I know it will go up a little more once we hit the flat, but still, barring divine intervention, we're not going much farther than Reno. We need a plan.

Soon we're racing across the flat lands of the desert, and into the suburbs and casino neon is popping up everywhere. As we pass the WELCOME TO RENO sign, Ollie screams suddenly, "Pull the car over, *now!*

Star, pushes him roughly. "What the hell are you talking about?"

"Pull over!" he screams again.

"What are you talking about, you freak?" Zen yells toward the back.

"Pull the car over *now!*"

Frightened, I obey. Perhaps he's getting sick or something.

Elvis coasts to a halt on the shoulder of the freeway while Star cusses him out.

"Did you see that Tom Jones is playing at Harrah's?" Ollie asks, excitedly.

"That's what this is about?" I ask as Walter starts laughing. Star is not amused.

"Have you ever seen him live?" asks Ollie. "When I was nine years old, we were on a trip through the Sierras and he was playing up at Tahoe. My mom talked Dad into taking us. To this day, it was one of the best live shows I've ever seen. Did you know that *Delilah* was one of the biggest hits?"

"You gonna come up with the tickets?" I ask.

"We can just hang out in the back of Harrah's," he begs. "A roadie might let us in. It's happened to me before."

"But Ollie," I say, "the show probably doesn't start for a couple of hours."

"Angus?" Star asks. "Do you have a plan? Does anybody?"

Zen laughs, shaking his head as he looks at me. "How much money do we have left in the band fund?"

Why did you have to ruin a perfectly good moment, Zen?

"None," I say, quietly. "I should have told you awhile ago that we weren't gonna have enough money to get home on but with all the distractions and stuff…" My voice trails off. Elvis rocks silently in the wind of passing cars and trucks.

"We're out of money?" asks Star quietly. "You lied about the money, too?"

"Star," I say, "I never lied about money. I just never told everybody how much we had. We might be in a little better shape if we didn't drive back and forth across Oregon a few days ago looking for Angel. I had the credit card as a back up, but thanks to Sunny and the Boss, it's all a bit irrelevant. I'm only trying to live in the moment so cut me some slack."

Zen estimates that we have about five gallons of fuel left in Elvis which might get us another thirty five to forty miles depending on traffic. We sit contemplating our situation and now Ollie's plan doesn't sound quite as goofy as it did a few moments before.

"What were you gonna do, just drive until we ran out of gas?" asks Star in disbelief.

"As a matter of fact, Star, I was trying not to think about it. I figured we'd deal with it when it happened."

Star just shakes her head, socking Walter on the shoulder. "Can you believe this guy?"

He laughs, and when he does I know things are gonna be all right. Maybe that's the secret. One needs to laugh a lot at everything. After all, almost everything in life is hilarious if you know how to look at it.

We pull back onto the freeway and soon we're driving back through the neon flash and glimmer of early evening Reno. All the cars on the street seem new and shiny. Horns blare and each green light is greeted with thundering acceleration—like there's not a second to be wasted when all that luck and good fortune are on the line, all those casinos with their perpetually smiling dealers begging for your hard-earned cash.

After several wrong turns, we pull up next to Harrah's. The giant marquee with blinking white and red rotating lights reads: An Evening With Tom Jones Tonight 8:00 P.M.

Ollie is very excited; besides, what else is there to do? Go run out of gas out in the desert somewhere and then get my head kicked in by Star?

There's a long line of shapeless, well-dressed couples stretching for almost a block. The men all seem to be wearing baggy shirts and slacks; all seem to have a little glow about them. Knowing that their wives will soon be swept away by the charismatic, tight-curled gentleman wearing an open neck shirt and shimmering silver medallion, this could be their lucky night.

We finally park Elvis, but we're a good five blocks away from Harrah's and I'm hungry. Nobody talks about food as we saunter up the humid street. Ollie has a certain cockiness about him. Here we are in Reno: flat broke, dressed like slobs, hungry as hell and on our way to a Tom Jones concert, where rather than tickets we have, in our midst, a musical shaman with amazing powers and a damn keen sense of irony. People seem to stare at us as if we're from a foreign land. In a way, I suppose we are.

"Sure beats last night."

"I'm hungry," says Star. "I knew I should have brought my credit card. You really blew this one, Angus." It's almost as if she's now saying it out of habit, resigned that we are now forced to live moment to moment and that trying to sneak into a Tom Jones concert in Reno beats getting murdered by a bunch of morons.

As we cross the street to Harrah's, Ollie leads us up the block and away from the crowd and we enter an alley in back. He takes us to a couple of iron doors with a staircase adorned with cheap red carpet leading up to them. "We'll wait here," he says. There's no one else around, which is surprising, and Ollie believes that Mr. Jones has already arrived and is inside. Still, we must be patient, he says.

We wait for about twenty minutes with no action. Star is growing visibly agitated. Then one of the doors opens and a brown-haired kid in a ponytail and a trace of goatee emerges with a bucket of ice water. After excusing himself, he pitches it onto the pavement. He turns back to the door when Ollie kind of blocks his way. The kid looks frightened.

"How's it going tonight?" asks Ollie, as we all stand in silent amazement.

Thirty

Pretty good," the kid says, obviously trying to conceal his nerves. "I don't think you're supposed to be out here. They're only letting people in the front."

"Don't worry, we're not dangerous or anything," whispers Star. "We're just here meet Mr. Jones. He knows we're coming."

"Yeah, right," says the kid. "You and a thousand others."

"We're a rock band from Bellingham, Washington," says Ollie. "Do you know where Bellingham is?"

"I think I've heard of it."

"Yeah, we're just north of Seattle. You know about Seattle? Home of Pearl Jam, Soundgarden, and Nirvana?"

"Yeah, Seattle's rad. I'm down with the Northwest, dude. You playing somewhere in Reno?"

"Not exactly," says Ollie, who then proceeds to tell the kid how we went out on tour to get famous while Frank Strong was pitching us to the major labels and things didn't go so well mainly because I lied about the tour to keep Frank from pulling the plug, but it didn't matter anyway since we ended up getting screwed over in Arcata, the Oregon Country Fair, and Rock City, although we never really did have a gig there to begin with and that I had told everyone we were going to play The Whiskey à Go Go in Los Angeles where the Doors used to play before they got famous, and by the way, would the kid believe that Ollie actually met Jim Morrison on Bellevue Way in 1970 the day after a Door's concert at the Seattle Center and that Morrison knocked him down after they got into an argument?

He rambles on about getting mugged and being down to five gallons of gas with no money left and noticed that Mr. Jones was playing tonight and was there any way the kid might let us in for free to watch the legend himself?

The kid says, "Well, you need sixty bucks or a rad story to get in here. And that's a rad story. So, sure!"

Star says, "We've got more rad stories but we're really hungry. Is there any food anywhere we might wash dishes for?" She winks at Ollie.

"I'll hook you up." He motions us to follow him through the doors, which we do gratefully. Ollie looks back at me, smiling, and it's like he's somehow set the whole thing up in advance. I'm even more impressed when I smell roasting garlic and peanut sauce. We walk down a long corridor with white walls and red carpets and the walls are adorned with signed black-and-white framed glossies of celebrities like Johnny Carson and Willie Nelson.

We round a bend and the smell of dinner is even stronger. As we walk through a couple of metal swinging doors into the well-lit dining area we stand dumb-struck at this sudden twist of fortune: there is the legend himself, Mr. Tom Jones, tearing at a filet mignon with a steak knife. He looks up at us, and says in a heavy Welsh accent, "Can I help you with something?"

"We're kind of hungry, actually," says Star, unaware of whom she's talking to. "We're hoping to catch some of Todd's show tonight. He's a legend, you know." She looks at Walter and ribs him in the gut. "Eh, Walter? The legend, Todd Jones?"

I wince as Ollie stares at Star in disbelief.

"Star, this is *Tom* Jones," says Ollie. Zen laughs out loud.

Star gasps. "I know, you idiot. How's it going, Tom? Or should I call you Mr. Jones, sir?"

He looks at her, his mouth working over the meat between his clenched teeth. Gradually, his face warms a little. "Tom. You can call me Tom." His stare lingers for a few moments before his attention is turned back toward the petite Barbie-type with poofy hair sitting across from him. Our host friend waves for us to sit at another table in the opposite corner of the room.

We follow him and, once we're seated, the kid promises to bring us some dinner and disappears through a couple of metal doors.

"Way to go, Star," says Ollie staring back across the room at Tom who seems to be intentionally not looking at us.

"What?"

"*Todd* Jones?"

"Lighten up before I crack your skull open right here in front of your big idol." She is smiling, but a little unsteady. She needs some food. Low blood sugar and Star's ego is not a good combination.

"Ollie," I say, "you are truly amazing. Forty five minutes ago, we were driving into Reno with five gallons of gas left in the tank with no destination and now we're sitting backstage at Harrah's right across from Tom Jones with a waiter who's about to bring us all dinner. You're all right."

"Thanks," says Ollie. "You never know how things are gonna turn out and I just figured that it was time for our luck to change. We've paid our dues; don't you think? I remember one time when I met Steve Martin on a chair-lift in Vail, Colorado…"

We're mercifully spared the rest of the story when the kid bursts through the doors with a giant platter of food. Yet I get the feeling it's Ollie's night. Even Star eyes him with reverence. Walter's been quiet; he seems tired.

"That was sure quick!" I say as plates of salad, prime rib, quiche, prawns, rama tofu, and a strange-looking whole cooked fish are placed before us. The talking stops and the devouring begins. And devour we do. Star actually picks up a piece of prime rib in her hand, and begins tearing at it, muttering to Walter something about caribou. "I really got to get me a bow and arrow," she says after one steak is gone. "This is the way it's done."

Zen eats quietly, as does Ollie, who keeps on staring over at Tom Jones across the room. I notice Tom staring back and I wonder if Ollie is making him a bit nervous. Maybe we all are.

"Did you know that *Delilah* sold seven million copies?" says Ollie.

"Ollie," says Star, hanging a large, butterfly prawn over her mouth, "I'm really into this food now, okay? You are a really interesting person and I think that you're probably a genius but you're irritating the hell out of me right now, even though I've come to grow quite fond of you. Does that make any sense?"

"Sorry," says Ollie. "I must really drive you guys crazy."

"As a matter of fact, you really do," says Star, which causes Zen to blow peanut sauce through his nose, which causes Walter to start coughing uncontrollably and now we're all red-faced, choking and laughing. A couple of young guys with goatees, white shirts and silk pants come over to our table.

"Sorry," says one, "but we're gonna have to ask you to leave now. You weren't supposed to be in here to begin with."

"Okay," laughs Star. She then picks up the fish by its tail, hanging it over her head. "Chinese-style fish, eh?"

"I said we're gonna have to ask you to leave now," says the other guy, a bit more stressed.

"All right, then ask away," says Star, taking a bite out of it. "They say in China that you never want to turn the fish upside down or bad luck will come."

"You've got to leave *now*," says the first guy, and I stand up as does Ollie, Walter and Zen, but no one knows what's gotten into Star. It's as if she's possessed by the spirit of Angel.

Tom Jones, meanwhile, is still sitting with Barbie and trying not to look at us.

I put my hand on Star's shoulder, and I can tell she's tense. I think she's probably having a bit of a post-traumatic stress. Walter reaches over and helps her out of her chair while we all stuff ourselves, knowing it may be awhile before we get to eat again, especially a meal like this one.

Tom Jones is still communing with Barbie and I feel a hand on my shoulder. It's the kid who let us in. "Sorry. I wasn't supposed to let anyone back here; I thought it would be chill but Tom wasn't down with it at all and now he's really sketched out. Don't take it personally."

"No sweat," I say. "Star's had a rough twenty-four hours. Tell Tom we're sorry if we caused too much trouble."

"He's chill," sighs the kid.

We start to exit the big dining room doors, but Ollie's not with us. He has approached his idol. "I don't know if you remember me or not," he says to Tom, "but I met you about twenty-six years ago up at Lake Tahoe. I was only nine years old at the time, and it was actually my mom who was a big fan of yours but I swear, I've never seen a live show that's topped what you pulled off that night and I think you're the best, but I have a couple of questions: I saw you on—"

"If you ever want some sax, give me a call," says Star, materializing at Ollie's shoulder and interrupting him. "I'm pretty hot up in Seattle, and I can definitely give you and your band some good sax."

Our backstage friend has gathered us again, trying one more time to lead us out of the cafeteria. "He's got a whole back-up horn section."

We wave goodbye to a now smiling Tom Jones who waves back to us, wishing us luck in our travels.

"Did you all get enough food?" I ask.

Star nods, laughing as she pulls out a butterfly prawn from her pocket with gobs of pocket lint all stuck to it. "I'll have this for a midnight snack."

"You should be careful," says Ollie. "Seafood spoils very quickly. I read one time where a guy's kidneys' shut down due to paralytic shellfish poisoning brought on by—"

"Please, Ollie, not now," I say, realizing I haven't a clue as to where we'll sleep tonight. It's kind of liberating, this living in the moment business.

Just when I think the kid's going to show us the back door he opens a set of doors that lead to the stage area; beyond it are probably eight hundred people seated at various tables having dinner, anticipating the big show tonight.

"You mean you're not kicking us out of the theater?" I ask, surprised.

"No way!" says the kid. "I'm quitting this job and going surfing for the rest of the summer. The people who run this place are all about greed. I'm all about real people. What's the Indian dude's name?"

"Walter," I say. "We won't forget what you did for us."

"Yeah, thanks," says Zen. "This is really cool."

Walter shakes the kid's hand and the kid's impressed. He then passes some tickets out to us. "For drinks, and more food," he says. "I'm down with what you guys are about. You haven't told me much, but I think I know." He disappears back through the doors and I silently wish him a good life with lots of big, warm waves.

"Pretty cool to have dinner in the same room as Tom Jones, huh?" asks Ollie.

"Nothing surprises me anymore," says Zen, though he's thrilled as we all are. "I'll never understand how you always meet these bizarre celebrities."

"Simple clairvoyance," says Ollie. "If you're open to it, anything can happen."

We order a round of beers and the numbing effect is welcomed by all except Walter who nurses a diet cola. I wonder if he didn't exert a vast reservoir of energy playing the thug charmer last night.

After an hour-and-a-half, and a pretty good buzz going, the lights go down and Tom Jones walks out on stage. He's wearing a glittery black shirt and tight slacks; his face is ringed by tight black and gray curls. The late-middle-aged women shriek like teeny-boppers in a surprising burst of regression. In seconds the whole place is thundering with applause and foot stomping.

Now that Tom's back-up band and five-piece orchestra have taken their places he says, "Good evening ladies and gentlemen!" which elicits even more approval. "You know something? It's not unusual…to be *loved* by anyone!"

The crowd is in freak mode, anticipating this big hit and all the others that are coming. When the band kicks the first chord, the fans erupt. It's like a Beatle's concert during the Hollywood Bowl years. The ladies, and even some of the men, scream the whole time. Even when the song ends and he's taking a bow—sweat pouring off his blockish roman nose and long face—the decibel level remains the same. I never knew KOA nomads and white-haired mall rats could scream so loudly.

"Too bad we pissed him off earlier!" Ollie yells to me as the rest of the band stares in awe. "He's great, isn't he?"

"He sure is, Ollie!" I yell back, unable to contain my laughter. "I owned a K-Tel record of his best stuff about twenty-five years ago!"

Ollie smiles back at me while my heart swells with love. I wish the world knew how strange Ollie really is. He's a celebrity in his own right.

Mr. Jones band sails into *I Who Have Nothing*, and the audience is screaming, crooning along, not missing a single word. Then it's *What's New Pussycat?* then *Whoa whoa whoa, She's a Lady*…. As he belts out the words, I wonder what became of his woman friend. Perhaps he has suffered as I have.

"I *love* this song!" bellows Walter as Tom sings *The Green, Green Grass of Home.* Zen gives a drunken thumbs up as well and I can tell he really misses Linda and I'm hurtling into darkness as I contemplate the end of my relationship with Lily.

It needs to be over, yet everywhere I look I see her. The screaming crowd is closed out and pushed away and I can barely hear them. Go back, I say to myself, trying to escape the airtight vacuum in which I'm enclosed. Like a life ring thrown to a man gasping his last breath, somewhere in the hazy periphery, I hear familiar notes and words, beckoning me back to gliztville, to safety as Lily's hand that clutches my arm grows weaker as she tells me with brown eyes brimming that she still loves me. She loses her grip, falling away as Tom's screaming voice suddenly bursts through the vacuum, flooding me with light and sound, screaming, "I'm never gonna fall in love again..." and I'm pulled back into the current of reality while Lily's fading face is swept away like misty morning vapor in an autumn wind.

Yeah, Tom. You understood before I could, and I cheer for you. You have filled me with such passion, anguish and hope. These songs bring people back to certain times and places when life had magic, romance and possibility, a time when you could fit in as a dreamer in a world of vapid, fleeting comfort. No one does get out of here alive, but thanks anyway, Tom. Thanks for playing your important role. We're all just frogs sitting around a pond and everyone must join the big song. It's all starting to make sense now. You take your place and do what you do without worrying whether or not you're doing it right. Just be true. Be true to yourself and everything else will happen, as it should.

~

As we join the legions of Tom Jones fans pouring out into the street and the warm, Nevada air, I regret having earlier offended Mr. Jones. But that's what happens during stress attacks.

"It was sure nice of that kid to let us into the concert, huh?" I ask my mates.

"Did you ever get his name?" asks Star. "He was sure cute."

"I think it was Mitch or something," says Zen rather absently.

"Did you have fun, Walter?" I ask.

"He makes me homesick," he says a little sadly. "He was good."

The warm air is scented with the smell of folks lighting up, and everywhere, there are couples drifting away into the night, some giggling, some hardly talking, but all in an obvious hurry to get somewhere, fast.

As we're trying to figure out which direction to go to get Elvis, Star asks if any of us have seen Ollie.

I turn around and scan the busy sidewalk. Finally I see him, standing stationary on the sidewalk about forty yards behind us, staring off toward something. It's in the direction of the front entrance. "What's going on, Ollie?" I ask as we come up to him.

He doesn't acknowledge us at first. He only stares very intensely, and now I believe it's at a middle-aged balding guy with wire-rimmed glasses and a foofy-looking Hawaiian shirt making a phone call.

"Yeah, Ollie," says Star, pulling a lint-drenched butterfly prawn from her pocket and popping it in her mouth. "Who is it this time, Merv Griffin?"

Ollie is unfazed. He only stares, his rugged blue eyes peering over the wire frames. "You're not gonna believe this," he whispers.

Who it is I cannot imagine. We wait patiently for the guy to get off the phone, which seems to take forever. Star and Zen have come up with a top five list of possible candidates including a former studio musician on a Tony Orlando Album, or perhaps a music writer for *The Rolling Stone* during the summer of 1972.

The guy seems to be wrapping up the conversation and notices us watching him. He's acting all nervous like he might want to make a break for it, but judging by those thin legs holding up his massive beer gut, he'd likely fall over if he started running.

"Come on, Ollie, you're making the dude nervous," I say. "Who the hell is it?"

Just then, the guy places the phone receiver back in its cradle and turns to us. He looks angry with sharp, black cunning eyes and a very small nose that looks like it was flattened years ago. For some reason, he reminds me of a bison. Ollie approaches him and the dude stiffens a bit. "What do you want?" he asks.

"Are you Bill Armond?"

The guy looks at Ollie, squinting hard. "*Yeah*. Do I know you?"

"Yeah," says Ollie. "My name's Ollie. We were taking a leak together in the State of Oregon's Talbot Rest Area washroom late one night last week. You were telling me that you were looking for a band to play at the grand opening of your car lot."

The guy just stares at Ollie in disbelief.

"Remember?" Ollie continues, "I told you that we were on a West Coast tour and were gonna play the Oregon Country Fair, and the big gig at Arcata to save the Redwoods?"

"Yeah," whispers the guy. "I do remember you…vaguely."

"Well things didn't really go the way we planned. In fact, we lost one of our band members during that very pit stop." He goes into a lengthy explanation of how we left Angel there and drove a couple of hours south before Zen noticed that she wasn't in the rig, and by the time we made it back to Talbot, she was gone.

"Yeah," says Bill. "I do remember some black-haired girl in a purple hat throwing an absolute fit outside. She kept yelling out this fella's name…Sounded like Angus if I remember. A lot of cars left during that racket. She was a band member, huh?"

"Yeah but she hooked up with Groovetribe a few hours later and quit our band," says Ollie. He then goes on for the next ten minutes filling Bill in on one disastrous turn of events after another, while Bill listens with a look of suspicion, awe and sympathy.

"So you guys want to play my grand opening the day after tomorrow?" he asks, and suddenly, his up-beat-car-dealer persona shines through with depth and insincerity.

"You still need a band?" asks Ollie.

"I sure do," he says. "I'll even pay you two hundred and fifty dollars for doing it. Sounds like you guys could use a paying gig." He laughs loudly. "I'm assuming you guys are good."

"Fuckin-a we're good," says Star. "I'm the most kick-ass lead guitarist in the Pacific Northwest."

"The most humble, too," I add.

She stares at me with indifference. "We don't have any money left or a place to park Elvis," she says. "Do you have any suggestions?"

Bill stares back at her and I pick up on his horny vibe.

"Hell, you all can come over to my place and stay there there a couple of days," he says. "Then after the gig, you'll be on your way back to Seattle."

"Sounds great!" says Zen. In spite of my suspicions, it seems that things might be getting better. Perhaps Ollie is right. We've paid our dues and now, at last, our fortunes are beginning to change.

Thirty-one

We follow Bill through downtown Reno and Elvis is charged with excitement. We have a ticket home. Living in the moment is cool.

"Wow, our first gig of the tour," I say.

"Ollie, you are amazing," says Star throwing her arms around him, and in a rare display of vulnerability and intimacy, plants one on his cheek.

"How'd you remember the guy?" asks Zen.

"I don't know," says Ollie. "We were walking out of Harrah's and I looked over at the line of pay phones, and there he was, Bill Armond."

"You never forget a name, do you?" I ask.

"Or a face," he replies.

"He's selling Mitsubishi cars," I lament. "Do you all know that Mitsubishi is one of the worst corporations in the world for destroying tropical rainforests?"

"I didn't know that," says Star.

Bill's pearly white Mercedes weaves gracefully through the traffic and we're hard-pressed to keep up with him.

He's now a couple of cars ahead of us as we're approaching the edge of town; soon we're on an open highway heading out into the high desert. Elvis's gauge is barely above empty, but it doesn't matter. Bill knows our situation and it's always easier to forgive a sleazball when he's offering cold cash and a place to stay. I may judge the actions of Mitsubishi, but I probably shouldn't judge his. He's the little guy. He's not even the middleman. Hell, I've even heard they're pretty damn good cars.

Bill turns left onto a long, gravel driveway and we follow it toward what looks like a space ship, looming in the distance.

"Pretty impressive," says Star, as we approach his very large house with every light turned on. When we're within a hundred yards, a garage door opens magically and Bill glides in, killing the engine. We park outside.

As we follow him up the steps I'm lost for words. Perhaps this how rock stars live. I wonder what kind of home Neil Young lives in.

"This'll work out great for all of us," says Bill as he fumbles for his house key. "I can't believe this coincidence."

"It's no coincidence," I say. "This happens to Ollie all the time."

He opens the door and we are standing in the main vestibule on marble floors with an indoor fountain gurgling in the center of an exotic plant oasis. He leads us through plush hallways and, at the end of one, there is a large portrait of Samuel Moore Walton hanging on the wall. Ollie and I look at each other.

"So, you live here by yourself?" Star asks.

Bill turns to her and whispers, "I haven't found the woman of my dreams...yet."

Star looks at him a bit suspiciously, but says nothing. He shows us all of our rooms, each with it's own shower and when we're done with the tour, he mixes drinks for us in the kitchen and asks us more about the history of our band and what's happening with Frank. I haven't the energy to get into it, but Ollie does and soon they're speaking like old friends. There can be something bonding about urinating with strangers in rest stops and Ollie is now showing us the fruits of it all.

"Are you comfortable here, Star?" I ask quietly as Ollie and Bill converse.

"It'll be fine," she says with resolve, and I realize that I'm exhausted. I excuse myself and once inside my room, I lie down for a second, just to catch my bearings. The rest is history as I fall into a deep, dreamless, and hassle-free sleep.

~

I awaken to the smell of bacon, eggs and coffee. I roll from the bed and, as my feet touch the floor, it occurs to me that I have no idea where in the hell I am. I hear voices echoing far away and, in the midst of it all, Star's shrieking laugh. It all slowly comes back to me and I wonder if it's part of a dream from which I'll awaken.

The voices are getting closer as I wind down the long hallway. My bare feet are silently absorbed in each step by the sponge-like carpet. I scan the pictures adorning the walls and notice that several are of blonde, swimsuit babes. At the end of this hall is a glossy of Henry Kissinger. Bill's definitely a Republican and, so far, a generous one. After all he's paying us real money to perform live in his new car lot.

"How'd you sleep?" asks a beaming Star as I enter the giant kitchen trimmed out with exotic tropical hardwoods and adorned with every appliance imaginable—including a large Vegomatic standing by the sink. There is a middle-aged Mexican man cooking up a storm. Ollie and Zen are slurping coffee.

"Great," I say. "Where's Bill?"

"He had some business in town and said to make ourselves at home. He'll be back in early afternoon."

"He's trusting us all alone in his place until he gets back?" I ask as I notice a black video camera mounted on the ceiling above the entrance.

"Yeah, he trusts us," says Star. "Angus, this is Pedro. He's the caretaker here."

Pedro says, "Hola Senior. Como Estas usted?" He has a thin mustache and tight, curly hair.

"Muy bien. Y tu?"

"Bien."

"I didn't know you spoke Spanish," says Ollie.

"There's a lot about me you don't know," I say, having just exhausted my entire Spanish vocabulary on this one interaction.

"You gotta check this place out," says Star, taking my hand. While Pedro continues his breakfast masterpiece Star and I embark on a journey through Bill's high-desert monstrosity. "Look at this," she says, opening a door. On the other side lies a sun room with a hot tub embedded in a redwood deck. Beyond, a giant aqua green swimming pool with two diving boards ringed by palm trees basks in the morning sun.

"This guy's loaded," I say. There are several patio loungers with umbrellas adorning the fringes and a few inflated beach balls buzzing lazily around the pool, pushed aimlessly about by a light desert wind.

"I took a hot tub last night after everyone crashed," sighs Star. "It was so wonderful." She looks at me wistfully, her blue eyes far away. "Wouldn't it be great to be famous and to have all of this shit?"

"Star," I say, noticing another black video camera mounted above the hot tub. "I can think of better ways to spend money. Did you know that the Colorado River doesn't even reach the Gulf of Mexico anymore thanks to this kind of lifestyle. You ought to read *Cadillac Desert*."

"You're starting to sound like Ollie," she says, defensively. "There's nothing wrong with enjoying pleasures like these. I talked with Bill for a long time last night. He worked his ass off for years before he got this place. When you take risks and get some breaks, why shouldn't you flaunt it a bit?"

"What did he do for years to earn this place?" I ask Star, and she smiles ironically.

"Get this: he actually worked at Sony back in the early eighties."

"No shit?"

"That's what he said. He wants to talk with us all later on about what we're doing. He's got some ideas."

"Did you take the hot tub alone Star?" I ask, feeling brotherly.

"Actually, I did, though Bill tried to join me. You know, I think you've got to deal with your contradictions. Deep down you're no different than anyone else. If you had the chance, I bet you'd have all of this and more. There's nothing wrong with it!"

Her words stun me. I cannot deny that it would be quite nice to take a dive in that pool and to lounge about, just drinking cocktails every day. "You're right, Star," I confess. "I'm a hypocrite. Bill's bending over backwards to help us out. It's just that I can't think about doing music for this. To me that's selling out. I hope that by staying true to myself that people will love me for who I am, buy my music unconditionally, and I'll then receive millions of dollars as a result. See the difference?"

She looks at me strangely, and then there is a gonging sound coming from the kitchen. "Breakfast time," she says and we leave these thoughts behind as we head for food, coffee and a new lease on life.

Back in the kitchen, Zen and Ollie are devouring platters of bacon, eggs, and hash browns. Walter nurses a cup of coffee, an untouched piece of toast in front of him. He's not hungry and I can tell he's not feeling so good. In fact, he seems to be sweating a bit. "How are you today, Walter?" I ask, and he only nods his head, smiling a little.

Pedro serves the food, and after breakfast we all converge on the patio by the pool with nothing to do until Bill gets back from errands. We lounge, swim and take hot tubs for the next few hours. By early afternoon Bill is back. He comes waddling out in a pair of neon-green shorts to join us at the poolside. He's got a drink in hand and soon Pedro has everyone supplied with cocktails. Bill's beer gut hangs like an giant, over-ripe squash and he just doesn't strike me as a guy who once worked at Sony.

"Hey, Bill, this is really great," says Ollie, lying on a blue, inflatable brontosaurus. "Thanks for all the hospitality."

"Yeah, Bill," I say. "You didn't need to go to all this trouble."

"No problem at all," he beams. "I was just down at the lot and the boys are building you guys a stage. I hope you're ready to rock."

"Oh, we'll rock," says Star. "Your car lot will never be the same."

"Where's the Indian?" asks Bill, suddenly.

"You mean Walter? He's lying down," I say. "He's not feeling so great."

"Sorry to hear that," says Bill, insincerely. "He's not from around here, is he?"

"No, he's from Alaska."

"I figured that. I got nothing against Indians and Lord knows some of 'em have been given a raw deal, but there's been a lot of trouble out at the test-site by some red-skin welfare babies who seem to have got nothing better to do than protest the nukes. Can't trust 'em for anything. Where's Chief Wahoo lying down?"

"That's not very nice," I say, feeling molten rumblings from within.

"Boy, Tom Jones was sure great last night, wasn't he?" asks Star, glaring at me.

"He's the best," says Bill, taking her cue while I approach the boiling point. "Actually know him personally. He's been out to the ranch a few times."

"Here?" asks Ollie, looking sheepish.

They banter on shallowly while I fight to keep my mouth shut. To people like Bill, minorities are too lazy and dishonest to work for a living. Bill, on the other hand, what an honest guy—working as a broker for the Japanese corporate Mafia.

"Star tells me you used to work for Sony," I finally manage to say.

"Yep, I was in marketing during the early seventies."

I look at Star. She looks away.

"Oh, really?" says Ollie. "So you helped Paul Simon jump from Columbia to Sony in '72?"

"Well, sort of." He sighs. "Paul definitely had a mind of his own about him, and he was ready to jump ship anyway. Columbia didn't have a clue how to handle him so when we offered him a seven-record contract the deal sort of did itself."

Geeze, I think. This guy *is* for real.

"See," Bill continues, "in those days it was about the art of making and promoting good music. These days it's about making a quick buck and getting out. That's why I quit. I had to do something with integrity. Something that made me feel like I was actually making the world a better place. Everybody needs a good car to drive and I'm a much happier person for my small contribution."

Bill orders Pedro to bring us another round of cocktails with some more crab dip and olive bread, and I'm afraid that I'm starting to tie one on.

"So have you heard about Mitsubishi's logging of tropical hardwoods in places like Borneo?" I slur, unable to censor myself any longer.

Bill looks long and hard at me.

"Why don't you not worry about it?" Star whispers through clenched teeth. Then she turns to Bill, pulling out her can of chew and tapping it. This serves as a well-timed diversion as Bill asks Pedro to bring Star a silver bowl to spit in. His eyes seem preoccupied with Star's modest cleavage revealed by the skimpy, polka-dotted bikini she's wearing.

"Corporate America is ruining everything," I say. "Soon we'll all be shopping at one big store."

Bill laughs, but I can tell he's furious. "I'm concerned about your allegations against Mitsubishi. There have been some local protesters sending me hate mail over this new car lot I'm opening and I've read their literature. I even called the company headquarters to get their side of things. Far as I can tell, it's all a bunch of hogwash. Bunch of spoiled college kids who've never had to work for anything coming around to stir up trouble. Fact is, Mitsubishi has a few experimental forests in the tropics. Know your facts before you start shootin' off at the mouth."

"Yeah, Angus," says Star, "don't you think it's a little rude to be discussing this stuff given that Bill has just opened up his home to us and is paying us to perform at his grand opening?"

"It's true, Angus," chortles Zen. "Know your facts."

"No offense, Angus, but we need the gig," chimes Ollie. "You have some valid concerns though. Bill, did you know that only ten percent of the earth's rain forests are left and that if current trends continue all the rain forests in the world will be gone in a mere twenty years. There's a great article in the Atlantic Monthly about—"

"Yeah, every day is Earth Day, right Ollie?" hollers Zen.

"Bill," says Star, trying to deflate the tension. "Would you mind rubbing some sun-screen on my back?"

Bill's angry gaze toward me lingers, but Star's ploy has worked. He empties a whole bottle of cream onto her back and begins rubbing with it furiously with his chubby hands. She wrinkles her face in disgust, winking at me.

"I'm sorry if I offended you Bill," I lie. "I think it's nice that you've hired us for the grand opening of your car lot and I was actually trying to speak rather objectively on the issue since I always like to hear both sides. But I can see how what I insinuated might have been interpreted as a personal attack, though I assure you, it wasn't."

Bill pauses from his massage to slurp his drink. "Just know your facts, Angus," he says.

The conversation eventually drifts back to music and the state of pop culture today—and, of course, whether or not Bill might have any useful contacts for Star's soon-to-be-solo career. Bill actually does know what he's talking about, though I'm still not sure if I believe that he ever worked for Sony Records.

Walter never does come out to join us; he must be really tired. After a half dozen cocktails, I'm ready for the mat myself. Bill gets Pedro busy on the dinner project and though I can't deny Pedro's cooking is other-worldly, I feel an enormous amount of liberal guilt over taking part in his exploitation. He doesn't seem to like being bossed around by Bill very much, but damn is he a good cook.

Eventually, around seven, dinner is served and Walter comes out to join us. Ironically, we are having buffalo with potatoes and gravy. Bill is polite enough to Walter and I'm relieved that I'm not going to have to rush to his defense over anything. I'm wasted from sitting in the sun all day and glad for this brief layover.

I eat and retire early and, as I recline in on my soft feather bed, I can't deny that this luxury business is kind of nice. It's all in one's perspective I suppose. I'm glad that we'll be on the road tomorrow evening with our ticket home. I'm still not ready to give up the good fight just yet. I've got a feeling that things can still happen and that our luck, like Ollie said, is finally starting to turn for the better.

I notice a television remote control next to my bedside table. I reach for it and turn on the tube. The first thing I see is Tom Brokaw's bloated head and I flip through the channels until I find Discovery. I watch porpoises underwater drifting aimlessly in an aqua-green soup and it makes me think of Angel who used to tell me about all of her telepathic experiences with dolphins off the coast of Baja and how she believed they had chosen her for some special purpose. I swear off tuna as my eyes grow heavy, though I can still hear laughter and splashing out by the pool and the late evening sun still garnishes the distant rocks in a red comforting glow. Tomorrow will be a fresh start and sleep will be a welcome friend.

Thirty-two

I awaken and have no idea where I am. There is a violin coming from the television. Discovery's off the air but there is a frozen image of a gorgeous mountain range basking in alpenglow. I stare at it as everything is slowly coming back to me. Once I've finally figured out where I am, I observe the time on the digital clock. It's only a little after midnight. It feels like it should be later.

I absently pick up the remote control to turn off the screen and press what I believe to be the off button. Yet when the Discovery channel suddenly disappears it is replaced by a green blank screen. How strange. It's as if I've turned something else on. I switch channels, perplexed. Same green screen.

I switch again and now I can't seem to turn the damn thing off. I try it one more time and I'm looking at some shirtless man bouncing up and down on a stool in front of a mirror flailing wildly at the air. Is this a commercial for MTV or an anti-perspirant ad? The man is shaking his head and screaming like he's in front of twenty thousand people. There's something very familiar about him. Holy shit! I feel a chill creeping up the back of my legs as I realize that it's Ollie.

I can't believe my eyes. How the hell did he get on television? At the peak of his frenzy, he begins singing the words to *Delilah*. I look up at the camera mounted above the door and it's starting to make sense. Bill's got a home video monitor security system hooked up. Ollie stops after awhile and sticks his left pinkie in his ear and twists. He pulls it out, examining it closely and I change the channel.

Now I see a partially clad Zen, furiously doing push-ups. After awhile he stops and stands up in front of the camera, sweat dripping from his face. He pulls forth a near-empty bottle of whiskey and in seconds it's gone. He throws the bottle down, wobbling uncertainly backwards before flopping back on the bed.

I change the channel and stare in shock. Star is playing electric air guitar buck-naked in high-heels in front of a large mirror. She goes off gyrating on some riff puckering her lips all serious-like before laughing like she's sharing a joke with her best buddy. Then she jumps up on a chair, thrusting her butt toward the mirror before leaping off, à la Pete Townshend. As she hits the carpet the heels buckle beneath her and she tumbles to the ground swearing unintelligibly. After a little while she gets up and puts down the guitar, examining herself for injuries. She walks to the mirror, a slight smile on her lips. Then she thrusts her naked hips forward as if taunting someone. "You're playing with fire, little boy. Oh, so you want me back now? Isn't *this* all you really want? It's what *all* you boys want. Admit it. Maybe you weren't as special as you thought, huh? It's *over* you wuss! Nobody plays games with the goddess. Didn't your momma ever tell you that?"

I can watch no more. I change networks again and see myself watching television. I gaze up to the black camera eye staring at me and I wink. "Hi, Bill," I say. The screen goes blank and the show's over for the night. I never do get to see what Walter's up to.

I pull the blankets over my head, cursing Bill Armond. Oh well, tomorrow we'll play the gig, grab the cash and head north back to Bellingham where we can get on with life. But first our date with destiny at a black strip of asphalt owned by a local car shark met by Ollie in a bizarre meeting that took place in the middle of the night at a rest area called Talbot…

Thirty-three

I can tell it's going to be a scorcher before the sun's even partway up. It's one of those days where you can smell the heat coming. As I gaze at my band mates I can't help but smile to myself at the thought of their late-night behavior.

We sit around the breakfast table ironing out the details of our set. We will play from 1:00 to 3:00 with a new car give-away happening during a fifteen-minute break in the middle. Bill's crew will be providing a stage, power and a tarp to shield us from the sun. We'll provide the sound system and music. Bill's very excited, though he keeps looking at me, smiling a little sheepishly.

We're showered and saying goodbye to Pedro at about 11:00 and, to my surprise, even Ollie is ready. We talk over our set lists and decide to pull out a few covers that might be good icebreakers before we launch into an environmental tirade about saving the trees. I've always dreamed of playing Pink Floyd's *Wish You Were Here* in a Reno used car lot. Maybe we'll be the first to pull it off.

As we follow Bill back through Reno toward the site of our concert, I ask the crew if I ought to call Sunny.

"Before we decide that," says Ollie, "I'd like to know if we're still a band."

"Good question, Ollie," I say. "Are we still a band, and if so, are we still taking orders from Sunny and Frank?"

"Let's do the gig and see how we feel," says Zen.

"I'm with Zen," says Star.

"Don't you think Sunny and Frank should at least know about this gig?" questions Ollie. "Maybe they could have some label people come out to hear us."

"Yeah, right," I reply. "Check out The Cosmic Poets at Bill Armond Mitsubishi and get a thousand dollars cash back on a brand new car! Get real, Ollie."

The first thing I notice when we arrive at the lot is a good-sized stage assembled for the occasion, green and yellow flags hung everywhere. Adorning the back of the stage is a sign that says: Drive Home A Bargain Today. There's a picture of Bill standing next to it, exuding a joyous, pearly-white smile. I find it perfectly ironic to see a large, blow-up doll of himself floating in a suspended, surrealistic wind-dance thirty feet over the asphalt lot, adorned by so many shiny new and semi-new imports made from one of the most evil corporations in existence. Telling him to go screw himself would have new meaning but hey, everybody's got to make a buck.

After hauling our gear onto the stage, we're all sweating like crazy. While Zen begins assembling things, I notice Bill standing about thirty feet away, talking to a few suits. Across the lot there is a group of kids around a helium tank blowing up dozens of colored balloons while laughing in high-pitched voices. What a festive day. The thought of actually getting paid overrides the feelings of acute despair at playing in a Reno car lot.

There are a few clusters of people scattered about; cars and trucks roar past on a busy street adjacent to the lot. Bill comes over and introduces us to some of his employees and friends who are all superficially beaming with joy. Then my stomach knots up and I hear an audible gasp as I notice a certain colorful group of people with dreads and tie-dye who have gathered in the far corner of the lot, between the street and sidewalk. Judging by the signs they're holding up—saying things like: Mitsubishi Kills Rain Forests—they are not here for Bill's new car give-away.

"The freak show's here!" someone yells, and I notice Bill suddenly on a cell phone. "Get over here and help me deal with this! Now, before the media shows up!"

He turns to us, flustered, and asks Star how soon we'll be ready to play. She turns to Zen who informs her that we're about a half-hour away.

More hippies are gathering; there are now about thirty of them. "Forest Rapers!" a woman screams. I cringe. We are taking money from the enemy. We have sold out. Or have we? What is a band in our circumstances to do? I wish I could explain our situation to them, but I can't. They wouldn't understand. As it turns out, it wouldn't matter.

In a scene that unfolds remarkably like one I was involved with in Bellingham a few years back, someone who works for Bill has connected a large hose to a fire hydrant. In moments, the hippies are drenched and screaming. The high-pressure blast of water decimates their signs, rendering them useless masses of soaked pulp on sticks. Bill's lackey unhooks the hose just before the cops arrive; in moments the soaked protesters are being led away. Judging by what I know about Nevada, they are probably offered a deal they can't refuse. They go rather passively and all that's left is a large area of soaked pavement that's quickly evaporating in the hot sun.

We continue setting up in silence. In fifteen minutes, we're sound-checking. Walter stands by, sweating profusely. Hard to adjust to this heat coming from Alaska, I imagine. I try not to think about the poor hippies.

There is now a crowd of about forty well-dressed, superficial people staring at us. Bill approaches the stage. "Are you ready to start?" he asks.

"We're close," I say, then add: "That was a pretty shitty thing of you to—"

"We need to be professional about things," says Star, cutting me off.

"It's my big day," says Bill. "I put a lot on the line to make this happen, and those welfare brats were on *my* property."

"They were on the sidewalk," counters Ollie.

"No they weren't," Bill argues. "I hired you guys to play music, not to argue politics."

"We got a job to do fellas!" yells Star.

Bill scans the stage and goes back to his friends who are obviously conferring about something important. We are now tuned up and there are about a hundred people who have now gathered. We are ready to rock and I embrace the possibility of an artistic experience.

"You ready?" Bill asks, as he jumps up on stage with us. There is a television crew that has arrived, and all the balloons are filled and distributed throughout the lot.

"Yeah, we're ready," Zen says.

We all stand there, ready for Bill's opening words and the big introduction. But instead of addressing the audience, he looks at me and asks the same question again.

"Yeah," I say. "We're ready."

"You sure?" he asks, looking at Walter who's standing across the stage on the side and then back at me. "What about the Indian?"

"Walter?" I ask.

"I didn't hire the Indian to play, no offense."

"He's our support crew," I say. "You're not being very nice, Bill."

"It don't look good having some Indian up on stage here. I hired you. Not a fucking redskin." He looks at Walter who gazes back, expressionless.

Star's face has turned pasty and she's looking deadly, kind of like when she almost broke Ollie's neck a couple of nights back. She throws her arm around Bill's neck, jerking his head close to hers. "Walter stays. You hear me, Bill?"

His eyes are undecided for a moment, then he nods his head, eyes big with sudden fear. Passion and triumph rage. As Walter smiles at Star, she smiles at me. We are fired up and ready to rock. After we get paid, my plan is to slash Bill's tires. I smile to myself at the thought.

"Are we on?" Bill asks Zen while tapping the microphone. Zen nods. "My name's Bill Armond!" he bellows. "I'd like to thank you all for coming out today to the big grand opening of Bill Armond Mitsubishi! We've got deals and we've got deals! Today only, we're practically giving these cars away at forty-percent off the regular sticker price!"

Cheers scatter throughout the crowd as the gleeful, ambulant consumers look on.

"The guys in green will all be on hand to answer questions and get you all familiar with our new line of cars that have just come in, and while we get started we're going to be treated with music by one of the Northwest's hottest bands…"

More cheers spatter about.

"During the intermission we'll do the draw for our grand opening new car-giveaway, a beautiful Mitsubishi Eclipse!" More cheers. "And help yourself to the free corn dogs and other refreshments," he says pointing toward a table set up by the main building. "Now, without further ado, let's give a warm, Reno-style welcome to: The Cosmic Poets!"

People clap and cheer while the cameras roll. As we crash into our first song there is a rage in our music that I've never before felt. Walter stands off to the side of the stage, staring at us, and in a little while he is smiling and tapping his foot. I look to the crowd and people seem to all be into it, grooving along with us. We finish the song and everybody's cheering loudly. They like us!

Here we are, playing our first real paying gig of the tour in a Reno car lot. Life could be worse. Thanks to Zen's artistic mastery of electronics, the sound is excellent and as we progress through our set the crowd seems to be growing significantly. In fact, after playing a few songs it seems as if several hundred people have gathered. Where are they all coming from? I notice after awhile that we must be quite a sight from the busy street and the endless stream of people in cars going by are staring and smiling. They are pulling over, too.

I'm seeing the wisdom of Bill's plan to draw people. We are helping to make it an event. At the half-way point of our first set I call for our song about global, ecological collapse due to rampant consumerism, deforestation and the widespread burning of fossil fuels. People seem to be really into it, too. This is fast becoming a monster gig.

The parking lot has been transformed into an outdoor rock festival and there are at least five hundred people grooving along with us. I doubt Bill has enough corn dogs to go around.

Walter is smiling now as he watches the scene unfold, and we are tight in a way we've never been before. I feel everybody listening to each other and we're all one, integrated organism. We rock. People freak. We rock more. More people are pulling over. The crowd swells. We rock. The masses dance and sway. We sing, unabashed and suddenly…it's time to take a break for the new car give-away.

Bill takes the stage and his expression is one of wonder. "I had no idea!" he says before turning to the crowd. "How about these Cosmic Poets!"

The crowd, which is now around a thousand, goes wild. I look at Star, Zen and Ollie and we're all bewildered at this suddenly awesome gig. "We rock!" I say.

"No shit!" says Star.

Zen stares out at the crowd as Ollie's fingers twitch away.

The crowd seems restless during the giveaway, kind of like they just want to rock out, but when Bill announces the number of the winner, a chubby fellow with a high-pitched feminine voice screams as he works his way toward the stage, waving a piece of paper above his head. As he stands on the stage with tears streaming down his face, the place goes wild. It's like he's just been baptized by Oral Roberts. While people yell for the music, Bill barks orders for more corn dogs.

We open the next set with the Neil Young cover, *Into the Black*, and we can do no wrong. The entire parking lot is full of people, and there are the suggestions of a mosh pit developing before us. After a few songs, Bill appears behind Star and wanders over to the edge of the stage, standing in front of the mosh pit, which is now full on. He looks out over the crowd, laughing and making goo-goo eyes at some particular girl while clapping his hands. As Star sends the crowd into a frenzy with all of her sound effects engaged at once, Bill flexes his arms for the big dive. No doubt he's waited a long time for this moment, and the waiting is over. His time has come.

He turns back to the audience, flashes an uncertain smile at Star, crouches like a Sumo wrestler and leaps into the crowd, a graceless, gelatinous mass of flailing arms and legs. His illusions of safety evaporate as quickly as the mosh pit before him, forming a black hole into which he's sucked and his scream is as audible as the crunch of his body smacking the asphalt.

He is almost instantly back on his feet, held up by dozens of arms and he smiles as blood spurts from a gash in his head. Some movement catches my eye off-stage. Walter has just fallen from his chair—doubled over on his side from laughing so hard. I have to look away or I'll lose it, too. Someone has placed a towel over Bill's bloody head, though he seems to be still trying to dance.

Throughout the mayhem, I keep noticing this dude in tie-dye, Carharts and a ponytail. He has clear, brown eyes, a crooked, yet handsome nose, and a small chin. He's grooving away below the right hand side of the stage, staring into my eyes. *Sorry, dude, I'm straight*.

"Can you believe it?" Star yells over the thundering crowd. "Our biggest gig ever!"

We are now fully engaged in the ultimate, rock-n-roll apocalypse, absolutely going off while the crowd swoons in this car-lot love affair. We rock…the crowd swelters…we groove…they sigh…we rule…they worship…and suddenly, I hear something very different. I look at Star who looks back at me, confused. It's the sound of a well-played harmonica going off with Ollie and Zen.

The audience screams as Walter struts out onto the stage playing the most awesome blues harp I've ever heard. I stop strumming, stunned. Star steps back as well. Zen and Ollie pound out a riff that quickly evolves into a bluesy swing. I hear myself screaming at the top of my lungs; Star, too, is yelling. Life is beautiful again. He goes off like a pro, stomping his foot to the beat while swaying back and forth to the groove and people are really worked up now. Humble, quiet Walter. Loser Bill is standing to the side of the stage holding the bloody towel to his head and I laugh at his look of bewilderment.

The handsome dude with the crooked nose is still smiling, but has that look of awe that tells me that we are in the zone, and I wonder if he's a new car customer turned music fan. I try not to look at him.

Walter, meanwhile, looks over at me, laughing, and as the song concludes in a great, thrashing climax, the crowd's roar is deafening. It's time to call it a show. Leave 'em wanting more as they say in the biz.

We leave the stage while they cheer us on, calling us back for more.

"You son of a bitch!" I yell as Walter and I embrace.

"I had no idea!" screams Star, giving him a high-five. "Where do you get off being so humble?"

"Let's give 'em one more," says Zen, and we charge back onto stage.

I try to explain the song we'll do, but Walter waves me off. It's as if he knows the song by heart and when we finish the masses are screaming, just like I'd always believed they would.

I laugh to myself because it doesn't matter to me anymore. There is nothing left to prove and Walter has just placed a major exclamation point on that one by pulling a musical rabbit out of his baseball cap in the shape of a "D" harmonica. What a way to end our big West Coast tour.

When I see Star embracing Walter backstage and Ollie and Zen standing arm in arm talking with some of our new fans, I feel pretty damn good. And Bill, despite a serious monkey-bump on his head, seems to be in business. I'm sure that he knows that he scored a good deal having us play for only two hundred and fifty dollars. I let the glory soak in and laugh at our futility in following Sunny's lead. But now a new possibility has emerged, though I'm not sure at this time what it means. As I turn from the beautiful, back-stage scene I jump a little, startled at the fact that I almost bump into the smiling dude with the crooked nose.

"How's it going?" I say, as I prepare to begin breaking down our gear for the big trip home.

"Great," he says. "You guys are fantastic."

"Thanks," I say. "This was a blast."

"Wow. And you're from Bellingham?"

"That's right."

"My sister lives in Bellingham!" He laughs.

"Oh really? Well, they do say that Bellingham's the cosmic center of the universe. Nothing surprises me anymore." There's something familiar about this guy, but I can't put my finger on it.

"I really like your sound. Kind of reminds me of The Who."

"Yeah, I've been told that before," I say, wanting to excuse myself. "Sorry to cut you short, but we got a long way to go tonight."

"That's cool," he says dreamily. "What's your name?"

"My name's Angus Keegan and the name of the band is The Cosmic Poets," I'm beginning to get irritated. I want to be done with this. Only out of politeness I reciprocate by asking, "And yours?"

"My name's Rod Ames," he says, extending his hand while still smiling. "I'm with A&M Records."

Thirty-four

I take a seat on an amplifier, trying to steady myself. My head is reeling and my eyes are spinning in and out of focus.

"Are you all right?" he asks, concerned.

"Yeah, I think so. You're really an A&R rep, huh?"

"I am," he says. "Is that hard to believe?"

I look around me. My band mates are scattered about, talking with various people. "Yeah, actually it is. I began to doubt whether or not you guys even existed."

"We do, Angus. I just happened to be driving to the airport on my way back to Los Angeles and I heard you guys. In fact, I can't chat very long or I'll miss my flight. You have a CD or a demo or anything I can take with me?"

"Yeah, right here," I say, reaching for my gig bag. *Don't go,* I scream inside. *There's so much I want to ask you. So much I need to know.* I hand him the tape and he looks at it for a few moments.

"Cool," he says, putting it in his pocket. "Are the songs you played today arranged the same way on the tape?"

"Basically," I say. "Though there's nothing like a good live gig."

"No doubt," he smiles. "You coming to California anytime soon?"

"No, our tour's over and we're headed back to Seattle for a gig at The Showbox."

"Really? When?" he asks.

"The day after tomorrow. The twenty-seventh of July, I believe. It's a battle of the bands."

"Hmmmm. I'm supposed to be in New York, but I'd really like to bring some people up for that one. I have some friends I'm gonna play this for, and if this tape sounds anything like what I heard today, I can't imagine why they wouldn't come to Seattle. You guys are fantastic!"

"Really?"

"You really are. And man, you had the crowd going. Very professional."

"Thanks, Rod."

"What are your goals, by the way?"

"That's a good question," I say, basking in the suddenly cooled waters of reality. "I used to think that touring with U2 would be really great, and I think it still would, but I'm contractually bound to Sunny Rickshire and Frank Strong, and quite frankly, I want to get back to art for art's sake. Do you think you can help us?"

After looking at me for a long moment, he says, "I'm not sure. It's a weird time to be working for a record company. We're downsizing, but to be honest, I'm really dissatisfied with the few bands that are being signed. I saw how the crowd responded to you and I liked what I heard a lot. Don't stop doing what you're doing. I'll try my damnedest to be up on the twenty-seventh; hopefully I'll have some people with me."

He shakes my hand and leaves me with his card that contains a direct e-mail and phone number to his office. In doing so, he leaves me floating on a cloud of drunken ecstasy. I now believe that we're destined to be huge. These are the kind of breaks that come along once in a lifetime to only a few people. And what else am I going to do with my life?

The only other option besides playing music I've considered is starting my own charismatic cult—though I question the ethics of channeling a fifty thousand year-old percussionist, even if it is in support of the arts. No, this Rod Ames is worth a shot. He's for real and the Fates have finally dealt us a break. A damn good one, too. My only question is whether or not I should inform everyone of my meeting with Rod. For now, I'll keep it to myself. Sometimes it's better not to talk too much. I've talked too much as it is. I'm finally starting to see the wisdom of living in the moment—and for the moment, our destiny is finally back in our hands where it has always belonged.

Thirty-five

It takes well over three hours to break everything down and clean up. The car lot is a mess, but in spite of the ragged gash on Bill's head, he's ecstatic. Not only have we helped him sell thirty cars, we've made his grand-opening into a city-wide media event; he's even fawning over Walter. In fact, he asks Walter to pose with him for a picture. When he's reminded of his rather unsightly wound, he yells to the cameraman, "Just scan it out later, Ted!"

Star and Walter have already posed for several pictures with different fans and if we had released our demo as a CD last year, we'd have been in fine shape after a gig like this. Ollie and Zen pose, shirts off, with a couple of grandmothers, while the miracle meeting with Rod has sent my brain into overdrive.

I know it's going to take my best sale's pitch ever to convince the group that we need to play The Battle in Seattle. Can I convince them to do this one last show without telling them of my meeting with Rod? I think so. We just played our best gig ever, but only because the band had split up. Now we're on a roll and I must keep it going. If we play The Battle with the attitude we had today, there will be no stopping us. None. If only I knew this basic truth before signing on with Sunny.

As I think of her I sink into a leaden despair. She's coming to The Showbox with Frank Strong and his contacts and things may get dicey. Already she's destined to see Angel playing with Groovetribe and when she and Frank realize that we're not the same band that his friends down in Rock City saw, there may be trouble. I sure don't want Rod to have to deal with all that conflict stuff, but he's probably used to it. Maybe I'll have time to explain it all to him before there's a big scene.

Besides, Sunny doesn't *own* us. We signed a contract that gives her control of everything *if* she or one of her colleagues scores a record deal. That says nothing about me scoring independent of her. I can just hear her threatening to sue for breach of contract. Breach my ass! She's all about setting herself up for life at our expense. She's already got my life savings as a deposit. I doubt a lawsuit by her would stand up in court. Any judge with good sense will see that she's a psycho. Things will work out fine, I think, and I'm already feeling better.

We follow Bill's white Mercedes through downtown Reno. Elvis is electric with excitement as we recall Bill's magnificent belly flop onto the hot asphalt. Walter is telling us a few missing details from his life. Namely that he won the Alaska State Blues Harp competition five years in a row and had his own kick-ass band called Walter Simon and the Nomads. But he got tired of doing it for money and was having too many personal problems to keep it together. He came to associate his harmonica with drunkenness, and it became too much for him. "I can let it go," he says. "And it doesn't bother me. I'm like a television set with a giant satellite dish hooked up outside. Music is only one channel to me."

"Walter," says Zen, slapping him on the shoulders, "you're so damn humble."

Star spits into a paper cup. "I can't believe you've been hiding this from us. It makes me wonder what else you've been hiding."

He smiles again, but a bit sadly this time.

"Can you believe Bill?" I ask. "What a racist bastard."

"It happens all the time with Indians," says Walter.

"He doesn't know how close he came to the death grip," says Star.

"He's pretty lucky," says Zen.

"I can tell he wants to get me in the sack," says Star. "But that's all right. I haven't kicked the shit out of a male in a couple of days. I need a fix."

We all laugh, knowing she's serious about it. We might just stop by the car-lot with a sack of sugar and some sharp tools on our way out of town…These thoughts and others are on my mind as we pull in behind him on the driveway to his house. Pedro's

Ford Fiesta isn't where it's usually parked and I wonder if he's gone home for the day.

Bill is standing by waiting for us, scowling.

"What's the problem?" I ask.

"These illegals are so undependable!" Bill spits, his gash making him look even more mean. "And there for awhile I thought I had a good one." He's now fumbling for his keys as we climb the stairs and I'm feeling my internal volcano starting to rumble again.

"This is the last straw, I swear," he says.

"You are really *mean*, Bill," I say as we stand at the top of the stairs while Bill fishes for his house key.

He turns and glares at me. "If you wanna get paid, you'd better shut up." He turns back to the door, puts the key in the lock and turns it. "I guess it's frozen fish sticks, kids."

But Bill Armond is wrong. There will be no frozen fish sticks tonight for Bill, or any of us for that matter. In fact, there's to be no dinner at all. A dark government-issue sedan has just pulled up behind us. Two men in suits and black ties get out. One is pointing a badge at us.

"Bill Armond?" he asks. "I am Special Agent Fred Coltrain with The Federal Bureau of Investigation. You're under arrest for the distribution of child pornography with intent to sell."

~

"What about our money for the gig, Bill?" I yell as they're stuffing him into one of several unmarked cars.

"Don't sweat it," he laughs, "they got nothin' on me."

"That's what you think, Armond," says one of the cops before roughly shoving his head down through the door and into the back seat.

"I hate you, Bill!" yells Star. "You're the scum of the earth."

"I knew he wasn't with Sony Records," whispers Ollie to me as they drive off. "Paul Simon wasn't even on Sony."

"Why didn't you say something?" I ask.

"Oh, I don't know. Would it have mattered?"

Star just kind of stares at him without speaking.

Another Fed named Bruce questions us for an hour or so before we convince him that we are just a bunch of dumb musicians who got a little side-tracked. Walter, however, seems to cause them much concern. What is it about the FBI and Indians, anyway? They hassle him for awhile before finally escorting us all away from the crime scene.

They are not concerned in the least that Bill owes us two hundred and fifty dollars—desperately needed in order to keep our date with what is now our biggest gig ever. Nor do they care that we've had nothing but bad luck on this entire tour. They are even ambivalent about the fact that we almost got murdered on the other side of the mountains. But the worst of it all is that they are convinced that, this time, Mr. Armond will not be seeing the light of day for a long, long while.

Their sting operation has netted some hard-core kid-porn, fresh in from Asia, and besides confiscating some CD ROMS, they have discovered an extensive home surveillance system with some very interesting video tapes of scantily clad musicians—in particular, a naked woman playing the electric guitar in front of a big mirror. Nothing illegal, however, though one local cop asks if he can dub the video for his personal collection. Star looks at him in disgust.

Our big break with Rod now seems destined to be torn as violently from us as a geoduck's neck on a public beach at low tide. Our chance of a lifetime looms in two days at a club in Seattle called The Showbox; we have to be there. We can't let some car-hawking child molester who owes us money stand in our way. We'll find a way. It will happen. And when it does, this will all look very funny in hindsight. Another chuckhole in the washed-out dirt road leading up a lonely mountain called success. We've navigated chuckholes before and we'll do it again. We just have to stay in the moment. Walter will keep us on the straight. We have forty-three hours before the big Seattle showdown. We'll figure something out. Besides, I laugh bitterly to myself, things like this are bound to happen to a band with a name like The Cosmic Poets.

Thirty-six

Spare change?" I timidly ask a woman dressed in bright clothes as she bustles by us and up to the entrance of the giant Smile Mart store that looms before us.

She stares straight ahead not looking at me and I want to lunge for that fake alligator purse of hers.

"This isn't working," says Star. "Maybe we should find a freeway exit and stand with cardboard signs at the bottom where all the cars have to stop."

"That's a pretty good idea," says Zen. "I know folks up in Bellingham who make a good living that way."

"That doesn't sound so good to me," I say, knowing Star might use it as an opportunity to desert us.

"Should we try busking again?" asks Ollie. "I'll try some Sinatra this time."

"Ollie," I say, "busking is all about location." Zen and Star sit dejectedly, staring out across the sweltering parking lot. "Busking doesn't just work anywhere. People here have one thing on their minds, and that's finding bargains."

"Isn't that true everywhere in America these days?" asks Walter, smiling slyly.

"I'll show you how it's done." Star jumps angrily to her feet. About thirty yards away a couple is getting out of their new Lexus and they jump back noticeably in fright as Star quickly approaches them. I hear voices talking over the distant roar of traffic, and then the man steps between the woman and Star, who screams at them to no avail. The couple head toward the big neon bargain jackpot, busy as a vacuum cleaner sucking people in one orifice and spitting them out the other.

"Doesn't anybody give a shit about anything?" she screams.

I myself have been asking that very question for years; it's good to finally know that I'm not alone. Oh well. We can't have everything just the way we want it here in the land of critical thought and self-restraint.

Star comes back to Elvis. "That was so pathetic!" Tears of rage film her cheeks.

I contemplate posing like parking lot security and charging people to park or camp here. Some of the enlightened Bellingham youth do pretty well with Canadians up in our giant K-Mart lot back home, but we can't wait another night. The clock is ticking and by my estimations, we're looking at a twenty-hour trip back to Seattle under the best of circumstances. At this moment making it back for the big Showbox showdown doesn't look good at all.

"You know," says Zen, "we ought to wait and see if Bill gets let out on bail. Then we'll get the cash and head home."

"Yeah, what's the hurry to get back?" echoes Star. "Maybe while we're waiting Ollie can score us some tickets to *Let's Make a Deal*."

"Did you know my father knew Monty Hall when they were in the army and I actually got to—"

"You mean you guys don't want to play The Showbox tomorrow night and honor our last commitment?" My voice is shaky. "It's the last gig of the tour; I think we should do it."

"Yeah, right," says Star sarcastically. "I'm having a hard time believing we even have a gig there, the way you lied about all the other ones and all."

"I'm with Star," says Zen. "I really need a break from the bullshit. Aren't you sick of it?"

"Of course I am," I say. "But I really think we should do The Showbox. There's still a chance we can score. I swear we've got a gig there."

"I'm with Angus," says Ollie. "Didn't you say Frank was flying out with his contacts?"

"Yeah, but Frank's contacts thought The Caustic Poets were us," counters Zen. "It's all a big joke now. I don't even know if Frank really exists. Have you ever talked to him?"

"No," I confess. "I don't blame you guys for doubting me, but I swear this gig is really, really important. Frank doesn't matter anymore. This is bigger than Sunny and Frank."

At this point, Walter breaks away from us, laughing as he wanders across the parking lot.

"I know you think we're all pathetic, Walter!" I cry. "But it's about commitment!"

The sound of distant harmonica shimmering in the heat waves is his only response.

"You need a break from this," says Zen to me. "We all do. The Showbox is gonna suck. I just wanna get back to a life where people are real and music's fun."

"Yeah, to hell with Sunny and Frank," Star says with tears still dribbling down her face. "They're both full of shit if you ask me, and besides, why are we even having this conversation? We're out of gas, money and food—and I'm almost out of chew."

"I think we should do the gig," says Ollie. "It's my fault that I recognized Bill at that pay phone. If I hadn't, maybe things would have turned out better. I wish for once I could do something right."

"No, Ollie," I say, "nothing is your fault. I'm the one who lied about the tour, but there's something you all need to know about The Showbox." They all turn to look at me and I know the time has come to lay all the cards on the table. I take a deep, shaky breath before I begin.

"It probably doesn't matter anymore, but before I tell you guys what's going on there, I just want you to know that you really mean a lot to me and no matter what happens, I'll always believe that we were one of the best rock bands that nobody's ever heard. I'm proud of you guys and I really believed when we met Sunny that she and Frank were gonna get us signed and Lily would come back to me. But I realized after Twin Bridges that I'd been doing music for all the wrong reasons. So get this: after our killer set at the car lot a guy came up to me saying he was from A&M Records and that he wanted to bring some people to hear us at The Showbox. He loved us."

"You've got to be kidding," says Star.

"I'm not," I say. "He was really down to earth too."

"Just what we need, more promises," says Zen.

"That's the point, Zen. The guy didn't make any promises. In fact, he said that few bands are getting signed anymore and just about all of them suck! The fact is he liked us, and he's canceling a trip to New York to be in Seattle tomorrow night."

"You're not lying again, are you?" asks Star. "Why didn't you say something before?"

"I was afraid that if I did, you'd all start getting self conscious again. I was hoping I could just get you guys to The Showbox to play with the attitude we displayed last night. If we do that, we'll be unstoppable. Whether that matters anymore to you guys is a different story."

"It matters to me," says Star, hurriedly.

"I've always been in," says Ollie. "You know, I think I saw the guy you're talking about. Was he wearing a tie-dyed shirt with long hair and a kind of crooked nose?"

"He was," I say.

"I'd do it," sighs Zen, "except that we're out of money. You guys keep forgetting that we're out of money."

"What's money got to do with anything?" asks Walter who has quietly come back.

We all look at him standing there. His eyes seem to burn and I love him. "Walter," I sigh. "Money does help to put gas into the tank. Plus some food would be nice."

"Didn't you learn *anything* from me?" he asks, irritated.

"What are you talking about?" asks Star. "We're trying to solve a problem here."

"A problem that you've invented for the occasion. You can't seem to tell the difference between an opportunity and a crisis."

Just as he says this, a Smile Mart security truck with a flashing yellow light comes pulling up and a short, fat little guy with his pants drooping low on his thighs waddles over and informs us that there have been numerous complaints against us for loitering, and that Elvis will be towed away unless we vacate the premises immediately.

"Very funny," says Star, sarcastically. "We're out of gas and have no money."

"Sorry, but I don't make the rules. I just enforce 'em."

"What do you suggest we do?" I ask, looking at the digital clock across the street, knowing that each passing minute weakens our hopes of making it back to Seattle in time for the showdown. Twenty six hours and counting…

"There's a mini-mart up the block," he says, pointing a pudgy finger towards a characterless food and gas mart. "Go park it there. I don't care what you do as long as you get it out of here."

Even if we manage to push him that far, we're only transferring the problem to another parking lot. Yet move we must. Any change of scenery from this Smile Mart Empire built on the bones of dead children will be welcome.

"You are so rude," I say. "I'm never shopping at Smile Mart again, and I'm gonna tell everyone I know not to either."

"Why don't you tell someone who gives a shit," he laughs.

He informs us that we have fifteen minutes to move Elvis before the tow truck shows up. Then he hops in his little mall security truck and drives away.

"What do we do now?" asks Ollie.

"Walter steers while we push," I say, not wanting to give Ollie the chance to weasel out of some manual labor.

It looks like we can get Elvis rolling down hill to about the half-way point and then it's going to be a hump to get him up to the far entrance of the lot, but if we can get enough momentum, we might get close. Then it will be a matter of pushing him out into oncoming traffic before swinging him around and into the mini-mart lot.

I explain the plan to everyone and even Zen seems to agree that it's our best one so far. After giving Walter a quick lesson in driver education, we're ready to rock. Or, at least, to roll.

"One, two, three!" I yell, and we heave forward, two people per side in the back. We grunt and shove and it feels like we're pushing a brick wall, but slowly the wall is starting to give.

"Geeze," sighs Star next to me. "This thing's a tank."

"Watch your back, Zen," grunts Ollie, but soon Elvis is rolling on his own.

"Push harder!" I holler.

Walter's doing a fine job of steering as we slowly weave through a maze of parked cars and we're quickly drenched with sweat. Elvis is rolling about five miles an hour when we reach the bottom of the dip. Now we're two-thirds of the way to the south entrance of the lot and the mini-mart looms like a castle in the clouds—

minus the clouds and medieval architecture, of course. The hissing and puffing is growing ever more profane, and we've now lost some momentum though we're still moving. If we can just budge Elvis over the little hump, we'll be home free. "Push!" I bellow as Walter is now outside pushing too.

There's no telling if we'll make it or not. Elvis is still moving, but with not more than five feet to go before the top of the rise the weight of him sinking backwards becomes too much.

"Out of the way!" I scream as Elvis begins rolling backwards. Walter jumps aside and Zen runs up to the driver's side. Just before Elvis crunches a green Pacer, he manages to jump in and engage the brake.

"Shit," mumbles Star. "So close."

"It'll never work," says Zen.

"We gotta try again," I say, panicked. Just the act of doing something feels like progress.

"There's no way we're gonna push this thing up and over that hill on our own," says Zen.

"We need more people," Star says with resolve as she jumps to her feet and runs across the parking lot to a couple of skateboard-types walking out of the store, one with a new basketball under his arm. She says something to them and immediately they are on their way over to us. Introductions are brief, though one of them begins asking a lot of questions about Walter's lineage and life growing up in Alaska. We line up behind Elvis to try again. We have got to break the curse.

There is a noticeable difference with six bodies versus four, and these skateboarders are in pretty good shape. Elvis slowly starts to move forward and soon we're pushing him up the slight grade in the lot. He's getting much heavier, but it looks like we're going to make it.

"*Push!*" someone grunts as Elvis is sinking back, getting ever more leaden though we're within five feet and I feel every muscle in by body screaming as it winds tightly to the snapping point. "We're gonna make it!" I yell but he's slowing down and now it's down to inches.

"Push!" yells Zen, in the midst of much wailing and gnashing of teeth. We're almost there. "Push! He's gonna…He's not gonna…He's gonna…Look out!"

Elvis has stopped within inches from the top of the rise There is a mournful groan as he slowly rolls backwards.

"Out of the way!" someone screams while we jump aside and watch in horror as Walter tries desperately to steer him. Picking up steam, by sheer luck he misses another car, reaching the bottom of the dip before rolling over a little island of bark and juniper.

"Shit!" wails Star, and I hear the sound of laughter. I look and see Walter standing by the driver's door, just cracking up.

Elvis now appears to be high-centered and now we're not going anywhere. Zen stares in quiet rage while Ollie is off in some other dimension playing air drums with his fingers. "So Groovetribe's playing The Showbox, too?" he asks, oblivious to the present situation.

"What does it matter?" I ask.

Star is a crumpled, sobbing mess. Walter just walks around Elvis blowing his harp and laughing.

"What's the problem Star?" I ask. "I'm surprised you're so upset."

She looks up at me with tears dribbling down her cheeks. "I wanted to be famous."

"That can still happen Star," I say, calmly. "Just not with this band."

The yellow security truck reappears, screeching up. This time chump-cakes has someone else with him. His walkie-talkie crackles with static. He waddles over to us with a swirl of self importance and looks over Elvis before smirking. "Nice job."

The other security guard laughs dutifully, knowing that it pleases chump-cakes immensely to be admired for his authority.

Chump-cakes mumbles something into the radio about bringing a tow truck and just shakes his head, muttering, "Tourists."

"We're not tourists," replies Star, angrily. "We're musicians on tour."

"Sure you are," he says, sarcastically.

"Hey dipstick," Star says. "I'll tear that smirk off your face and stuff it in your mouth."

Suddenly he's on his radio in a panic "I need back-up! Now!"

"Oh, come on," I say. "She's only kidding."

"No, I'm not," Star snarls.

"I told you to move your rig fifteen minutes ago. Now you're starting trouble." Pointing accusingly at Star, he says, "You better keep her in line."

She glares at him as a cop car comes pulling up with blue lights flashing. Following it is a white tow truck with red lettering. As I read the logo, I can't believe my eyes. It says: Smile Mart Towing.

"You guys have your own in-house towing department?"

"You got it," says chump-cakes.

The real cop asks if there is any trouble and before he can answer, Star says, "Yeah, this rent-a-bozo is harassing us."

"Me?" he asks, shocked. "People have been complaining all morning and afternoon about these trashy panhandlers. They've been threatening people who don't give them money. I gave them fifteen minutes to move their rig and they're still here."

"I told him we were out of gas," says Star to the cop.

The cop just kind of looks at us all before glaring at chump-cakes, saying, "You called me for this? I've got a real job to do." He gets in his car and drives off, glaring at all of us while shaking his head.

This is a real blow to chump-cakes, whose skinny little buddy just kind of looks down. "Don't try anything funny," he says, trying to gloss over his embarrassment.

The tow truck driver wearing Smile Mart overalls begins hooking up Elvis to the tow bar.

"Pretty soon Smile Mart's gonna own everything," says Ollie. "Do you ever wonder about Smile Mart's effect on the little guy trying to stay alive?"

"I don't recall saying anything to you," chump-cakes snorts back, and suddenly I think of Rod from A&M Records. I've got to call and tell him that we're not gonna make it back to Seattle before he leaves Los Angeles.

"What are you so afraid of?" asks Walter.

"I'm not afraid of nothing, chief," he snorts, looking shocked.

"You act like you're very frightened," says Walter. "You must've gotten picked on when you were a teenager."

Chump-cakes just stares at Walter. So much for illusion, title and appearance. He shakes his head and mumbles something hopping in his truck with the other moron.

"Have a nice day, dipstick," taunts Star.

As he drives off, he flips us the bird.

The towing dude hardly seems any more human as he finishes hooking up Elvis. "It's gonna be one hundred and fifty bucks to get your motor-home back," he says. "Aisle 9. Ask for towing."

"We don't have any money," I whisper.

"Loan department's on Aisle 7. Good luck." He hops in the truck and engages the tow bar that raises slowly while Elvis groans a bit. He pulls forward cautiously, disengaging Elvis off the island. Then he heads toward the south side of the massive building. Like our dreams, Elvis gradually fades in size and definition until the heat waves make him appear like a mirage. And that's the last we see of him before he disappears.

~

"What now?" asks Zen.

"I don't know," I say, looking at the digital clock across the street, which now reads 5:45 P.M. "We'd probably barely make it back to Seattle as it is, even if we left now."

"I'm thirsty," says Star. "I need water."

"And I'm really hungry," announces Zen.

"Let's go to the mini-mart and get some water," sighs Star. "Maybe we could bum some popcorn off of them or something."

"There's a pay phone," I say, noticing it tucked in the corner of the giant lot in the direction we're going. "I'm going to check my messages."

"I hate Bill Armond!" Star cries. "I hope they lock him up for life."

"Should we try to call him?" asks Ollie. "Maybe he could wire us our money from jail."

"I doubt it, Ollie," I reply, watching Walter smirk. "The cops said he'd be in the tank at least a week. Why are you in such a good mood, Walter?"

"You're very funny." He sighs. "Everything you need is right here. But you just never learn, do you?"

"You got a hundred and fifty bucks to get us back to Bellingham?" I ask.

He laughs. "You never learn," he says again.

I dial in the calling card number and the phone rings once before the automated voice comes on, telling me that I have five new messages. With great trepidation, I punch in the secret access code.

First message left Monday at 8:03 P.M.: "Did you hang up on me or did we just lose our connection? I'll assume that we just lost the connection. Anyway, sweetie, Frank called and he'll be flying into Seattle Friday morning for the big Showbox gig. I am so excited I can't even sleep. I went see my psychic again and she says that your luck is about to change. Frank's friends from RCA will be meeting him at 1:00 at Pier 84. I'm coming down for the meeting and you have to be there. They're all looking forward to talking to you. Frank also said that he'd be calling you personally for an update. I told you we were on the threshold. Remember, Angus, don't fuck it all up."

Next message left Tuesday at 3:32 P.M.: "Hi Angus, it's Angel. Sorry about what happened at Rock City. I had no idea that you gave the boss five hundred bucks to warm up for us. You gotta admit though, that was a pretty stupid thing to do. It's funny, later on he was buying everybody drinks and here I thought he was so generous. I didn't know the drinks were really on *you*! We don't have any record deals yet, but some guys who said they were from RCA were there and they really liked our set. Get this: they're flying out to check us out at the Showbox. They said they were out to hear The Caustic Poets, but they liked us just as much. Sequoia and Matt think we're close to a deal and I had another visit from the dolphins. I think I'm finally understanding what they've been trying to tell me for the last year. I can't explain it right here; I'll tell you about it when I see you since it pertains to you, too. Sorry things didn't work out for you, but you know if you weren't so selfish, I'd still be in the band. Oh well, it's all for the best. By the way, I'm looking for my hat, and I think that I left it in Elvis. If you even do make it to the show, can you bring it for me? I hope there are no hard feelings anymore. I've forgiven you for what you did to me. Sequoia teaches me a lot about myself. You could learn a lot from him, too. Did you know that he's published a book of his teachings? He says that we've got to let go of all emotion and pain in order to be in the moment. It's all about 'being' when you think about it; please remember the hat. Bye."

Next message left Wednesday at 8:08 P.M.: "Angus? Frank Strong here. I just wanted to make personal contact with you before I fly out to Seattle. I know y'all are still on tour, but can you call me when you get this message? My friends from RCA really loved your set up at Rock City, but they have a few questions for you. Evidently there's been some confusion regarding the name of the band, but that's club owners for you. Sunny's been keeping me informed of the band's progress and it sounds like you've had a really good tour. I think we're close to something special my friend. I'm looking forward to meeting you in person. Call me as soon as you can; I'm flying out on Thursday at 5:00 from Florida. If you don't get this before I leave, call Sunny as soon as you do. We're having a meeting Friday at 1:00 in Seattle."

My hand is shaking so hard I can hardly control it. The clock across the street reads 5:55 P.M. Frank's been in the air almost an hour. I cannot seem to get a grip on anything, much less the receiver of the phone. My hand is so sweaty that the damn thing keeps slipping out. Maybe I should stop squeezing it so hard.

Next message left Wednesday at 11:36 P.M.: "I just want you to know that I've hardly slept in days. You made me so angry, but it's all so confusing, too. I didn't mean to offend you or make you think you need to be *fixed* in order to be with me. *Zen and the Art of Motorcycle Maintenance* really opened my eyes to a lot of things in myself, and I was only suggesting it as a resource shared by one friend with another. You freaked out and I got mad. I'm sorry for telling you to fuck off, but if I didn't love you so much I wouldn't have said anything. I know you don't want to hear that, but it's true. Angus, I love you more than anyone else I've ever known. I know it's hard for you to take, but you need to bear it in mind during this difficult time. I'm really sorry about hanging up on you and I hope you can forgive me. I assume you're going to finish the tour and all, so I'll see you Friday night at The Showbox. I hope we'll find a way to talk then, and I hope we'll be able to spend some quality time soon. Bye, love…"

"Yeeeaaah!" I scream. My momentary elation is short-lived when I consider Elvis locked inside Smile Mart's towing garage. It's funny how one can feel really good and excited about things when reality isn't taken into consideration.

Next message left today, at 4:30 P.M.: "Angus, this is Rod Ames, from A&M Records in Los Angeles. I met you yesterday in Reno at the car lot. I'm calling you from the airport and I'm hoping that you check your messages. I was able to postpone the New York trip 'til next week, so I'm flying out to Seattle tonight with a couple of friends of mine to catch your gig tomorrow night at The Showbox. We listened to the tape and all thought it was pretty good, but I convinced them that your live show is the real deal. I'm not making any promises, but we do like what we hear. Hope to chat with you a little before the show if there's time. Otherwise, have a great set and we'll talk with you afterwards. See you tomorrow."

"What? What's the matter?" asks Star. I realize that I've hardly noticed my band mates plus Walter standing before me the whole time I've been listening to the messages.

"Oh, nothing." I press the replay button of all the messages before handing the phone to Star for her and the others to hear while I walk past them to the curb, crumbling in a heap so I can have a good, long cry.

Thirty-seven

Can I help you?" asks an old hippie with long, gray hair and dark circles under his eyes. He looks like he hasn't slept in quite awhile.

"Can we have some water to drink?" whispers a ragged-looking Star as we all file in behind her.

"It's twenty five-cents for the cup," he says, nervously. "The water's free, though."

"Mister," says Star, trembling a bit. "All I ever wanted to do was become a rock-n-roll star."

"Isn't that all anyone wants, really?" asks the clerk. "I mean, when you get right down to it."

"What's your name?"

"Jake."

"Well, you don't understand, Jake, that we have had a really rough West Coast tour and in spite of it all, Rod Ames from A&M Records along with Frank Strong and all of his contacts are coming to our gig tomorrow night at The Showbox and we just got our bus towed away by your friendly, neighborhood Smile Mart Corporation and, on top of that, we're out of money and if you really want to hit us up for a stupid cup of water then go ahead, but if you do, you know something? You'll be the biggest jerk I've ever met!"

"I'll buy you a cup of water, Star," Ollie says, pulling out a couple of lone coins from his pocket.

"Nah," the clerk says, shaken. "The water's on me. Sorry you've been having such a rough time."

"You've been holding out on us, huh, Ollie?" I ask. "I thought we were all out of money."

"These two quarters are all I have, I swear," he says, showing me the two quarters plus a few pennies.

Star gratefully accepts the extra-large cup of water filled with ice, and now Walter's in the store, and the four of us pass it around refreshing our parched throats while Ollie wanders over to a magazine rack before something more interesting seems to catch his eye.

I want to scream at the Fates, cursing our bad fortune. But what's the point, really? Shit happens and we've been dealt a lot of excrement on this journey.

The sound of jingling catches my ear. My first thought is that someone is playing pinball close by until it occurs to me that there are no pinball machines in this store. In the back a man in a Hawaiian shirt is playing a slot machine, Ollie standing behind him watching in fascination. It's a quarter machine, and in a span of about five minutes he pumps in about forty quarters, coming up empty each time.

That's the thing about Nevada. You're never very far away from your lucky break; there's always a casino within spitting distance, and if you're not really into that scene, you can always throw your money away on the slot machines, located in just about every store and public place.

The guy in a Hawaiian shirt is really getting pissed and keeps yelling at the machine, but to no avail. He yanks back furiously on the handle while it keeps swallowing quarters, though every once in awhile it spits a few out, just enough to keep him going. Finally he curses the machine before storming past us and out of the store. "These machines are rigged!" he yells.

"What do people expect?" the clerk asks.

I turn my attention back to Ollie who is now standing before the machine, studying it. He then pops a quarter in and pulls the lever. It comes up, strawberry, banana and peach.

"Save your money, Ollie," I say. "We'll need whatever we have." Rod and Frank are both on airplanes headed for Seattle to check us out and here we are stuck in some Reno, Nevada, mini-mart with no money left to our name. Maybe we would qualify for a Smile Mart Loan, I think, trying to suppress the agony. It could have been a great gig with break-through potential. I look at the clock. It's now 6:32.

I'm shaken from my daydream by the sound of coins pouring out of the machine. Ollie is standing back, surprised at the sudden good fortune his last quarter brought him. "I bet it's ten bucks," he says and, after counting it up, I realize that he's right.

"Hey, you guys," I yell over to Star, Zen, and Walter. "Ollie just won ten bucks."

Everyone wanders to the back of the store to watch Ollie counting his quarters.

"All right, Ollie," says Zen. "Food and beer money."

"Not so fast," Star says. "Let's win some more." She steps in front of the machine and says, "Give me some quarters, Ollie."

"Star?" Ollie replies, "I won these quarters, they're mine, and I really think we ought to quit while we're—"

She whirls toward him like she's going take his head off. "Give me some fucking quarters!" He immediately hands over a fistful, and she starts plugging the machine and yanking the lever.

Could she be our ticket? I mean, what better script could be written? The Cosmic Poets, broke and despairing, a day and nine hundred sixty-seven miles away from their biggest gig ever, their car in tow, hit the big jackpot in a Reno convenience store. We all stand around Star, cheering her on while she keeps losing. *Go Star*, I think while she white-knuckles the lever, yanking on it. "Come on baby, give me another peach, give it to me now…"

When she's down to the last quarter, she demands that everyone step back. Then she pulls several cans of Spam from the shelf next to her and places them on the floor in a circle in the middle of which she places the last quarter. She bends over it uttering strange, unintelligible incantations while we stare on in amazement.

"Star," says Ollie, "Those were my quarters and I'm mad that you—"

"Shut your mouth, Ollie. Can't you see that I'm trying to *manifest* something?" She mumbles a few more words, kissing the quarter before flipping it high in the air. She catches it, popping it in the machine while turning her head away and pulling the lever. The image spins while she brakes on each one…peach…peach…banana!

She wails and falls away from the machine. "These machines are rigged!"

"That was our dinner, Star," Ollie says, bitterly.

"What is it that's so funny, Walter?" I ask, looking at him standing behind us, grinning.

"You just don't ever learn," he says. "After everything I've taught you."

"Please explain it to me because I don't see anything funny about this at all," I reply.

"White people always need things explained or written down for them. My grandmother always told me that white people would give me the gift of patience."

"Humor us, Walter," I say as Zen and Ollie head toward the front of the store.

"If I try to explain it to you, it will ruin everything."

"Yeah, but everything's in ruins, anyway," I reply as shouting erupts from the front of the store.

"What's going on?" says Zen. It's Star and Ollie, locked in another wrestling match. When Zen and I manage to break them apart they're both panting, staring at each other like wild dogs.

"You bastard," Star says to Ollie. "I thought I taught you not to mess with the goddess."

"You got a lot of nerve, Star," pants Ollie. "First you lose my ten bucks, and then—"

"Oh, you would'a lost it yourself anyway. Why don't you take responsibility for your—"

"Why don't you quit trying to change the subject," Ollie says. He turns to add: "She's been holding out on us." He pulls out an unopened can of chew and holds it up for all to see. "First she loses my money, then I catch her trying to buy *this*. She's got money." He turns to her. "You're the one with a lot of nerve. And, by the way, did you know that the tobacco industry literally controls the entire House and Senate and—"

"It was my last three bucks, Mr. Conspiracy. And I swear, you do not, and I mean, *do not* want to be around me when I'm out of chew! If you thought I kicked your ass before, you don't even have a clue as to what I *could* do to you!" Saying this, she bursts into fresh tears. "I'm sorry I lost the money, but three bucks at this point isn't gonna make much difference. Let me keep the chew, please?"

"Star," I say. "This isn't just about you anymore. We're all in this together. We need the three bucks."

"No," she wails, surrendering the can to Zen who presents it to the clerk.

"Can we have our money back?"

Our hippie-clerk sighs while he presents Zen with the refund. "Why can't everybody just get along?" he asks no one in particular.

"It's for the best, Star," I say, examining our dinner options. A bag of cheese puffs, three bean and cheese burritos that have been roasting for days under a heat lamp, and a box of milk duds. That totals $2.69.

"You guys like bean burritos?" I ask the crew. Star wails in response.

"Give me the totem," Walter says to me. He is not smiling anymore. In fact, he looks very intense.

"What are you talking about?" I ask.

"Just give it to me."

"What?"

"The totem I gave you before you dropped me off at Chemewah. Remember?"

"Oh yeah, *that* thing." I fish around my front pocket until I feel the smooth, ivory little block buried at the bottom. I pull it out and hand it over to him. "How the hell did you make such an intricate carving on such a small piece of ivory, Walter?" I ask.

"Always needing an explanation," he says, blowing it off. He then goes over and hands it to Ollie. "I made a mistake. This really belongs to you."

"Thanks, Walter," Ollie says, examining it. "This is really neat."

"Yeah, thanks a lot," I say, sarcastically.

Ollie looks at me, puzzled.

"Give him the money," Walter says to Zen. Zen looks at me. I can only shrug my shoulders.

Just then, a big guy with a straw hat and sunglasses comes in and pays for his gas. He stares at us like we're part of a freak show.

Meanwhile our hippie-clerk just seems amused by the whole thing and has said very little. At least he hasn't asked us to leave, which is a good sign. People like us probably help him pass the time.

Zen hands Star's three bucks to Ollie.

"Make change and try again," Walter commands.

"What?" Ollie asks, confused.

"Get some quarters and try again."

"Are you sure, Walter?" he asks. "I know three bucks doesn't go very far anymore with inflation and all but you know if we were in Canada right now, with the value of their dollar and all, we might, in fact, be in pretty good shape, but—"

"Get some quarters!"

"Sure, Walter," he says, submissively. Star looks on, intrigued.

He gets thirteen quarters and we move to the back of the store. Walter studies the slot machine very closely. "I want you to hold the totem in your left hand while you play," he says to Ollie.

Ollie dutifully pulls out the totem and holds it in his left hand.

"Now *play!*" says Walter.

Ollie plugs a quarter in and pulls the lever. The cylinder swirls and Ollie pulls the lever three times, coming up empty. He looks at Walter, forlornly.

"Go again," says Walter.

He does it again with the same result.

"I'm telling you, these machines are rigged," I say.

"Keep playing," says Walter.

Ollie does and he keeps losing. When we're down to two quarters, he says, "Are you sure, Walter?"

"Play," he says.

Ollie plugs the machine and engages the cylinder and then applies the brakes...peach...peach...peach! Quarters pour from the machine, and suddenly they stop. We count five dollars.

"Play," says Walter. "Don't stop."

Ollie plays, and of course, starts losing again, and I conclude that even winners will never make more than ten to fifteen bucks at best. But Ollie is obsessed. He talks, plays and groans each time the machine swallows another quarter. Finally we're down to just three left. He takes one quarter, blows on it, jams it into the machine and yanks. The cylinder purrs and he brakes one at a time. No luck. He tries again with the same result, and now we're down to our final quarter.

Suddenly Walter is cracking up again. He's laughing so hard he falls to his knees. We all look at him and we're finally able to see for the first time, the absurdity of our entire situation.

First it's Star who starts laughing and once she starts, she's doubled up and falling over which causes Zen to lose it and now

244 | Tim McHugh

I'm on the floor too, hardly able to breathe. Everything is funny—
Rod Ames, Bill Armond, Tom Jones, the pull-tab morons, the Boss,
Rock City, Groovetribe, The Oregon Country Fair, Frank Strong
and this. And here, in the cultural heart of Nevada, we're having
a ten-year laugh. To hell with all of the bullshit. It'll be a long
hitch back to Bellingham, but so what? At the very least, we'll all
have to get real jobs in order to bail Elvis out of the slammer.
Maybe we'll even rent a house and stay here for awhile. Who
cares anymore?

Now the hippie-clerk is standing over us, concerned. "I'm afraid
you're gonna have to leave now," he says. "My boss is showing
up soon."

One by one we climb to our feet, dusting ourselves off, still
laughing.

"Thanks for the water," Star finally says, rosy-cheeked and
spent.

"No problem," he says.

Just then, I hear Ollie pop his last quarter in the machine and
without hesitation yanks hard on the lever and engages the brakes
almost simultaneously; suddenly the machine lights up as sirens
go off like a ten-alarm fire and we turn in shock as all hell seems
to be breaking loose.

Thirty-eight

There's a commonly held belief that serious gamblers who come to Nevada don't waste their time with slot machines since the pay-offs are usually on the small side. Most people who'll spend a few hundred bucks to fly in for a weekend on some special, package deal have one thing on their minds: winning big. This usually means cards and roulette, with slot machines providing a nice break from the stress of concentration. Big jackpots in the slot machines might be few and far between, yet even with their small pay-offs, nothing beats the sensory stimulation of a slot machine in action.

We watch with wonder as quarters pour out of the pulsating machine, colored lights flashing, an endless river of silver chiming against the hard floor, a giant pile growing larger and larger with each passing second, stray quarters rolling everywhere throughout the store. It's as if we're witnessing a sacred moment in the history of civilization. Hard to know how long this avalanche actually lasts; it seems like it goes on forever.

Finally, when the noise dies down and the stream of quarters becomes a trickle, it lurches, belches, and vomits another silver pile.

Star's face bears an angelic glow. Ollie and Zen just stand there, staring. Walter is cracking up. The show ends; before us stands a mountain of quarters maybe two feet high.

"I've never seen anything like this," says the wide-eyed hippie-clerk.

Star goes over to Ollie and grabs him in a bear hug, lifting him high off the ground. "I love you, Ollie!" she yelps, while he just hangs limply in her arms. The heavenly floodgates of luck and good fortune have rained down upon us and I realize that I'm crying. We all are. The hippie-clerk brings us cotton sacks and we begin filling them up with quarters. There's another bald-headed, fifty-something dude now standing in the store. He's evidently played this machine before. He stares at us and his eyes are filled with awe, jealously and amazement. "I can't watch this, Jake," he says before turning to leave. "Some people have *all* the luck."

It's hard to know how long it takes to bag up the quarters, but I would estimate it's at least an hour. When we're done, we've got fourteen full sacks.

"I'd estimate that it's about six thousand-dollars," says the hippie-clerk.

"Can you believe this?" yells Star.

"Unbelievable," says Zen. "It's like out of a movie."

"Ollie, you did it. You saved us all," I say. He beams with charisma and power.

"No, it was Walter. Or at least the lucky totem he gave me."

Walter only smiles.

"What is that thing, Walter?" I ask. "Some magical totem that has been in your family for generations, meant to protect and bring good luck and fortune?"

"Nah," he says, indifferently. "I bought it in a Fairbanks gift shop a few months ago. Here, let me see it." Ollie hands it to him. He turns it over in his hands while squinting. "There," he says. "Check it out."

I take it from him and turn it over in my hand reading the fine print carved in the bottom. I laugh out loud. "You won't believe this," I tell everyone. "The damned thing was made in China."

~

As we lug the sacks of coins out of what is now our most favorite mini-mart in the entire universe, it occurs to me that we are going to be an easy target for robbers. It also occurs to me that we're being protected by unseen forces. We're near the edge of the lot when Star suddenly drops her sacks, grabs a fistful of quarters and says, "I'll be right back."

We wait, exposed, vulnerable and nervous, yet full of hope. I'm trying to estimate the time it will take to drive back to Seattle once we reclaim Elvis. Star emerges from the store, her bottom lip hideously swollen, packed with more chew than I thought the human lip could take. She smiles. Her eyes are clear.

I lug three sacks myself, which feel like a hundred pounds. Once we're a third of the way across the big parking lot with the evil Smile Mart Empire looming before us, I need a break. "Damn, lugging all this money around sure is draining."

Walter smiles, but says nothing.

"I don't mind problems like this," says Star, spitting with joy.

"You know, Star," I sigh, "some day you're gonna lose all your teeth if you don't quit that stuff."

"You're about to lose all your teeth right now if you don't lay off me," she says, smiling. "I'll quit after the tour's over."

We've worked up a dripping sweat. Cars roll past, some of the gawkers pointing. We must be quite a sight, too, dragging several thousand dollars in quarters across a Smile Mart parking lot. Since the hippie-clerk was ill prepared to deal with changing all those quarters, there is no alternative. Not to mention it should be very satisfying to pay Smile Mart one hundred and fifty dollars in quarters to reclaim Elvis.

At the front entrance, the gratuitous, eighty-something Smile Mart zombie lady gives us the surreal, "Welcome to Smile Mart," greeting. She doesn't even seem to notice the bags of change we drag with us. The first thing I notice is the George Michael Muzak pumped over the store's intercom system.

"The towing department, please," I say.

"Check Customer Service," says a way-too-friendly guy in a Smile Mart shirt.

"Have a nice day," I say to the old lady.

"Welcome to Smile Mart," she repeats as if seeing me for the first time.

I grab a shopping cart, which we load up with our small fortune. The going is much easier now. I'm feeling cocky and powerful in ways I've never felt before. We weave our way through the human ant farm and everyone seems to have the same glazed, passive, lifeless eyes; I half expect Rod Serling to pop out from behind one of these aisles.

"They must learn," I say to myself.

"What?" asks Star.

"We must teach them," I repeat and Walter, Zen and Ollie laugh out loud before Star catches on and laughs, too. The customer service center where we'll pay our impoundment fee looms thirty yards ahead and closing.

"Watch this," I say to everyone, then zero in on an everyday-looking American male who's scanning a coupon book on aisle eight. "Excuse me sir, but do you know where I might find the meaning of life?"

"What?" He recoils, his comfort zone fearfully invaded.

"You know: that thing we all used to have before being brainwashed into believing that freedom is one's ability to choose between a variety of low paying jobs, specialized careers and slave-labor made products and I was just wondering if you know on which aisle I might find the meaning of life?"

The man just looks at me. "Are you lost or something?"

"No, sir!" I holler. "I'm alive! You're alive! We all have real choices about how to live meaningfully!" He stares in horror for a moment before running away. Other people have stopped momentarily from their work and are looking at me with eyes of concern. I can say nothing more and the glassy look soon returns as they go back to their business.

I hear a familiar blend of voices singing. *"Oh beautiful for spacious skies for amber waves of grain…"* It's Walter and Ollie. A second later, Star and Zen are joining in, as am I.

We stand singing and, in moments, dozens of shoppers have gathered with us, all singing along enthusiastically. Some old lady is actually crying. As we drown out the George Michael song on the intercom, I am overwhelmed with a feeling of pride and patriotism. I know in my heart that if ordered to I would kill for these shoppers.

We finish the song and people are cheering throughout our part of the store. I run over to Walter and grab him in a bear hug. "You people have no idea what has happened to us and how much we learned on this tour! I love you, Walter!"

Walter tries to wriggle away from me. "Let's not take this too far," he says, winking at Star.

"Wow, Angus," says Star. "I've never seen you so…so dangerous."

"I've never *felt* so dangerous! I don't care what happens to the band up in Seattle anymore. I don't care if we score with labels; I just want this feeling to last forever."

"Speak for yourself," says Star, turning serious. "I'm ready to blow Groovetribe out of the water."

We're finally at the customer service desk and I'm amazed at how huge this store is.

"Can I help you?" drones a middle-aged woman with streaked hair.

"Yeah," I say, amazed that they've hardly noticed the commotion. "We're here to pick up Elvis."

"Elvis?" she asks, suddenly excited. "You've seen him, *alive*?"

"Elvis is our tour bus," says Star. "One of your rent-a-cops had him towed."

"Oh, right," she says with disappointment. "I know what you're talking about." She starts leafing through a pile of papers, and eventually pulls one up. "Yep, right here. That'll be two hundred thirty-seven dollars to get him back."

"What? The towing guy said a hundred and fifty bucks."

"Yeah, but we have to charge you for destroying one juniper and messing up our landscaping. We have to re-plant and re-bark the island because of you people."

"Just pay it, Angus," says Star. "We don't have any more time to waste."

I heft a bag of Ollie's quarters onto the counter. To the woman's astonishment, we begin counting the money for the bill.

Once we've paid our impoundment and wilderness restoration fees—which have hardly dented Ollie's pile of coins—we are taken to the back of the store to be reunited with Elvis. We load him with the coin sacks while Zen volunteers to run back to the mini-mart with a new, Smile Mart gas can to fetch us a few gallons of petrol.

The towing guy seems a bit skeptical of our story about the jackpot, but still seems surprised to see us.

"What time is it?" Star asks.

Ollie looks at his watch and replies that it's now 9:46 P.M.

"I don't know if we can make it," I say. "We've got less than twenty-four hours, and we still need to eat dinner. I'm starving."

"So am I," says Ollie.

"We'll make it," says Star. "I know we will."

Zen is back sooner than I would have expected and we gas Elvis up. As the back freight doors open, Zen fires the engine. Elvis coughs and sputters, spewing a blue and white death plume that envelops the garage. Store employees are running everywhere, choking and complaining loudly.

"Get it out of here!" bellows the towing guy.

"We've gotta warm him up first," yells Zen back at him and I take great satisfaction watching the smoke spread everywhere.

We're all aboard now as Zen slowly pulls Elvis forward and out into the open air and fading sunlight. Our date with destiny is once more tangible. We've bucked off the Fates hell-bent on destroying us. As we glide through the parking lot heading toward Interstate 43, Star yells out, "Hey there's my favorite rent-a-cop!"

Sure enough, there is chump-cakes parked in a stall munching a hamburger with mayo, mustard, and pickle juice running down both sides of his face. He stares at us in astonishment. His window is open.

"Stop, Zen," Star says. "I want to say goodbye."

Zen stops, and Star slides open the side window while the poor moron just kind of stares up at us, hurriedly wiping his face with a napkin. He seems a little embarrassed. "What do you idiots want now?" he asks.

"The bitch just wanted to say goodbye." Seductively, Star mashes her chest against the window. Chump-cakes' eyes get big. "And to tell him that she is sure gonna miss him…How about some lubrication for the road there big fella?" With the marksmanship of a pro, her lips pucker and her cheeks tremble, flexing iron-hard muscles before launching a dark stream of chew spit that, like a heat seeking missile, finds its target with lethal precision, splattering a brown mess squarely in his crotch. The last thing we hear as Zen pulls away is a weird kind of screaming that doesn't even sound like a human being at all.

Thirty-nine

We're about twenty miles north of Reno. Earlier we stopped for a luxurious dinner of fries and ice cream. Star wanted lobster and made Ollie promise to take her out to the Chuckanut Manor once we get back to Bellingham. Zen drives and I now realize that I am completely exhausted, though I cannot seem to tear myself away from the Atlas. It's doubtful we'll get back in time, though Zen promises to try.

There is much chatter and excitement and Ollie is fully engrossed in counting the money. It's like we've just robbed a bank or something. It seems so strange that we're going home to what may be the biggest gig ever. Everything is turning slow and syrupy...I try to stay awake...Which side is real? I'm afraid that the whole thing is a dream and I'll wake up on a logging road cursing Sunny or the boss. Walter's laughter echoing off a mountain ridge jolts me awake and I hear Star talking. But I'm falling again and this time I cannot stop myself...

~

I'm in a huge crowd...a sea of lighters with a giant stage set up in the distance and there is a thunder of feet stomping...thousands of feet, perhaps millions. I hear my own voice yelling, so frail, so close, so faltering, swallowed up by the mayhem and excitement. In the midst of them all, I am alone. Suddenly the ceiling lights go on, flooding the arena with bright light while the lights on the stage go off. As a man comes walking out on the stage dressed in slick, black clothes, the crowd din dies down. In fact, it becomes very quiet.

"Welcome, friends," he says over the PA. I look around me and see that the crowd I'm in is all aspiring musicians, just like myself. We're all staring attentively at the stage while some hold up signs that I cannot read just yet.

"I would just like to inform you that we're reviewing material to be released by our record company and, unfortunately, only about three or four of you are going to be successful." His familiar-looking face is now being broadcast via mega-giant screen and he pouts his lips as if to say, "Sorry suckers."

The place absolutely erupts in pandemonium. Yet I can hear individual voices in the thundering din screaming to get his attention. A David Bowie look-alike next to me hollers, "Look at me! I've got pop sensibilities like nobody's business!"

He's immediately countered by a Sheryl Crow look-alike on my right who shrieks, "My hooks will blow your socks off! And I'm sexy!"

"I'm better than you," yells an Eddie Vedder clone. "You're a fake. I've been authentically tortured by society and a fucked-up family."

"You're the fake," roars a Joan Jett clone. "I'm the true punk!"

"Yeah?" says an Elvis Costello fake. "I'm the best poet I've ever heard of and my guitar playing is kick-ass, but it doesn't even come close to my clever, wry wit. I'm very funny, actually."

As these aspiring artists argue amongst themselves, they do not look at each other. They only stare at the suit, standing on the distant stage.

One very bored looking folk singer holds a sign that says: Cutting Edge Pop with Innovative Jazz Textures and Stylistic Sensibilities…

A Courtney Love look-alike holds another sign that reads: Dark and Emotional, Raucous and Dynamic, Will Fuck for Contract! She is not smiling either.

A Sting clone holds a sign that says: I'm Fucking Mesmerizing!

"Fun-loving chick…look at *me*…"

"I'm a visionary…look at *me*…"

"Witty and ironic with a gritty edge…look at *me*…"

"I write beautiful melodies…*listen* to me…"

"Passionate and unique…*sign* me…"

"I'm fragile and sensitive…*look* at me!"

"Bold and innovative…*I'm* the best…"

"I play every instrument there is…try me…"

"Love me…"

"Like me…" They are now jumping up and down in a thundering rage, thousands of them all trying to get the dude's attention. Two Jimmy Page look-alikes staring at the stage are punching at each other but keep missing because they won't look at where they're swinging. "My licks are hotter'n yours, you fake!"

"You're all phonies!" I scream, though my voice is drowned out in the mayhem while the clamor only gets louder. The ringing in my ears is almost unbearable and I am now very afraid. I want to go back to Bellingham, but the crowd is suffocating me; hands are on my head, pushing me down and people are trying to use me as a footstool for a better vantage point and isn't that what it's all about, stepping on each other for a better shot at the prize…?

Somebody throws a compact disc at the stage; the jewel case cracks on impact. "Listen to *me!*" And now the air is full of flying CDs, all being thrown at the guy in a suit. As he dodges them, cases shatter and discs roll everywhere. He looks a little frightened.

"Remember who's in control," he laughs into the microphone. A disc hits his head. As blood begins spurting from a gash I recognize who he is: Bill Armond!

"You'll love me…I guarantee it!"

"It's all about *me!*"

Musicians are now climbing onto the stage while large men in yellow coats with long white sticks are smacking them on the heads and kicking them back into the crowd where they fall slowly, reminding me of maggots swarming over a rotten carcass. A human ladder has formed stage left and a security man is blasting them back with a fire hose. Bill is holding a small mirror in front of himself, trying to stitch his gash.

I hear the sound of wailing; flesh and fabric tear; two women are fighting next to me, scratching each other, blood pouring off of their faces. They look at me and start laughing. Then they're back at it, trying to eat each other alive. I turn to run, but can't. I'm being consumed by this slow-motion horror, hoping to God it's a dream…

I hear whimpering right next to me and I see this Marilyn Manson clone with tears and mascara running off his face holding up one of those cheap, hand-held digital pianos. He's crying like a baby who's been separated from his mother until a skin-headed Nazi rocker grabs him just under the jaw and, in one quick motion, rips the poor dude's head from the torso; he swings it several times before hucking it toward the stage where it lands bouncing and skidding up to the mountain of CDs spewing blood, right next to Bill Armond who's still bleeding himself, but laughing and jumping up and down while taking piles of discs and throwing them up in the air, watching them rain down. "Remember, only *three* are gonna make it. *Who* will they be?"

"Meeee...!" is the thundering response. The crowd is a mass of desperation, all lunging toward the stage. Black cameras are hung everywhere.

Thousands of hands and feet kick me and push me down. I scream but can't even hear my own voice. I'm on my back, but no one hears me and, even if they did, I wouldn't have a chance in hell. Then I feel the hand, a large hand, cool to the touch, tap me on my arm. I see a silhouette bending over that looks strangely familiar. I recognize it but can't place it in any context. I know that I must follow.

Instead of standing up, the figure begins crawling through the maze of writhing legs. I follow. *Who are you*, I wonder. He's slender and bears shoulder-length hair. The crowd of legs eventually thins a bit and there is more space ahead as a light comes up through a trap door in the floor. He enters and disappears. I follow.

There is a ladder leading down to another level where it is much nicer. In fact, it's spacious and comfortable, the roar of the crowd muffled and distant through the floor.

We stand and look at each other in the light. His face is soft, but his eyes are sad.

"Who are you?" I ask, thickly.

He doesn't answer, but motions for me to look around—which I do. There are actually quite a few others here as well. Many of them are playing guitars. I hear the sounds of beautiful singing as well as the sound of running water, and now I see that we're all next to a lovely stream with moss-covered banks, sparkling in the dimly lit stage lights that hang from the ceiling. Across the room is an electric fan, which makes for a nice breeze. I can hear the dullness of the crowd above us, still trying to get Bill Armond's attention. Here I feel safer.

Nobody notices me. People are just quietly strumming their guitars alone and in small groups, and off in one corner a guy sits by himself, playing the flute.

"Who are you?" I ask the shadow, again. "I want to go back to Bellingham."

He smiles sadly, shaking his head as he picks up a guitar and sits down in a chair. His hands are absolutely huge. He begins picking and a chill sweeps over me at the familiarity of the song, yet I cannot place it. Then Nick Drake begins to sing...

~

I awaken. Elvis is bouncing along and it's pitch dark and probably has been for awhile. Zen commandeers our road ship homeward, and I squint my eyes, trying to focus on a road sign, trying to get a clue as to what state we're in—or, for that matter, what state *I'm* in. I'm shaking quietly and feel fever sweats still flashing, dark images and sounds while I stare, alone in the world. Something has truly changed in me and this time I know what I must do. I notice a sign for Redding. Elvis's clock reads 4:57 A.M. It's going to be close, but I know in my heart it doesn't matter anymore. I close my eyes and slowly feel the heaviness of sleep coming on again. I pray that this time it's without images and meaning...

Forty

It's 6:33 P.M. Friday, as we pull onto First Avenue in downtown Seattle, looking for a place to park Elvis. Everybody pretty much stopped talking around Longview as it became clear that we were going to make it back for the big show. Even Walter has become more quiet, brooding and intense than ever.

Somewhere back in Central Oregon, Walter filled the band in on more of the missing details from his mysterious journey down from Alaska. He had been notified that his ex-wife Victoria had passed away earlier this year and he had come to Seattle to settle some affairs and to at last make contact with his long, lost daughter, Celia. But he had no luck finding her since she had long since moved from her past address, leaving no forwarding one.

After exhausting his leads in Seattle, he had decided to go south to the Chemewah Boarding School in Salem, Oregon, where she had attended school. One administrator had informed Walter that last they knew she was living back in Seattle. Discouraged, Walter decided to hitch to San Francisco to look up some cousins, but when we showed up, he decided that our little journey sounded more interesting.

This prompted a confession from Ollie that after counting the jackpot twice, he figured that he had won somewhere in the neighborhood of $6871.25 in quarters from that mystical mini-mart in Reno. I'm amazed that there has been no argument from Star about the fact that it was her three bucks that was given to Ollie by Walter that started this whole thing. Maybe she knows that there's too much on the line now to worry about silly things like thousands of dollars. Maybe she doesn't care anymore. I want to believe the latter. I'm trying not to care either as I'm still haunted by a shadowy silhouette who called to me from my dreams, and I know I'm long overdue for a 3:00 A.M. *Pink Moon* session.

We drive south, past The Showbox, and the sign on the marquee reads: Northwest Music Extravaganza and Third Annual Battle of Seattle Featuring: Goon Squad, The Cosmic Poets, and Groovetribe - 8:00 P.M. There is a lineup a half a block long.

"What a surprise," I say, looking at the marquee. "They got our name right for once."

We missed our 1:00 P.M. meeting and Sunny will be furious. I don't dread seeing her anymore. In fact, I'm ready. We drive to the back alley and find the loading dock and there sits the Groovetribe Coach-Liner along with a couple of shiny BMWs pulled up next to it. No, there's nothing to worry about anymore. No crisis, only opportunity. I am ready for battle. We all are.

~

"Hi, you guys!" she says, sending my stomach into a half hitch. "It's *so good* to see you." Angel's words are, of course, directed at Star, Zen, Ollie and Walter. I just kind of hang out in back observing this heart-warming reunion with loathing and despair. While they engage in shallow banter, Sequoia and Matt oversee the load-in with indifference. Eventually Matt does seem to notice me sulking in the background. "You feeling better?" he asks.

"Yeah," I say, wincing at the memory of Rock City. I hear Sequoia make some wisecrack about a padded cell while the rest of them laugh. I pretend not to hear them.

"Did you ever find my hat?" asks Angel innocently, finally acknowledging my existence. She is dressed in flowing colors and has spent some time embellishing the unkempt, hippie look.

"No, Angel," I say, gazing into her penetrating eyes. "Sorry."

"I hope we can still be friends after all this, Angus. Did you get my message that I've forgiven you for everything you ever did to me?"

"Yeah, Angel. Thanks."

"Have you seen Sunny?" she asks. "She and this older guy have been looking all over for you. Just to forewarn you, she's really upset."

"Why?" I ask, rhetorically.

"Because of your stupidity and selfishness that forced me to quit the band."

"It was an *accident*, Angel. I didn't know that you went to the washroom at Talbot."

"Don't lie to me, Angus," she says. "You'd better talk to her. She insists that I sing with you in honor of the contract we signed. She even mentioned a lawsuit."

"Oh, did she now?"Just as I begin despairing, I remember the money I gave her and the despair turns back to rage that is fast approaching critical mass.

The inside of The Showbox is elegant: a huge ballroom with soft red lights, a hardwood floor, and an ornate bar off to the side. Yet in spite of its size, there is a intimate feel. The stage is quite large, adorned by black, velvety curtains, and there is that drummer with rainbow hair from Goon Squad setting up a trap set.

"Quite a tour I hear you've had." Her voice startles me, and I know I visibly jump at the sound of her words.

As I turn to face Sunny, I say, "It sure was." She looks older. Maybe it's the lights, but her hair seems white. With her is someone I've never seen before. He is an older man, slender, brittle eyed, thin lipped. The sight of them doesn't frighten me like I thought it would.

"Angus, I'd like to introduce you to Frank Strong." Sunny has a tense smile that cracks her caked-on makeup, making her face appear like a parched desert floor. She's smiling but I can see the secret pools of rage behind her eyes.

"It's nice to finally meet you, Angus," Frank says, snapping me from my daze. "Sorry you couldn't make our meeting this afternoon, but Sunny tells me you had some engine trouble down south."

I look at Sunny, who only stares at me with death and loathing dare I utter a word of truth.

"Yeah, something like that," I mumble. "Wow. Frank Strong. I was beginning to even wonder if you really existed."

Sunny laughs loudly. "He's such a Gemini, Frank."

Frank laughs, lightening things up a bit. "You didn't get my message about my two friends from RCA showing up, did you?"

"You know, I did, Frank, but you were already on your way here and I was hoping we'd just hook up at today's meeting. Sorry it didn't work out."

He looks at me and his sense of calm and politeness is calculated. "My friends Bob and June really loved your show down at Rock City."

"That's so cool," I say, feeling a heat flash.

He looks at me a moment. "Is something wrong?"

"No, Frank," I say. "Things are better than they've ever been."

We chatter superficially until Frank excuses himself to make some phone calls, telling me he's looking forward to hearing us, and to talking business. He sits down at a table by himself, pulling out a cell phone and a little black book.

"He's a gentlemen," I say to Sunny, staring at him in amazement.

"He sure is," whispers Sunny, "and don't you even think you're gonna pull any of your bullshit on me tonight."

"What are you talking about?"

She stares at me, trying to frighten me into submission. "Angel told me how you intentionally ditched her at the rest area and how you *lied* about the Oregon Country Fair, and you *lied* about Rock City and you *lied* about everything, stringing all of us along in hopes that somehow you could pull it all off. I've been in this business thirty years and I've never experienced the complete lack of integrity that you've shown. Let me tell you something, mister: unless you want your court papers mailed to you special delivery tomorrow for breach of contract, Angel is singing with you tonight. I told you that under *no circumstances* were there to be any line-up changes in the band. None. Nobody asked me if she could quit. Frank Strong knows nothing of this, and you'd better not even think of fucking with me or you'll be really, really sorry. I'm not kidding you."

I shrug, feeling a profound sense of detachment. "Sorry, Sunny, but Angel is already a full-time member of Groovetribe. She's not gonna quit them to come back to us."

"I've already thought about that, and I can convince Frank that she's just sitting in with them as a friend as long as she sings with you."

"Whatever you say, Sunny," I reply. My time to speak hasn't quite yet come.

"Now, we gotta get you ready to play," she says, suddenly business-like and friendly. "Can I buy you a drink?"

"Sure, Sunny, that actually sounds good."

"What do you want?"

"How 'bout a double lime margarita," I say, surprised at her generosity. "Thanks, Sunny."

"Anytime," she says, searching her purse. "Say, it looks like I'm a little short of cash."

"Here, Sunny," I say, giving her a handful of quarters.

"Thanks, sweetie. Quarters, huh?" She looks a little puzzled and I laugh. She heads toward the bar and I turn toward the back entrance.

Back on the loading dock, Walter and Zen are helping Ollie carry in his drum set while Star spits tobacco, telling Angel of our exploits with Bill Armond and Tom Jones and how she helped Ollie win over six grand in quarters.

"Hi, Angus."

The sound of her voice rips into my soul like an armor-piercing bullet.

"Hi," I say, heart clapping wildly in my chest. "How's it going, Lily?"

"Did you get my message?" she asks, her fawn-like eyes staring up at me.

"Yeah. Are you here with Nathan?"

"Oh," she laughs. "I can't be around Nathan right now. He wants to get serious again and I told him that we could only be friends. I'm not ready to be in a relationship with *anybody*, but if I was, it would only be one person…" She smiles longingly at me.

"Here's your drink," says Sunny, interrupting us. "I've been looking all over for you." She hands me a glass of generic beer, while holding what looks like a triple daiquiri in her hand.

"Any change?" I ask.

"Had to leave a tip," she says, smiling slyly, but as she notices Lily, her smiles fades. "Who's this?"

"Sunny, this is Lily. Lily, Sunny."

"Hello there, sweetheart," says Sunny, coldly. "I've heard a lot about you."

"No you haven't," I say. "I've never told you about Lily."

Lily looks at me, confused.

"Sunny's the one who's been shopping us to record labels," I say.

"Nice to meet you," Lily says, obligingly. "I've heard a lot about you, too." She looks back at me and smiles while Sunny stares at her.

"Bob and June from RCA are gonna want to talk with you," says Sunny. "I'll let you know when they're here." She grabs me around the neck and mashes her lips into my cheek. Then she shoots Lily a cold glance and says, "He's *my* hot property." She then heads off with her drink and I'm certain that she's under the illusion that she has most graciously purchased me this beautiful beer out of her hard-earned dollars.

"What a weirdo," says Lily.

"The biggest," I say.

"I've really missed you, Angus. Do you forgive me for hanging up on you?"

"Sure, Lily. I forgive you."

"What's the matter?" She looks worried.

"I don't know, Lily," I say, feeling transformed into truth's mystical orifice. "I love you, but I want to forget about what we had because I know we could never love each other as we are. We only love our expectations of each other and every time we fall short there's unbearable distance, and you start looking elsewhere."

"I'm not as shallow as you seem to think," she says, offended at my words. "Whether or not you're a successful artist doesn't mean I won't love you for who you are."

"Yeah, but does it mean you'll stand beside me when I'm struggling to find my way?"

"I told you that I can't say whether or not we can be together. But I'll always love you like no other."

"Lily," I say, possessed with a power I've never known, "that's not good enough for me anymore." I bend over and kiss her on the cheek, knowing my love for her doesn't matter anymore. "It's over, Lily."

"I don't want *that*." Her eyes are fearful.

"No, but I do." I feel the Power surging through me. "What I want from you, you could never give."

She stares at me, stunned. "I've never seen you like this before, Angus. Something's really changed."

"I guess it has. I may not know what I want, but I'm finally learning what I don't want, and nothing personal against you, but we really need to be apart."

"What about friendship? Don't you want to be friends?"

"Lily," I say, intoxicated with life, "friendship to me is based in love, trust and loyalty, none of which we have."

She is starting to cry. "Look, I'm sorry about *Zen and the Art of Motorcycle Maintenance*. I can see why you might think I'm arrogant. I *am* arrogant." She bursts into tears. "I don't know why I shut down with you. You are so strong and powerful when you're distant. I wish I could see that same strength when you weren't. You do deserve someone who's better than me."

"I know I do," I say, truthfully, and my whole being is suddenly lighter than ever.

"You teach me so much about *myself*." She throws her arms around me, but I pull away. "Angus, please be patient with me; I don't want to lose you."

"Why? So I can teach you more about yourself? Is it all just about *you*? Goodbye, Lily."

"You're the only one I'll ever love." She is sobbing and I wonder if she understands what she's really saying. I doubt it. As I walk away from the loading dock, her words fall away from me like dead leaves.

Forty-one

Just as we've finished loading in, a guy dressed in morbid, Leonard Cohen-style clothes comes up and introduces himself as Andrew Lord, radio personality for 106.7 FM, and emcee for tonight. He wins me over with a wisecrack about Groovetribe and their ridiculous tour bus while informing me that we've been selected to go on last. I smile to myself at the thought. We stand on the back loading dock while he smokes a cigarette.

"You know, these battle of the bands are really such bullshit," he says. "Just a bunch of assholes from *The Rocket* deciding who's cool in Seattle."

"They're the ones who decide who wins?"

"Yeah," he says. "There's about twenty of them here. A bunch of them are already tied-in close with Groovetribe. Don't get your hopes up for winning."

"I won't." I wish I could tell him of our tour and all we've learned.

"I'm so sick of Groovetribe I can hardly believe it," Andrew continues. "You know that Sequoia's father is the President of *Channel 7 News-at-Nine*, and has practically financed Groovetribe's whole shtick. He bought them all their radio ads on 106.7, but none of the programmers can stand these guys. They come up to the station like they own everything." He takes a hard drag off his smoke before continuing. "I guess being from the other side of the tracks I got a big chip on my shoulder—besides the fact that they're music's lame."

"What about Goon Squad?" I ask as Walter comes over to me. I throw my arm around him and laughingly say, "I bet you love a name like that."

Walter laughs, but seems a bit down.

"Great band," says Andrew. "Especially their cello player. I can't remember her name. Phenomenal musician, though."

I conjure up the dark haired beauty under the sultry lights of the Ballard Firehouse a couple of month's back. "So we're on last, huh?" I ask. "That's really cool. I finally broke it off with my girlfriend a few minutes ago and I feel better than I ever have."

"Congratulations," says Andrew. "It must have been for the best."

"Yeah, it was." I turn to Walter. "And I have Walter here to thank for teaching me that a crisis is only an opportunity in disguise."

Walter smiles a little.

"Has anybody talked to you about a sound-check?" Ollie asks, rushing up to me.

"Take a deep breath, Ollie," I say. "We're going on last."

"Last?" says Zen who arrives with him. "Did you see how many people are outside? There's about four hundred."

"I told you this would be a killer gig."

"I'm worried about the quarters," says Ollie. "I got over six grand in silver sitting on the floor of Elvis. I feel like we need to do something about it."

"Just throw a blanket over them," I whisper. "They'll be fine." But as I say this, I'm not so sure.

Zen looks past me as some of the color drains from his face while his jaw drops slightly. "My goodness," he sighs.

I turn slowly around and it takes a moment for me to recognize the woman buried under the post-grunge costume apparel. There is a set of smiling, painted lips beneath the tuft of hair bunched up straight over her head. She wears hot pants with zebra stockings and a vinyl leather coat. Her black silk shirt hangs loosely beneath and the platform boots she wears would make even Gary Payton think twice about taking the ball inside. It's Star's alter ego, objectified in her millennium-renaissance-wiccan attire. In her left hand she clutches her saxophone like she's posing for a cover shot of *Rolling Stone*. Her lower lip is swollen with chew. "Are you ready to rock?" she whispers.

"Star," I sigh, after a long, painful moment. "Don't you think you're being a bit extreme?"

Her air of invincibility wilts and she sighs. "I can't believe you guys. We gotta put on a show for 'em. That's what people want."

"If that's what you want to wear, Star, then go ahead," I say, feeling tranquil again. "It's ugly as sin, but go for it."

She looks at me strangely, as do Zen and Ollie.

"Rumor has it that the winner tonight will be playing at the Sasquatch Festival when it comes through the Gorge in a couple of weeks," she says.

"I never heard that," I say. "That's pretty huge, I suppose."

"Did you know we're going on last?" she asks, excitedly.

"I sure do," I say. "It's great."

"Groovetribe doesn't think it's so great," she laughs. "In fact, Matt and Sequoia are furious. I just heard them chewing out Andrew, but he won't budge an inch on it."

"Good for him," I beam. "It's about time those cry-babies got their due."

"Just to warn you, they want to talk to you about it."

"What's there to talk about?" I ask, gleeful at my newfound power. "I dumped Lily tonight! I told her there's nothing more to talk about. I'm through talking."

"Give it to me, baby!" shrieks Star, holding up her palm for a high-five. Then her smile vanishes.

There at the back stage entrance stand Matt and Sequoia. They are both grinning at me. "Hey, fellas," I say. "How's it going?"

They walk over to me, super-friendly like, and nod to my mates. "The question really is, how are *you* doing?" asks manager Matt.

"Great," I say. "I just dumped my girlfriend after things had dragged on for months. I was stupid for holding out hope."

"Happens to all of us," says Matt, unconvincingly.

Sequoia ambles around to the side of me. "Angus, I really want to apologize for what happened down at Rock City." He puts his hands on my shoulders and starts massaging me. "Are you *really* okay?" He gazes insincerely into my eyes before glancing over to Matt with a smile and a quick wink.

"Yeah, I'm really okay, Sequoia."

"That was such bullshit the way you guys were treated at Rock City," he continues while staring at my band mates. "I even told The Caustic Poets' manager Kevin that it was downright rude bumping you after you gave that dude the five-spot. I told him that I don't think we can gig with those guys after that."

"Hey, thanks for your sympathy," I say. "That's really nice of you to say that."

"Yeah, we Northwest bands gotta stick together…"

I look over and Ollie, Star and Zen are completely absorbed in this interaction. They look at me, and this time I know that I am the leader. "What do you guys *really* want?" I ask.

Matt and Sequoia look at each other, and Sequoia gives me a deep squeeze on the neck. He smiles. "My brother, it seems that there's been a mistake in scheduling the order of bands tonight. *We're* supposed to go on last."

"Really? I heard that *we're* going last," I say, smiling too.

"Andrew *thought* you were," Matt says, "but we're *really* the ones closing the show tonight. It's been set in stone for weeks. The first set's gonna be hot anyway."

"You know it is," says Sequoia. "It's probably gonna give you the most exposure."

"You know you can die of exposure?" I wink at Zen who smiles back.

"That's really funny," Sequoia says, faking a laugh. "Die of exposure."

"If the first set's gonna be so great, why don't you take it and we'll go last? We don't mind, really."

"We *can't* go first." Sequoia's manipulative appendages fall from my shoulders.

"Why not?" I ask.

"There's been an emergency with one of our band members." Sequoia's head falls forward a little and he whispers, "It's a personal crisis and I can't really get into it, but he can only play if we go last."

"You know what?" I ask. "I really want my band to go last. We've got label people coming out to hear us."

"You know that's not gonna matter at all," says Matt. "The label's will be here from the get-go and chances are that if you're first, you'll be more likely to be remembered."

My mates are standing by like grade school kids in the lunch line, just staring at me. They are my children.

"Sorry," I say. "Send me some promo, and maybe we'll do it another time."

Sequoia and Matt stare blankly at me, missing the joke.

"Look, I'll tell you what," says Sequoia with one last attempt at civility. "If you let us close things out tonight, we'll let you guys warm up for us at our next gig in Bellingham."

I stare at him as my rage builds. "Well that's mighty kind of you, Sequoia, but in case you forgot, Bellingham is *our* home. It's where *we're* from."

"Hey, we're not talking about the skanky 3-B," he says. "We're talking about having you open for us at The Mount Baker Theater."

"Sequoia, I don't play games anymore. You guys don't care about places like Bellingham or bands like us. Go first tonight, and just be glad you're alive, you spoiled brat!" My band mates erupt with enthusiastic applause while the Groovetriber's faces are white with fury.

"*We're* going last," snarls Sequoia, defiantly. "What do you care anyway? It's not like you're about to land a record deal."

"After some of the stories Angel has told us," snaps Matt, "I'm surprised you even found Seattle on the map!" They both burst out laughing and as I look over at my band mates, the collective expression is one of pain and humiliation.

"You guys are phonier than a Reno car dealer," I say. "And you're not going last. We are."

"You don't know who you're fucking with," hisses Sequoia. "We just played to twenty thousand people down in Northern California and we're on the verge of a record deal and besides that, my father is the President of *Channel 7 News-at-Nine*. I've got a lot of friends in this town who won't forget about this." Then some color returns as he realizes that he's gone over the edge. His eyes betray the fear of someone who has revealed too much truth about himself. "Come on, *brah*," he pleads. "Can't we work together on this one?"

"Tell you what," I say. "We'll flip a coin for it." I look over and see Star shaking her head mouthing the word, "Baaad."

"It's okay, guys," I say to them. "If it means so much to our friends here, then the least we can do is make it fair. I *know* they'd do the same for us." I look at Sequoia and Matt who are still very angry. "Fair enough, fellas?" I ask. "We'll flip a coin and if you lose then you will shut up, right?"

"Sure," says Sequoia after a long pause. "Matt gets the flip."

"Ollie flips," I say. "You pick the coin, but Ollie flips."

"Matt flips!"

"We'll flip to see who flips." Turning to Zen, I say, "Go get Andrew as our witness." With a big smile, he obliges.

We stand silently, all looking everywhere but at each other. It seems to take forever for Zen and Andrew to get back. Finally we hear voices in the hall, then they're standing in the room with us. Andrew looks perturbed. "What's this about a coin flip to see who goes last?" he says, scowling at Sequoia and Matt. "It was already decided that you're on first."

"These guys agreed to do a coin flip, Andrew," says Sequoia, softly. "It's only fair."

Andrew stares coldly at Sequoia, then turns to me. "That's *okay* with you guys? You don't have to."

"It's okay," I say. "Just one question: what about Goon Squad? They should be flipping too."

"No," says Andrew. "They want the middle spot. It's just between you guys."

Everyone gathers around as Andrew prepares the coin toss between Matt and Ollie to see who gets to flip the coin. Sequoia seems to be chanting something quietly.

Andrew looks at me wistfully and then tells Matt to call it in the air. He flicks it perfectly and, as it whirs upward, Matt yells, "Heads!"

The coin lands, spins, and rolls before coming to rest as all crowd over. "Tails!" yelps Star.

"Let me see!" Sequoia shoves Star and Zen aside. "Fuck," he says, disgustedly.

My mates clap loudly and Star is squealing with delight. As Andrew prepares to give Ollie the coin that will determine the evening's fate, perhaps the very fate of our band, Star says, "All right, Ollie, baby! Do it again!"

"Everybody ready?" asks Andrew, obviously enjoying his role in this. He hands the quarter to Ollie who polishes it on his shirt before examining it carefully.

"Wow," he says. "A 1967 quarter. Did you know that *Light My Fire* was at the top of the charts for thirty five weeks between February and September, and that was the year that—"

"Flip the coin Ollie you crazy motherfucker!" yells Zen and, startled, Ollie tosses it high in the air.

"Tails!" he yells as it bounces twice and rolls around in a slowly diminishing circle before finally coming to a standstill. Everyone but me crowds over. The sound of a kick drum thumping through the sound system two rooms away tells me that Goon Squad has started their sound-check. It also sounds like a large crowd is beginning to brew. This should be a killer gig no matter what, and—

"It's tails!" screeches Star as she grabs Ollie around the neck, planting a big kiss on his cheek.

Matt just shakes his head in disgust. Sequoia turns to him and, in a surprisingly calm voice, says, "Let's go finish setting up, Matt. It's not gonna matter anyway." Turning his lifeless eyes to me he quietly finishes his thought for all to hear. "We're gonna bury you losers. You'll see."

Forty-two

As we enter the ballroom once more, I am surprised to find that it's already damn near two-thirds full. There is a low-level buzz of voices and clinking glass and I notice that Goon Squad is now in the process of pulling their gear off stage to accommodate the sullen looking Groovetribers standing by. We'll sound-check after them, then hopefully, leave most of our gear set up.

"It shouldn't surprise me that you're pulling all this crap now, Angus," snarls Angel from behind me.

"What are you talking about, Angel? We flipped for it. Groovetribe lost and we won."

"That's not what I heard. Sequoia told me that you paid off Andrew, just like the Boss at Rock City. You're just a big shmoozer and you're only using people to get what you want. I know all about your tricks."

"Angel," I say, "I didn't pay anybody anything and you know something? You're starting to sound a lot like Sunny. Besides, I thought you forgave me for all the pain I caused you."

"I did, but that's in the past. I'm talking about *now*! We've got labels coming out to hear us and you seem to act like you're the only one in the world who matters."

"What are you saying, Angel? I really don't understand you."

She doesn't answer. Instead she sticks her tongue out at me and stomps away.

Now Andrew approaches me and tells me that Groovetribe, in fact, will not be sound checking, and since we are last, we will set up our stuff for a quick test. Luckily he's already informed the rest of the band, since rounding them up quickly would be a losing proposition. We only have a few minutes, and they want to clear all musicians off the stage by 7:45. Ollie is already setting up his drums, and Zen and Star are assembling their stuff too. Wow. It's time. I scan the crowd quickly but there's no sign of Rod Ames, or Sunny and Frank for that matter. I feel sad. I don't want people to hate me.

After about five minutes of plugging in cords and placing amps, we are ready for a quick blast of sound. We test the monitors and play a few measures before the sound engineer, Jon, gives us a throat cut and thumbs up. "Sounds good," he says coming up to me. "You're ready to go."

I head for the bar. The place is getting packed and it's an interesting mix of punks, gen-exers and young hippies. I order a local microbrew and glance up at the old clock behind the bar. It's almost eight. I turn, jumping back a little in fear.

"I thought I told you to stop playing games." Her eyes are death and rage boiled over.

"What are you talking about, Sunny?"

"You know exactly what I'm talking about," she hisses, violently rubbing her nose while motioning for me to follow her to her table. As I do, I notice Frank Strong sitting with Peaches and two other people whom I've never seen before in my life. They stare at me not looking at all happy.

"Hello," I say to everyone, feeling my voice shake.

"Hello, Angus," says Frank, softly. "This is June Farrow and Bob Stills from RCA Records."

"Hi," I say to a stiff-looking female and a gerbil-eyed fellow who hardly looks twenty-one.

They nod their greeting to me, but I feel a distinct coldness. They say nothing but look back at Frank. I feel Sunny's eyes penetrating the back of my head. The feeling reminds me of being in the principal's office.

"Angus," sighs Frank, almost sadly. "Did you really think you could get away with this?"

"What are you talking about?" Waves of guilt wash over me.

"I'm talking about the name of the band. Did you really think that you could get away with calling yourselves The Caustic

272 | Tim McHugh

Poets?" Frank sucks air through his nose and his face trembles a bit. "You're playing games with the wrong people, Angus."

Meanwhile, Peaches just kind of sits there smiling.

"What do you mean?" I ask, knowing damn well what he means.

"Did you guys meet down at Rock City or not?" Frank asks his two colleagues, while staring at me.

"We've never seen him or his band before," says Bob, the gerbil-eyed young man. "We saw a band at Rock City called The *Caustic Poets* who were wonderful. We came up to Seattle to hear *them*, not these guys."

"But it was our demo that you liked that led you out to see them," I retort.

"The demo we heard wasn't even *close* to what we saw live," says June. "We base almost everything on the live performance. Live music sells albums. We can make anybody sound decent in the studio." She turns to Frank and says, "This is a waste of time. We've g t to be in Austin tomorrow morning. You might as well take us back to the airport."

"You should just hear us before you leave," I say. "We've been through an awful lot on our tour, and have worked so hard to get where we are, and all we ever wanted was a fair shot." The words mechanically tumble from my mouth. I'm realizing that I don't really care anymore and this gives me a rush of joy. Their opinions of me are not half as precious as my experiences on this tour, and I wouldn't trade them for all the quarters in all the slot machines in Nevada. Angus Keegan has been going through the motions all along.

I sit down and calmly tell the whole story about how I tried to organize a West Coast tour to complement the timing of Frank's promotion, but we couldn't seem to get gigs, though we did manage to secure a spot at the Oregon Country Fair and Redwood Summer where Ollie and Walter stopped a riot by singing *America the Beautiful* but the fear of Frank and Sunny pulling the plug on us led me to lie about the rest of the tour in hopes of pulling off a miracle and I knew it was wrong but did it anyway and after the Rock City disaster I kind of bottomed out and realized that I was playing music for all the wrong reasons but thanks to Walter Simon who saved us from getting murdered by angry rednecks while teaching us about the power of living in the moment and finding satisfaction in playing music for music's sake and not for someone else I learned some important lessons that I've found to be more valuable than a record contract by some company that only views music as a junk-food commodity and doesn't and never could get people like Walter and Ollie.

I do not tell them about Bill Armond, or the six grand that Ollie won as I can just imagine Sunny staking her claim. Yet they seem interested in my story. When I'm finished, June says that it sounds more like a movie script than real life while Frank and Bob just kind of shake their heads in amazement.

"You know, y'all really should hear these guys live," says Sunny in a last ditch effort to keep control. "I know Angus is delusional but what artist or musician worth anything isn't?"

"Good point, Sunny," says Frank, sadly, "but I had no idea what I was really working with. I'm a very, very busy man. So are my colleagues here. I told you long ago that I only work with bands that are *ready* to take that next step. I told you that maturity, integrity and open, honest communication are essential factors that determine whom I represent." He then turns to me. "You tell a very interesting and rather entertaining story, I must say, but do you realize that you've made a mockery out of this entire process, and your lack of integrity is a poor reflection on me to my friends here?"

I wince, nodding my head.

"Frank," pleads Sunny, "I had no idea that Angus had lied about the tour and I was under the distinct impression that everything was above boards. But, please…Please listen to their set. They are really, really *good*."

"There are a lot of really good bands out there," interrupts Bob. "Just being good isn't enough anymore. You have to be ready to take the next step. It isn't like it used to be, is it Frank?"

"No, it isn't, Bob," says Frank.

In a maternal tone, June says, "See, Angus, the days of developing raw talent are over. Overhead in record companies has gotten to be so much that I'm not allowed to twice make the mistake of signing a band that doesn't sell. It's nothing personal; it's just reality. We have to take other things into consideration besides how good we think the music is. It's almost like a marriage.

You wouldn't want to marry someone based only on looks. Good sex is also a very, very important factor. You get what I'm saying? I'm sorry, but from what we're seeing, there's no way we're going to 'have sex' with you. Hopefully you'll learn something from this experience and we wish you the best of luck. It's no easy road."

Frank sighs again, shaking his head. "I'm sorry Sunny, but we need to get back to the airport. We're meeting with a band tomorrow in Austin." He turns to me. "Not that this would have made a difference, but you did miss a very important meeting today."

"Please, just *listen* to them!" yells Sunny. "Groovetribe's playing too. You guys liked Groovetribe, didn't you?"

"You know," says Bob, "I did like them live, but their manager was too pushy. Bands like Groovetribe are a dime a dozen."

"I'm sorry, Sunny," says Frank as he gets up from the table, prompting June and Bob to do the same. "We've already wasted enough time here."

"Do you fucking know who I am?" Sunny turns to me in a swirling rage. "You've made an ass out of me, Angus Keegan!"

"Where's my four thousand bucks, Sunny?" I retort, glancing at Frank, Bob and June, who are now standing up. "Did you and Mr. Harvey have fun snorting it up those vacuum cleaners you call noses?"

Sunny looks at me, stunned.

"Hey, Mr. Harvey," I say to Peaches.

"Heeey, Aaangus!" His face lights up, then frowns as if he's trying to remember something. He turns to Sunny, perplexed.

"I don't know what he's talking about," she says loud enough for Frank and company to hear. "It's just part of the big delusion, isn't it, Angus?"

"Yeah, the delusion that I became a part of. The delusion that allowed me to hide the band's real identity. The delusion that allowed me to forget why music is important to me. But you know what I've learned through all this? I wanna be a real person who plays real music, not some fake. You accuse me of lying and maybe I did, but you're the one who made Frank think we were bigger than we really were. I failed trying to complete the lie, but I'm not lying anymore, Sunny. I want to be real. And that was really shitty of you to steal another grand from me."

She stares at me, trying to burn a hole in my soul.

"When we were on tour," I announce to Frank and company, "Sunny asked me to wire her a thousand dollars off of my emergency credit card so she could move out on Peaches because one of his multiple personalities was threatening to cut her into little pieces."

"He's talking about part of my share of advance money held in trust," she snaps back to them while staring wildly at me. "And let me tell you something mister, a thousand bucks doesn't even begin to compensate me for what you've put me through. You keep fucking with my reputation and I'm gonna get a lot more than that by the time I'm done with you. You obviously don't understand what *breach of contract* really means, but I'm sure a good lawyer will get it through your thick skull."

"You owe me four thousand dollars, Sunny," I say feeling giddy. I know I'll never see the money again, but I do not care. Sunny no longer holds power over me. Frank Strong and his musical mystery meat from RCA have lost their mystique. They are corporate robots who are all about covering their own butts while keeping the airwaves flooded with mindless mediocrity. They have no concept of what's important. Or worse, if they do, they do not care.

I stand there in silence, studying each face, quietly rejoicing in the fact that after this night, I will never, ever see them again. Soon I am laughing so hard I'm crying. "You're all absurd," I manage to stammer, while they can only stare. "Excuse me, but I've got one last gig to get to."

As I work my way back through the crowd, I hear Sunny screeching something nasty. I wave to her and, as I turn back to continue on my journey to the backstage and a new beginning, I hear the people behind me beginning to cheer.

Forty-three

When the house lights go off, the crowd roars. A single spotlight graces the stage and out comes Andrew to introduce the opening act. I sit near the front with Walter and by the sound of the crowd, this is going to be a really big gig. In fairness to Groovetribe, this isn't gonna be a half-bad time of night for them to be playing music. A shirtless Sequoia walks out dressed in his sweat shorts, his long dreads tied back with flowers.

"Ladies and Gentlemen," says Andrew, smiling, "thank you for coming out to support the fourth annual Battle of Seattle benefiting Children's Hospital." Sequoia smiles, blinking both eyes at some girl in the second or third row. I try to see who it is, but I can't tell.

"We've got a killer line-up for you tonight with Seattle favorites Goon Squad and Groovetribe." As he says this, Sequoia chatters like a howler monkey, waving his hands in the air. "...And from Bellingham, Washington—you all know someone who lives in Bellingham—fresh off their West Coast tour, we have, closing out the show, The Cosmic Poets."

There is clapping, but I know that most people here have never seen nor heard us, so the chances of us winning even if we wanted to are about nil.

"...The winner will receive two thousand dollars and a trip to play the Gorge when the Sasquatch Festival comes through in two weeks." Sequoia stands next to him, smiling and clapping like he and Andrew are old buddies. Now Angel, in her elegance, comes out and stands behind her organ. The percussion ensemble lines up behind their instruments. Everyone looks so happy and at ease. If only people knew the truth…

"Ladies and gentlemen, we have up for you first…Do you have any words you would like to say before I introduce you and your Groovetribe?" a smiling Andrew asks Sequoia.

"Well, Andrew, I'd just like to give a heart-felt thanks to the bands Goon Squad and the…uh…What's the band from Bellingham? The Spastic Poets…The Cosmic Poets, sorry…And to say that whoever wins isn't important. This concert isn't about egos and competition. It's about helping the *children!*"

As he says this the crowd goes wild. Fuming, I writhe in my seat. Walter elbows me in the ribs, laughing loudly.

"…We must listen to the children and the elders…That's what the Great Grandfather says…Thanks so much for coming out my friends! Namaste!"

The crowd erupts as bass and drums kick in, drowning out the rest of Andrew's introduction. The battle is underway.

Just like at Redwood Summer, the wall of percussion kicks into a funky, tribalesque groove, Kimta spanking out a really snappy bass line while Sequoia screams into the mic: "Here's a song for ya we're gonna dedicate to the children of the world…it's called *Remember the Children!*"

The crowd titters a bit as dark silhouetted heads begin to sway and I'm yet again filled with a poisonous, unspeakable jealously— especially as I suspect that the girl Sequoia is making eyes with in the front middle section might be Lily.

I leave Walter so I may roam; I have to know. I hope to God I'm wrong. It's so much easier to dump someone when a third party isn't involved or waiting in the wings. Standing to the left of the front section and kind of back a little, I'm able to determine the unmistakable silhouette of Lily, grooving away in the second row. What nerve! She's supposed to be in mourning, and I would hope that she would follow standard feminine protocol by waiting at least two days before jumping into another hot and heavy relationship. Is it presumptuous of me to assume that she's the one Sequoia's eyeing? I have to resist a panic-filled compulsion to go running up to her, throwing myself at her feet in a teary, hysterical froth, begging for her to beat up my heart some more, that her abuse is worth the price of my love and sybaritic, ruttish incontinence. But I don't; I won't; it's over. Isn't it?

When I return to my seat, Groovetribe's well into a jam, and the whole place seems to be swaying and rocking out. I know we don't stand a chance in hell. Angel looks powerful under the lights, and these guys are tighter than I want to admit.

"They got good rhythm, eh?" asks Walter, nudging me.

"They're okay." I sigh.

For about the first twenty minutes Groovetribe is invincible. Their on-stage banter is witty, casual and relaxed; their songs flow from one to the other, and each one seems to elicit more applause than the last. I can't believe Lily would go for someone as phony as Sequoia. People are cheering loudly... Groovetribe's gonna be a tough act to follow. Angel is on; they all are.

But alas, everything good must come to an end; Murphy's law is always the great equalizer, even for bands like Groovetribe. When considering these realities, it's no surprise that somewhere well into the set, as the Groovies are getting ready to play their seventh or eighth song and while Sequoia is delivering a heart-felt eulogy to the Children of Mother Earth, there comes the crackling of thunder and this weird, low-level electronic buzz. A colorful flash of movement catches my eye. It's Angel, slapping at her keyboard and rocking it back and forth. My goodness, it must be that bad cord that she never bothered to change.

I wince as I watch her growing more panic stricken with each passing second, and now there's the audible sound of her voice coming over the PA system, "Fucking, piece of shit...Don't fuck with me now."

Sequoia now seems to be whispering something to her as Kimta has walked over and is fiddling with the back of her keyboard. The crowd is growing restless and I feel Sequoia's pain—which makes me giddy. He now seems to be pleading with her about something before turning to the rhythm section and yelling for them to start the next song.

They do, and soon the music is grooving along again, Angel standing behind her organ, playing a tambourine. But I also recognize her I'm-gonna-kick-your-ass-when-this-gig-is-over death smile—pointed directly at Sequoia. Somehow he seems to have risen above it and is back in the mythical Adam groove while

Eve looks on with languid, vapid eyes, sullen in momentary defeat. Very momentary. The song finishes and she's back messing around with the cord again. Suddenly a familiar high-pitched electronic shriek fills the room. While people cover their ears in pain, Sequoia and Angel are having a heated little conference at the front of the stage.

The other Groovetribers recognize the deadly brew that's starting to bubble, and they kick in a little funk jam to lighten things up—but that's not going to work.

"I told you I was gonna quit this fuckin' band if I didn't get to—" Her salacious voice hisses to the beat of the music while the audience gasps.

"Go Angel!" I holler.

"It's not my fault!" she hisses as Sequoia reaches down and grabs a handful of cords at her feet and rips them out of their plugs. Smiling, he faces the audience.

"The curse of technology!" he laughs, while the other Groovies laugh with him, but I know sooner or later there's gonna be hell to pay. "It's all part of the big resolution!" He gyrates, searching for some words to somehow right this ship that's now careening ever closer to disaster. "Or did I say *revolution*? That's what we're talking about: a revolution where there can be no winners and no losers!"

I now notice manager Matt's silhouette standing off stage left, and he's trying to get Angel's attention, but she either doesn't see him, or is purposely ignoring him.

"...It's for the children...Remember the children..."

"...Piece of shit...It's not my fault..."

"...For the earth..."

"...Can't hear the fuckin' keyboard..."

"...Gotta save the children..."

"...You wanted me out of this band all along..."

Matt's up on the stage trying to figure out what to do, but it's too late. Angel's eyes reveal a lucidity I've never seen before. She looks out at the audience as if she's trying to analyze people's facial expressions. Things have become rather frightening. In a final act of rage and defiance, she hollers something at Sequioa and grabs hold of the doomed keyboard, flinging it up and pushing it forward, allowing gravity to finish her dirty work. As it topples to the stage in a mighty crashing and crackling, four hundred cheering people come to their feet. The tribal funk jam, however, continues on uninterrupted. She yells something at Sequoia before falling upon the dying keyboard, shrieking like an eagle landing on its prey.

It would be difficult for Groovetribe to top what just happened, and as the song ends, Sequoia thanks them for participating in this live art/theater demonstration about the end of technology and the return to tribalism that Groovetribe's been preparing to share for this event. They help Angel to her feet, leaving the stage to a standing ovation as I bite back my own feelings of jealously once again. Somehow, even in defeat, Groovetribe comes out on top yet again.

~

After a quick changeover, the dark-haired Indian cellist, the punk bassist, and rainbow-frizz drummer are assembled behind Andrew the emcee. It's 9:10, and during the short break, I walk around a bit to see if Rod Ames ever showed up, and to make sure that Sunny, Frank, Peaches and the zombies from RCA are really gone.

I feel a queasiness brewing in my gut, but that's what happens when one has hopes. What did I expect? Chances are Rod and company would be just like Frank's carpy cohorts. More lies, more disappointments.

Now that I've signed off on Sunny and company, as well as Lily, I know I don't need a record contract to be a success. Success is the music that pours out of your soul in spite of yourself. Success is making it through any given day. I may have one hell of a novel on my hands if I can manage to write all of this down, but who would believe it?

I haven't been able to find Ollie, Star or Zen, and I wouldn't doubt if they're out getting plastered before the gig.

I do find Walter and sit next to him. He is staring intently at the stage. "That's a cello." He sounds amazed. And I admit it is an unusual instrument to see in a rock band.

As the lights go down and the crowd quiets, Andrew says, "Ladies and gentlemen, it gives me the greatest pleasure to introduce one of the most original, under-rated bands in the Pacific Northwest. These guys have been at if for three years and just recently completed work on a new album that they hope to release this fall. Won't you please put your hands together for Goon Squad!"

The audience cheers as rainbow frizz begins thumping his kick drum while punk man thwanks out a fat bass line over it. As the young woman's ethereal-sounding cello fills the room, Walter leans over to me saying, "She's good, isn't she?"

"Yeah," I say. "We warmed up for Big Brother and the Holding Company with these guys a few months back. She's the real deal."

Her very presence is mesmerizing, even without playing. She is adorned with glossy black hair, a well-worn pair of jeans with the anarchy symbol etched above the right knee. She wears a simple, white dress shirt. The dark glasses she's wearing give her a dangerous mystique and the fact that she's slightly overweight somehow makes her even more appealing.

Punk man belts out a scratchy vocal. By the time they finish their first song the crowd is won over. Unlike Groovetribe, these guys say very little between songs, no proselytizing, no pretension. Their humility is charming. As they progress through their funky set, I sense a sadness about them.

When the lights go real low, I get this weird feeling of deja vu. It all starts when rainbow frizz and punk man leave the stage and focus is entirely on the Celia. She plays a few notes, then stops and walks over to the microphone. In a quiet voice, she says, "I just want everyone to know that we're not here to compete with anybody. Our manager thought this would be good exposure for us, so we took the gig. We don't care about winning."

The audience is still, though there is some moron somewhere in the back screaming about how the Mariners were going to choke in the playoffs. Someone tells him to shut up and it's quiet again.

"My mom passed away this past year but I never got to say goodbye because someone, somewhere determined ten years ago that she was unfit to take care of me, and since nobody had any idea where my dad was, I was forced to grow up in foster homes. As far as I remember, Dad was a drunk, but when I was young, he started teaching me this song about finding peace. He left before he finished teaching it to me, and all these years I've been trying to figure out an ending for it. Hey, Walter," she says, staring in our direction. "I'm glad you showed up tonight. I think I just finished that song."

Next to me, I hear Walter groan. His face is stiff with shock. As his daughter, Celia, begins to evoke beautiful sounds from her cello, she smiles at him. Walter extends a visibly shaking hand and places it on my shoulder. He slowly turns to me and now his eyes are brimming with tears. But he doesn't say anything; he can't. He knows that I finally understand.

Forty-four

About three-quarters of the way through Goon Squad's set, I leave Walter to head backstage to find the rest of the band in preparation for our final show. Sunny, Frank and the record people are gone, and I now know for sure that Rod Ames and company haven't made it to the gig either. It's no big deal. We weren't meant to be famous rock stars and a life of obscurity lived out in Bellingham isn't sounding half-bad to me right now. I am at peace. Besides, if anyone deserves to win and make it to the Sasquatch Festival, it's Goon Squad. Who knows, maybe Walter could join them in a guest appearance. Still, we have come a long way, and we must rock one last time.

As I walk down the hallway past the dressing rooms, I hear the sound of familiar laughter over the muffled vibrations of Goon Squad coming through the walls. The laughter seems to be coming from Dressing Room C. I now clearly hear a male and female voice. I stand there listening. Soft giggling, my name is mentioned...

I slowly turn the handle and, as the door creaks open, I am met with a pungent cloud of pot smoke. The lights are low, and I don't even see them at first.

"He just can't accept that it's over," I hear her say. "He's like a dog who won't go home..."

Sequoia laughs. "That dude depresses me, man. What a piece of work."

When my eyes finally adjust to the light, I groan. In the far corner of the room, half-naked, lying together on a small bed, are Sequoia and Lily. When she finally notices me, she screams and they are suddenly all commotion and swearing as they untangle themselves from each other. Sequoia looks at me and starts giggling.

Lily, on the other hand, glares at me, though her eyes can't hide the fear.

"Like a dog, huh?" I ask.

"You just don't get it, do you?" she snaps. "Go home!"

"I am going home," I say. "And by the way, I do get it now, Lily. I finally get everything. Thanks for setting me free." I hear her cry something out as I slam the door on yet another chapter in my life.

I have to take a few hard breaths to regain my poise before continuing my search for truth, meaning, and my rock-and-roll band. But first I need to make a trip to Ivar's for some chowder, and the walk might help alleviate some stress right now.

~

I still cannot find my band mates anywhere and Goon Squad has just finished their set, but going for chowder was a good move, and feeding the gulls always mellows me out. There is still quite a crowd milling about and I'm surprised to find that Ollie, Star and Zen have already set up their stuff during my absence. But they're still nowhere to be seen. I want to wreak havoc on this place. I want to offend people. I want to set this building on fire.

These thoughts and more are flowing through my head as I put my guitar on its stand, arranging my effects pedals. I finish, scanning the crowd. Again, no sign of Sunny, Frank and the rodents from glamville. No sign of Rod Ames, either. Where is everybody? Why am I so numb? Then I see her.

She sits with two others at a table off to the side of the stage, and she is staring at me with this gorgeous smile and teeth that light up the world. Her long brunette hair falls naturally and gracefully across her shoulders and her eyes are soft, olive pools of goodness that stare at me with curiosity. I have to look away. Unlike Lily, these eyes aren't trying to draw me in. They're just beautiful eyes, that's all.

"Hey, Angus, how's it going?" says a rough voice that's smoked way too many cigarettes. I turn to the source, and look at the person standing before me below the stage. I am stunned. It couldn't be, but it is...

"Larry?" I ask. He's got bushy hair and is wearing a leather jacket that's two sizes too small. At his side is his old Les Paul and he doesn't look like he's aged at all in the ten years since I've seen him.

"Can I jam out?" he asks.

"We haven't played yet, Larry," I say, laughing. "I never thought I'd see you again."

He smiles as he pulls out his guitar from its case. It's not a Les Paul; it's a vintage Strat. As if he's reading my mind, he says, "I got ripped off down in LA."

"Everybody gets ripped off in LA, Larry," I say. "You know I had a dream about you a few nights ago. You were my guitar tech for a really big gig."

He smiles, knowingly. "So can I jam out?" he asks, again.

"After the gig, Larry. Always after the gig."

"Two minutes," says Andrew as he comes up on the stage. "Is your band ready?"

"I don't know where the hell they are," I say. "I'll just play anyway. They'll show up eventually. We're The Cosmic Poets...It's hard to explain. Just introduce us like everything's normal."

Andrew looks at me strangely, then says, "Could you believe Groovetribe and their new organ player?"

"Yeah," I say. "Her name's Angel. She used to be with us, but we accidentally left her at the Talbot Rest Area. I love that crazy nut."

"Boy, did she ever do a number on that poor girl."

"What do you mean?"

"You didn't hear all that commotion? Where were you?"

"I went to Ivar's for some food. What happened?"

Andrew shakes his head. "Maybe she'll tell you when she gets out of jail."

"*What*?"

The lights flicker, and Andrew says, "You're on. I'll tell you all about it later."

"Oh, man," I say feeling sick.

The house lights dim and the room grows silent. I try to focus.

"Ladies and gentlemen," says Andrew. "We have for you now, that band you may have heard about from Bellingham who has just come off their big West Coast tour, and we're lucky to have them closing out the show tonight. Please give a big welcome to The Cosmic Poets!"

There is an obligatory spattering of applause while people stare, wondering what I'm going to do. I stand before the microphone feeling strangely tranquil, with my acoustic guitar slung over my shoulder. "I guess The Cosmic Poets got lost again," I say, which gets a few laughs. "You know what, people? I don't care if we win or not. In fact, I urge all of you music writers to do the right thing and vote for Goon Squad. I'm through trying to be someone else."

"Hey, you know any Dylan?" someone shouts from the back.

"Yeah," says another, "play some Dylan or something!" I see Larry off to the right of the stage behind the curtain and he's got his guitar out. He seems to be tuning it.

"No," I say, quietly, "I'll play what I like." My words seem to hang in the void, and I'm barely holding on, though I struggle to continue. The room is silent. "I'm not pushing anymore. I just want you to listen. Will you listen to me, tonight?"

For a moment the room is silent. Then a couple of people are clapping. Now a few more, and I hear Walter's laughter out there somewhere, but my head is swimming in a luke-warm dreamscape; far away I hear commotion but I do not want to come up for air ever again though I know I must, and when I finally do, bursting to the surface, the noise is louder, almost deafening. People are cheering, just like at the Reno car-lot, just like back home. It's still getting louder, and the first thing I notice as I turn my head is that Star is wearing a new black tank-top with white letters that boldly spell the word DOMINATE. The next thing I notice is that she has shaved her head. The gleam from the new silver nose ring with which she has just adorned herself sparkles under the colored lights. Judging by the way her bottom lip is swollen, she is ready to wreak havoc, too. Ollie sits a bit sheepishly behind his drums while Zen stands there looking at me, smiling, bass tuned, plugged in and ready to rock. He shrugs his shoulders.

"What happened to you guys?" I ask.

"You won't believe it, Angus," says Zen, laughing. "Groovetribe's tour bus just got towed and Angel was arrested for assaulting Sequoia and Lily. We had to move Elvis before the cops towed us too, and Ollie decided at the last minute to drag all of his bags of quarters inside. That's why we were late. Plus, Star decided she needed a shave."

"Good God! Is Lily okay?" I ask, stunned.

Star smiles wistfully. "She'll be all right, though they took her to the hospital. You should've seen the fight. When Angel caught'em kissing on the loading dock, she flat-out wasted'em. They're both gonna need big-time stitches."

"Lily's not gonna *die* is she?"

"Hell no, she's not," says Star. "Probably just a broken nose. She's just lucky I wasn't doing her. Can we please rock now?"

Finally, with all truth and sincerity I am able to say, "Yes, Star. Let us rock, now." My heart swells with love and affection for my comrades, and though I feel bad for Lily, maybe getting her nose broken by Angel will do her some good. One thing is for sure: this is the ultimate farewell gig and there will be no stopping us.

"Ladies and gentlemen," I say, "this is our last show together and we would like to rock, now." The place seems to come unglued, and as we slam into the first song, blasting them with a wall of sound, Star's electric guitar just seems to burn in her hands as she leaps around the stage. Zen just stands there, stoically thumping out the groove with Ollie and I pounding away, too. The song ends and the place is rocking. It's all becoming a blur as rage pours through my being and for once, I am connected. We hit 'em again, and I notice Walter and Celia sitting together at another table, watching and smiling, knowing that the purpose of our big tour has finally revealed itself to me. It was so simple and easy, but how could I have missed it? Ride the tsunami of life and to hell with the experts. Everything is right here and right now, just like Walter said, but I bet even he didn't even know how true that was going to become in the end.

As we sail through our set, I relish every song and each passing moment, knowing that this is the closing of something much more graceful than I could have ever hoped. I burn with love and passion, relishing the big letting go of it all in spite of that old, tiresome voice from within that whispers: "You gotta keep it together; you'll be huge."

That voice is dying, while the tears and sweat that are pouring off my face make it itch like hell. I'm sure we'll never catch bands like Groovetribe, but that's good because we don't need a scene to be heard. As long as the voice stays true that's all that matters—which is a big part of the revolution that most people never get. And it's so damn good to see Larry after all these years still carrying a guitar with him like he doesn't need a world to figure him out 'cause he's already figured out the world a long time ago and the simple truth that you've got to make your own world if you're gonna be able to live in it and I wish to hell Sunny wasn't back and staring at me 'cause that's the only thing that's keeping this from being a great, great moment...

We're all tuned up, and as I slowly start the last song that The Cosmic Poets will ever play together, I am really fighting back tears as I realize that Lily and I can never go back, nor can The Cosmic Poets, but my sorrow is tempered by my dream girl who stares back at me, filling my heart with new possibility, and I do believe I see tears on her cheeks as well.

"Hey, can I sit in with you now?" asks Larry who is standing next to me on stage.

"You know the rules, Larry," I say. "As long as you don't turn it up."

He smiles knowingly, sticks a guitar jack into a dead amp off to the side of the stage, and begins going off on some unimaginable lead. I laugh out loud, higher on life than I've ever been.

As I stare at my smiling, skin-headed electric guitarist, I know Star's going to put together her kick-ass, heavy-metal bluegrass band and dominate the Bellingham music scene for years to come, and that Ollie will someday write his best-seller about his strange encounters with celebrities over the past thirty years. Once she gets out of jail, Angel will certainly find fame and glory with her own band if she only learns to get out of her own way. And Zen...I wish Zen a happy and relatively sober life in the country with Linda and a whole flock of Elvis's descendants named after various rock icons...This is too much...I'm aware of a rumbling beneath us, and I realize that the gig is over. I don't even know which song we played.

"The winner of this year's Battle of Seattle will be announced in five minutes!" Andrew's voice thunders over the sound system.

I jump down onto the floor and it's all hugs, handshakes and high-five's with people I've never met. Larry's still up on stage going off, and by the contorted expression on his face I know that he's far, far away and for him, the song will never end.

"Great job, Angus."

I turn to the source of this familiar voice and jump a little. It's a smiling Rod Ames. Rod, from A&M Records.

"You *did* make it," I say. "I didn't think you would."

"I told you I'd be here. Unfortunately, my friends canceled at the last minute. I really wish they could have seen this."

"Yeah, it was really great, wasn't it?"

"Very moving, Angus. I relate to your struggle, being a musician myself."

"Really?"

"Sure. Most people have no idea what goes into keeping a band together. But the band is breaking up?"

"It sure feels that way, Rod," I say. "Why, are you going to offer us a record contract?"

He laughs. "I really like your sound, and just as importantly for me, I like you all personally. You guys seem authentic and original, dying traits amongst most artists trying to make it these days."

"Thanks, Rod," I say, sincerely. Yet even Rod holds no more power over me. He's just a normal guy thanking us for a good gig.

"Yeah, *thanks*, Rod," says Sunny, drunkenly. She has sneaked up on us, and as my weary eyes fall upon her I hear myself groan.

"My name's Sunny Rickshire, publisher, agent and manager for The Cosmic Poets." She glares at me with the slightest smile betrayed on her heavily painted lips. She reaches out to shake Rod's hand. As she looks at me her glassy, black eyes are not too drunk to see my anger. I notice Peaches somberly standing guard behind her. "All business affairs regarding The Cosmic Poets go through *me*."

"I'm not doing business with anybody tonight, ma'am," says Rod, gracefully. "I just came out to hear the band."

"Rod, we have a lot of labels looking at these guys," she says. "I just want you to know that."

"I understand," he says, now smiling.

"Oh, come on, Sunny," I sigh. "Do we really have to go through this *again*? I thought we ended things."

"Last I checked, I've got you under contract until fall of next year. Don't you remember me telling you that the ocean is full of sharks?"

"Sunny," I say, trying to take her aside. "It's over. I know you did your damnedest to score for us in the best way you knew how, and I accept responsibility for my contribution to this mess, but I want out. Now."

"Why, so you can kiss somebody else's ass for a record deal? After all I've done for you, all the sacrifices I've made in getting you to the doorstep, you're gonna try to jump horses in midstream, not that it surprises me, but since you've destroyed my reputation with Frank and our friends from RCA, you'd better know that I'm gonna get *something* out of this."

"You got four thousand bucks out of me, Sunny," I say glaring at Peaches.

"That's nothing!" she snarls. "Mere pocket change for what you've done to me."

"Sunny," I say, calmly. "You're fired."

She looks at me as if the words have stunned her. Her face slowly breaks into that cracked, desert floor smile which precipitates a rumbling laughter, emanating from deep within her tortured being. "You can't fire me; we have many months to go on your contract. Besides, *you're* working for *me*." Peaches starts to giggle while Rod looks on, fascinated.

"No, Sunny," I say as the illusory chains of bondage and servitude fall away from me. "I'm really sorry for breaking it to you, but you are fired. I hereby fire you right now, and now that you're fired, I want you to walk away from Rod and I so I never have to look at your fired face again. Does my former manager, agent and publisher who has hereby been fired understand that? Huh, my fired friend?"

She glares at me, then turns to Rod. "He'll have to buy me out," she says, quietly.

"What are you talking about?" I ask.

"Oh, you need a lesson in legalese, now? You just don't get it." She then turns to Rod who has been silently observing this melodrama unfolding. "If you really want to work with this pathological liar, then I won't stand in the way, but protocol calls for a buyout of the contract plus a share of publishing and speculated advance money."

"Miss," says Rod. "I've been in this business for twenty years, and I've never heard of such a thing. What's speculated advance money?"

"Oh, about one hundred fifty-seven thousand dollars with four thousand dollars credit given in good will by myself." She smiles. "See, I'm not in it for the bucks."

Rod stares at her in disbelief for a moment, and then laughs. "I see," he says, winking at me. "I'll talk to my people and we'll see what kind of arrangements can be made if we do in fact decide to work with The Cosmic Poets." He frowns at me, shaking his head while I just glare at Sunny. She smiles back.

"I'm through with her," I whisper to Rod. "She's a nut."

"Don't worry about it," he whispers back. "She doesn't have a leg to stand on."

"I heard that!" she snarls. "I'll see you in court. You've got my word on that. I'm not playing games with you anymore." She turns and stomps away while Peaches just lingers for an extra moment, glaring at us. "Seeee what you've dooone, nooow?" Then, shaking his green head, he follows her toward the bar where I'm sure she's looking for some other sucker she can charm into buying her a drink.

"I'll call you, Angus." Rod clasps my shoulder. "Great job."

"Thanks Rod," I say, feeling detached. "Aren't you going to stick around to see who won?"

"I already know," he says, almost sadly.

I watch him work his way toward the door, imagining myself standing before a judge as I'm being grilled by Sunny's lawyer over percentages.

"Hi," says a girlish voice startling me.

I turn and feel my face flush red. It's my brown-eyed, knockout dream girl. I expel Sunny and Peaches from my mind with a quick flush of my psychic power toilet. "Hey," I say. "How are you?"

She giggles a bit shyly. "I'm good. So, you live in Bellingham?"

"Yeah, I do," I say. "Why, do you know someone who lives there?"

"Well, *I* live there."

"You do?" I ask. "You know, I think I might have seen you around."

"Oh? Maybe you have. I can't stay, but…here." She hands me a rose from behind her back with a little note taped to the stem. I glance at it, noticing a phone number.

"Thanks," I say. "Can I call you?"

She smiles, turning scarlet and then she runs away into the crowd leaving me stunned, yet elated.

"Ladies and gentlemen," says Andrew, standing nervously on the stage again. "We have an unfortunate announcement to make. I have been informed by the fire marshal that we must evacuate the premises immediately. There is no reason to panic and we hope to let people back into the building for the announcement of this year's winner, but in case that doesn't happen, the results will be mailed to all participating bands. We regret having to make this request. Please evacuate the building immediately!"

It's an eruption of panic, screaming, and commotion as people head for the exits. Instantly, all musicians are on stage, grabbing armfuls of gear, instruments and cords, and even Ollie is headed for an exit, dragging some very familiar-looking sacks along with part of his drum set.

"What's going on?" I ask Andrew as he passes by, heading for the door.

"Someone called in a bomb threat. It's no big deal, but we still have to evacuate. What a way to end a great night, huh?"

"No big deal? Why do you say that?"

"Oh," he says wiping his forehead with his arm while smiling at me. "The cops traced the call to the pay phone at the back lobby and caught the woman who made the call. Funny, Angus, she claims that she's your manager."

Epilogue

The Pike Place Market clock reads 3:46 A.M. which tells me that it's too late to go back to Ivar's for more chowder. No worries, we're all pretty beat. Walter and Celia sit on the curb of an empty First Avenue quietly talking while the eerie sound of Star's saxophone floats upward into the summer night. Load-in eight-and-a-half hours ago seems like another lifetime, and as Zen, Ollie and I join Walter and his daughter sitting on the curb, I'm overcome with a sense of well being and emptiness.

Star remains by herself, playing something that sounds kind of ancient, like she's reaching out of a painting to lay the finishing touches on an almost-finished scene. There is something about a group of musicians sitting on a curb of a major city street in the wee hours of the morning that is peaceful.

There is a warm and salty breeze blowing in off the water and besides the occasional bus or taxi cruising past, we have the place to ourselves. The streetlights cast a mellow glow over the scene and make it appear far less menacing than it is during the mid-evening hours. No one seems in too big a hurry to be northbound. I do notice an occasional human shadow walk past on the other side of the street. It is a time of night for loners.

"Are you sure this is where you parked Elvis?" I ask.

"First and Pike," sighs Zen. "I'm positive."

"I'm just glad I'd stashed all the bags of quarters in the club," says Ollie.

We glare at him, recalling the effort it took to relay the bags *and* the instruments out on to the street. I don't envy him now, sitting on a sidewalk on First and Pike with his drums set up next to a pile of sacks containing over six grand in quarters. A pan handler's nirvana…

"Poor Elvis," I say. "He was so good to us. I wonder what will ever become of him."

"Let's not talk about it," says Zen. "It's too depressing."

"You know, auto theft is one of the most common crimes in the Puget Sound region," says Ollie. "In fact, I just read the other day—"

"You know," says Walter, artfully changing the subject, "that was a great tour. Thanks for picking me up." He and Celia seem to take their chance encounter completely in stride as if it's the most natural, expected thing in existence.

"You guys have a great band," says Celia.

"So do you," I reply. "I hope you make it to the Sasquatch Festival."

"Maybe we could all go on tour together some day," she says.

"Yeah, right," says Star from fifteen feet away, and we all laugh before drifting back into silence—save for the sound of saxophone and occasional spitting. Then Ollie gets up and starts messing around with his pile of quarters, before turning to me with two cloth sacks that he struggles to hold up. "Here's four thousand five hundred dollars," he says. "I counted it out on the trip up, but you might want to recount it just to make sure."

"Are you serious?"

"Yeah," he says. "It's for the deposit you left with Sunny plus the credit card. Credit card interest rates are such a crime. Did you know that it was considered a mortal sin during the Middle Ages to charge interest on money? And the way these credit card companies encourage people to go into debt, most of them will never get out of it as long as they live…I'm sorry, I'm babbling on, aren't I? Anyway, here. Don't even thank me. You would have done the same."

I stand up and give him a monster bear hug as he tries to wriggle away from me. "Ollie, if the world only knew about you."

"He's only trying to lighten his load," says Zen.

"I've got no problem hiking back to Bellingham with cold cash like this. Walter how in the hell did you help Ollie win that money?"

"I have absolutely no idea," he sighs, putting his arm around his daughter.

Star has now come back into our midst and even as she sits down with us, I can tell she's in another place. It doesn't matter. Every woman has her own way.

As we grace the curb of First Avenue, staring out of our own worlds that happened to collide along this epic journey, I notice a shadowy figure that has passed down the sidewalk across the street and who's now doubling back. We have, for some reason, caught his attention. He stands, staring at us, a black man in his mid-thirties, wearing a white shirt and jeans. As he crosses the street coming toward us, I feel everybody stiffen.

"How y'all doing tonight," he says, standing before us while he pants a bit. He's been running for awhile.

"All right," I say, while everyone else stares at him. "What's up?"

"Oh, man, you really wanna know?" he asks, his eyes welling with tears. "It's the devil. The devil's been chasing me and I just can't run fast enough."

"The devil?" asks Walter.

"Yeah, the devil," he sighs. "I just started using again, and now I've lost everything. My wife, three kids, they're gone for good this time. It's the devil, man, the devil…"

"Mister," says Celia with compassion. "Don't be so hard on yourself."

He stands there crying for a few moments until his sobs become more intermittent. "Can I ask you a favor?"

"Go ahead," I say, fully expecting him to hit us up for some cash.

"Can I sing you a song I wrote?"

Walter and Celia stare at him with huge eyes. "Please do," says Celia.

He clears his throat and almost comically straightens up his posture. Then his mouth opens and out of it floats a beautifully well-seasoned tenor. As he sings a stunning, heart-blistering piece, I'm filled with sadness that there is nothing that I can do to save him, though I sure won't mind giving him a whole bunch of quarters.

His voice echoes off the buildings and I hear the sound of gulls shrieking, aware of the force of gravity holding us to the concrete. The song is over and he just stands there panting, holding at bay the floodgates of grief. All I can think of is how I love the smell of saltwater.

"That was beautiful."

"Thanks," he says with sudden calm. He smiles, shaking his head as he sees me reaching for the moneybags. Before I can say anything, he's off and running down the block; in a matter of a few seconds his tiny shadow disappears into the grayish yellow of the coming morning.

We all stare wistfully in the direction in which he disappeared, and this is our cue to be on our way. Star stands up first. Picking up her saxophone, she blows it off a little while rubbing it on her shirt. She holds it outward as if examining it closely. Then she turns to Walter and hands it to him. "You'll be needing this," she says, and as if reading his dumb-struck expression, she says, "Don't worry, I have another one in Bellingham."

He turns it over and over in his hands looking back and forth between it and her.

"Just don't go selling it for seventy-seven bucks in any pawn shop."

He finally manages to say, "No, I'd want at least a hundred." He smiles back at her while his eyes glisten. Celia walks over and places her arms around Star and is soon followed by Ollie followed by Zen then Walter, and finally, myself. We all stand, swaying together, saying our last good-byes to Walter and Celia, wondering if we'll ever meet up again, but whatever words that are now being shared in this closing circle of a closing chapter, they're now being drowned out by the seagulls that are gathering overhead, circling above the mad streets, letting their mournful cries float upward as offerings and intentions made on our behalf as it's now time to leave Celia and Walter standing on the corner of First and Pike as we hail a cab to take us and our gear eastward to the bus station, or perhaps north, all the way to Bellingham. That depends on how generous Ollie's feeling right now.

"You know guys," I say, after we're all loaded up and sitting down, "the things that happened to us on this tour are bound to happen to any band with a name like The Cosmic Poets."

"Things like that will happen to any band who tries to transcend the physical and material realm by altering the nature of cosmic reality in pursuit of esoteric truth," says Zen.

"Maybe we should change our name," replies Star.

"Are we still a band?" asks Ollie.

"You know, I don't really want to think about that right now," says Zen. "I just want to go home."

"Don't you think we ought to go bail Angel out of the slammer, first?" asks Ollie.

"I was just thinking that," I say, suddenly missing her. "I owe her one for wasting Sequoia. What a sweetheart."

"Yeah," says Zen. "I love that girl. She's...Bellingham."

"Nobody like her," concludes Star. "No place like Bellingham, either."

As we pull away from the curb and wave to Walter and Celia, Walter's playing Star's sax, and I notice that there are now what seems like millions of seagulls swirling upward far above, fading into the golden light of the early morning. Even after we've traveled six blocks with the warm, early morning winds blowing through the cab's open windows as we head for the jail to get Angel, I swear I can hear Walter's saxophone still echoing off the buildings behind us...or maybe that's just his laughter.